World Cinema and the Ethics of Realism

Lúcia Nagib

BLOOMSBURY
NEW DELHI • LONDON • OXFORD • NEW YORK • SYDNEY

BLOOMSBURY INDIA
Bloomsbury Publishing India Pvt. Ltd
Second Floor, Building No. 4
DDA Complex LSC, Pocket C – 6 & 7
Vasant Kunj, New Delhi 110070
www.bloomsbury.com

BLOOMSBURY, Bloomsbury Academic India and the Diana
logo are trademarks of Bloomsbury Publishing Plc

First published in India 2014
First published 2011 by Continuum

This edition published with permission from Bloomsbury Publishing Plc,
50 Bedford Square, London, WC1B3DP, UK

British Library Cataloguing-in-Publication Data
A catalogue record for this book is available from the British Library.

Library of Congress Cataloging-in-Publication Data
A catalog record for this book is available from the Library of Congress

ISBN: 978-93-84052-88-1

For sale in the Indian subcontinent only

Typeset by Newgen Imaging Systems Pvt Ltd, Chennai, India
Digitally printed and bound in India by Replika Press Pvt. Ltd.

To Nagisa Oshima,
with profound admiration and gratitude.

CONTENTS

and Japanese cinema in general. Meeting him was a life-changing event for me, and for this reason I dedicate this book to him. No parts of this book have been previously published, except for Chapter 6, on the work of Kazuo Hara and Sachiko Kobayashi, first published in L. Nagib & C. Mello (eds), *Realism and the Audiovisual Media* (Basingstoke: Palgrave, 2009). The theme of Chapter 3 was approached in a very different light in my article 'Panaméricas Utópicas: Entranced and Transient Nations in *I Am Cuba* (1964) and *Land in Anguish* (1967)', *Hispanic Research Journal*, 8, 2007, pp. 79–90. The same is true of my study of João César Monteiro in Chapter 7, a filmmaker I have previously examined from a completely different angle in 'The Trilogy of John of God', in Alberto Mira (ed.), *The Cinema of Spain and Portugal* (London: Wallflower Press, 2005, pp. 188–197).

Special thanks are due to my dear friend and research partner Cecília Mello, an endless source of inspiration and encouragement in so many successful and unsuccessful adventures. This book shares its very genesis with her. Finally, eternal gratitude goes to my best reader and beloved husband, Stephen Shennan.

CONTENTS

LIST OF ILLUSTRATIONS

ACKNOWLEDGEMENTS

This book would not have been possible without the unrestricted support I have received at the University of Leeds. In the academic year of 2008–09, I was granted a fully funded sabbatical leave by the Faculty of Arts and the School of Modern Languages and Cultures, which enabled me to bring this book to completion. During this period, I was blessed with unfailing support from administrative and teaching staff, as well as graduate students at the Centre for World Cinemas (especially Tiago de Luca), who shared my duties among themselves and made sure the Centre continued to function as normal. The critical responses I received from both colleagues and students at CWC were also fundamental to the development of the ideas contained here. In particular, I must thank my colleague and friend Diana Holmes, who despite her busy schedule was always ready to read and make illuminating comments on whatever outlines and chapters I submitted to her. Paul Cooke was another insightful discussant, especially with regard to Werner Herzog and the New German Cinema. Max Silverman and Ismail Xavier made useful suggestions when the book was still at project stage. My heart-felt thanks go to Beto Brant and Priscila Prade for providing me with illustrations for *Delicate Crime*. Paloma Rocha, Joel Pizzini and Sara Rocha (Tempo Glauber) were extremely supportive in locating and providing illustrations for Glauber Rocha's films. Kazuo Hara and Sachiko Kobayashi (Shisso Production) assisted me with information, pictures and films. For contributing documents, information and help of various kinds, I thank José Carlos Avellar, Mika Ko, Mateus Araújo Silva, Peter B. Schumann, Dudley Andrew, Nicola Liscutin, Brad Prager, Teresa Borges (Cinemateca Portuguesa) and Beata Wiggen (Kairos Film). As always, Laura Mulvey gave me fantastic intellectual support.

Many of the films analysed here have been the subject of my attention for many years. Nagisa Oshima is someone I have regularly returned to (and this will not be the last time!), not only for the extraordinary quality of his films, but also for his exemplary courage and ethics as a filmmaker. Before he was forced by ill health to retire from public life, he unstintingly supported me throughout my research on his work and Japanese cinema in general. Meeting him was a life-changing event for me, and for this reason I dedicate this book to him. No parts of this book have been previously published, except for Chapter 6, on the work of Kazuo Hara and Sachiko Kobayashi, first published in L. Nagib & C. Mello (eds), *Realism and the Audiovisual Media* (Basingstoke: Palgrave, 2009). The theme of Chapter 3 was approached in a very different light in my article 'Panaméricas Utópicas: Entranced and Transient Nations in *I Am Cuba* (1964) and *Land in Anguish* (1967)', *Hispanic Research Journal*, 8, 2007, pp. 79–90. The same is true of my study of João César Monteiro in Chapter 7, a filmmaker I have previously examined from a completely different angle in 'The Trilogy of John of God', in Alberto Mira (ed.), *The Cinema of Spain and Portugal* (London: Wallflower Press, 2005, pp. 188–197).

Special thanks are due to my dear friend and research partner Cecília Mello, an endless source of inspiration and encouragement in so many successful and unsuccessful adventures. This book shares its very genesis with her. Finally, eternal gratitude goes to my best reader and beloved husband, Stephen Shennan.

INTRODUCTION

This book proposes to address world cinema through an ethics of realism. The juxtaposition of the terms 'world cinema', 'ethics' and 'realism' creates a tension which asks for the redefinition of all of them.

As regards world cinema, my intention is in the first place to offer a productive alternative to traditional oppositional binaries such as popular versus art cinemas, fiction versus documentary films, narrative versus non-narrative films, mainstream versus peripheral cinema. More importantly, I propose to break away from discourses of 'difference', which reduce world cinema to a victimized 'other' and risk replicating and perpetuating the very colonial partition of the world they claim to deconstruct. Instead, I hope to stimulate and legitimize the experience of world films through passion rather than compassion. To that end, I suggest the adoption of a positive, democratic and inclusive approach to film studies, which defines world cinema as a polycentric phenomenon with peaks of creation in different places and periods. Once notions of a single centre and primacies are discarded, everything can be put on the world cinema map on an equal footing, even Hollywood, which instead of a threat becomes a cinema among others (see Nagib, 2006). At the core of this proposal is the belief that different cinemas of the world can generate their own, original theories. They do not depend on paradigms set by the so-called Hollywood classical narrative style and in most cases are misunderstood if seen in this light. In multicultural, multi-ethnic societies like ours, cinematic expressions from various origins cannot be seen as 'the other' for the simple reason that they are us. More interesting than their difference is, in most cases, their interconnectedness.

My take on polycentrism has its precedents, of course. Nearly two decades ago Stam and Shohat, in their introduction to the groundbreaking book *Unthinking Eurocentrism*, formulated the concept of a 'polycentric multiculturalism', summarily dismissing as insufficient and ultimately wrong the world division between 'us' and the 'other', 'centre and periphery', 'the West and the Rest' (1994, p. 8). Their ideas found resonance in a number of other studies, and alternatives to the dual system and the Hollywood canon have proliferated ever since. Drawing on Franco Moretti's organization of world literatures into an 'atlas', Dudley Andrew, for example, draws an 'atlas of world cinema', which allows film history to be seen as a sequence of 'waves . . . rolling through adjacent cultures'. The obvious example he gives of this phenomenon is the French New Wave, which 'buoyed French film in 1959 and rolled around the world, affecting in different ways and under dissimilar circumstances the cinema lives of Britain, Japan, Cuba, Brazil, Argentina, Czechoslovakia, Yugoslavia, Hungary and later Taiwan' (Andrew, 2006, pp. 21–2). To approach world cinema through its waves is attractive above all for the supra-national and cross-temporal networking it enables. As regards the Nouvelle Vague, for example, one could see a previous crest of a wave a little earlier in the mid-1950s with the films focusing on the 'sun tribe' generation in Japan, which had a decisive influence on Truffaut. One could also look at the New German Cinema of the 1960s and 1970s in relation to how it re-elaborated elements of the Brazilian Cinema Novo (see Chapter 2).

More recently, Andrew came to think of world cinema as a 'phase', squeezed between the 'federated' national cinemas of the 1960s and the 'global' cinema of today. Notwithstanding this temporal containment, world cinema continues to be, in his view, characterized by waves, this time by the new cinemas of the 1980s, which he describes as 'coming from places never before thought of as cinematically interesting or viable', such as Taiwan, China, Senegal, Mali, Iran, Yugoslavia and Ireland, to fill in the gap 'caused by the retreat of the modernist art cinema' of the 1960s (Andrew, 2010, p. 77). Implicit in this approach is the realist component inherent to all new cinemas which by these means reconnect across history and geography with Italian Neorealism, which Andrew, following Bazin, acknowledges as the inaugural marker of modern cinema. Cinematic modernity falls outside the scope of my discussion, but realism is central to it, as it defines an ethical stance which animates cinema's peaks of creation across the globe. Indeed, my ethical hypothesis draws on the cyclical re-emergence of realist approaches to cinema around the world, in the form of physical realism (as examined in Chapters 1 and 2), social realism (Chapters 1 and 3), surrealism (Chapter 2), conceptual and medium realisms (Chapters 3 and 4), real sex on screen (Chapter 5), political and private documentary forms (Chapter 6) and the autobiographical genre (Chapter 7). However, I would stop short of subscribing to a possible dual system deriving from this phenomenon, along the lines suggested by Elsaesser, who defines world cinema by its higher degree of realism as compared to Hollywood (2009, p. 3). Even less useful to my approach would be the idea of narrative realism, or the 'impression of reality', a favourite target of criticism since the late 1960s for its alleged association with 'narrative closure', 'bourgeois ideology' and the so-called Hollywood classical cinema (see Nagib and Mello, pp. xvii ff). Rather, the realism I focus on relates to modes of production and address, and here my challenging of binary oppositions confronts me with a more sophisticated dual model, which is the understanding of cinema as a system of representation.

Realism, Presentation, Representation

Representation theories provide the tools customarily adopted by Cultural Studies for the assessment of cinema and other arts, and their use has proved effective for the deconstruction of ideologically biased portrayals of minorities. In Cultural Studies, artworks are seen as media of communication, that is to say, as languages, through which things acquire or are given meanings from which emerges, in Stuart Hall's words, 'a sense of our own identity' (Hall, 2003, p. 3). Though derived from the Platonic idea of reflective mimesis, representation, in Hall's view, differs from it insofar as it opens up to more complex, constructive approaches, according to which things found in the material world have no meaning outside of how they are represented (2003, pp. 6–7). This, however, has not prevented representational approaches from being regularly utilized in art criticism as a means to preserve, rather than abolish, the dual division between material world and its image, art and its model. As a result, the critic is invested with the role of a decoder who sets out to unearth from an artwork what underlies its treacherous appearance, that is to say, its 'real' meaning. The risks of separating appearance from essence, form from content, reality from its image are well known, among them the establishment of a hierarchy which ascribes a superior position to those who purportedly hold the knowledge of the real (the critic) as opposed to those who 're-present it' in an artwork (the artist). As a result, representation, as a method, often leads the critic to become judgmental rather than appreciative, normative rather than inquisitive, a moralizing preacher rather than a passionate learner, thus reenacting the very power relations Cultural Studies aspire to debunk.

But let me formulate this question in a different way: are all works of art necessarily (or exclusively) representational? The philosopher Jacques Rancière, in his illuminating book on cinema, would deny it, establishing instead a distinction between what he calls the 'representative regime' and the 'aesthetic regime' in art:

> The representative regime understands artistic activity on the model of an active form that imposes itself upon inert matter and subjects it to its representational ends. The aesthetic regime of art rejects the idea of form wilfully imposing itself on matter and instead identifies the power of the work with the identity of contraries: the identity of active and passive, of thought and non-thought, of intentional and unintentional. (Rancière, 2006, p. 117)

He goes on to suggest that 'the most abrupt formulation of this idea is to be found in Flaubert, who set out to write a book that depended on nothing external and was held together solely by the strength of its style' (2006, p. 117). It is not mere coincidence that Rancière resorts to a self-contained reality of the style rather than mimesis of the real to define an eminently realist writer, who for him is the best expression of the non-representative regime. This idea, I believe, acquires even greater significance when it comes to cinema.

Indeed the debate between presentational and representational modes in cinema goes back a long way and is inextricable from the question of realism. Noël Burch, in his pioneering assessment of early cinema, famously opposed what he called 'bourgeois representationalism' to a 'popular presentationalism', drawing from this division two very distinct phases of cinema, before and after the emergence of an 'institutional mode of representation', which he located around 1906 (Burch, 1990, pp. 186ff.). Burch's resolute stand in favour of 'presentational' filmmaking is best illustrated by certain strands of Japanese cinema, which he defined as eminently non-anthropocentric and indeed alien to all ideas of centres. He found in Barthes a common ground with this concern and praised his famous book on Japan, *L'Empire des signes,* as a

> first attempt by any Western writer to *read* the Japanese 'text' in the light of contemporary semiotics, a reading informed by a rejection of ethnocentrism – and indeed of all the 'centrisms' which have anchored ideology in the West since the industrial revolution and the rise of capitalism. (Burch, 1979, p. 13)

What would be the actual difference between 'representational' and 'presentational' cinemas for Burch? Basically, the fact that 'representational' cinema was directed towards producing an 'impression of reality', whereas 'presentational' cinema was quite at ease in acknowledging its own artifice. Burch's fundamental point, at least at that stage, was to counter the manipulative character of Hollywood cinema, whose aim was to produce 'illusionism', something both early and Japanese cinemas could dispense with. He was the first to connect early cinema's strategies to avant-garde and experimental techniques and, in so doing, severed the ties which had been carefully woven by evolutionist approaches between artistic improvement and technological progress. Original and farsighted though it was, Burch's approach was no less binary insofar as it subscribed to and reinforced the division between Hollywood and its emulators on the one hand and its contraveners on the other. As a result, his cherished anti-bourgeois cinema ended up with a negative definition, based on what it was not. In effect, Burch's brilliant book on Japanese cinema is constructed on the basis of how it systematically disregards Hollywood classical cinema rules of plot construction, camera placement and montage.

It seems to me that Tom Gunning made a step forward into a more encompassing understanding of presentational cinema when he formulated his theory of a 'cinema of attractions', which draws on Eisenstein's famous definition of a 'montage of attractions'. Similarly to Burch, he defined the 'cinema of attractions' as a prevailing mode in early cinema until 1906–1907, when it was supplanted by the arrival of Griffith's and other markedly narrative filmmaking modes. This, however, did not mean the end of the cinema of attractions, which survived by going underground and becoming a defining element of avant-garde cinemas and even a subtle, disruptive component of some narrative films. The distinctive quality of this cinema, according to Gunning, was its ability to 'show' something rather than 'represent' it. 'Contrasted to the voyeuristic aspect of narrative cinema analysed by Christian Metz', says Gunning, 'this is an exhibitionist cinema', in which actors are constantly looking at the spectators – that is to say, 'breaking the theatre's fourth wall', as Brecht would put it some thirty years after such films were made. For Gunning, the 'cinema of attractions' at its most literal would be the erotic films that thrived during cinema's early days (Gunning, 1997, pp. 56–62).

Presentational cinema became a privileged object of study for narratologists such as André Gaudreault, who defined cinematic narrative as a 'dialectical combination of the two basic modes of narrative communication: narration and monstration' (1997, p. 73). 'To monstrate', a literal translation of the French *montrer,* is another way of signifying 'presentation', for which Gaudreault found a perfect illustration in the figure of the live narrator who used to provide explanation for silent films before the advent of intertitles. They were to be found all over the world and were called, for example, *bonnimenteurs* in French or *benshi* in Japanese. The *benshi,* who were trained as authentic actors in the tradition of the kabuki theatre, became a prominent institution during cinema's early days in Japan, thus realizing Brecht's dream of alienation effects *avant la lettre,* by providing a neat separation between the real person of the actor-interpreter and the fictional characters on the screen.

More recently, presentational modes of address have been connected to the historical contingent, as in Willemen's approach, which formulates the issue in terms of 'representation (one thing standing for another) versus presentation (something manifesting itself even if only in a disguised, distorted or translated manner)', triggering the question: 'how do the dynamics animating historical change "present" in representations?' (Willemen, 2010, p. 252). Rancière replies to this question by defining the film medium itself as inherently presentational. As a mechanical reproduction of the real, he says, cinema 'revokes the old mimetic order, because it resolves the question of *mimesis* at its root'. He argues:

> At the origin of the cinema, there is a 'scrupulously honest' artist that does not cheat, that cannot cheat, because all it does is record. . . . Cinematographic automatism settles the quarrel between art and technique by changing the very status of the 'real'. It does not reproduce things as they offer themselves to the gaze. It records them as the human eye cannot see them, as they come into being, in a state of waves and vibrations, before they can be qualified as intelligible objects, people, or events due to their descriptive and narrative properties. (Rancière, 2006, p. 2)

Both Rancière and Willemen are actually rewording André Bazin's foundational concept of the 'ontology of the photographic image' and, in so doing, reviving the question of realism. In Bazin's famous definition, photography differs from other art forms in that the object is directly imprinted on the film emulsion without the mediation of the human being, as in the case of a death mask or the Holy Shroud. In his words, it is 'a mechanical reproduction in the making of which man plays no part' (Bazin, 1967, p. 14). Peter Wollen, in his influential book of the late 1960s, *Signs and Meaning in the Cinema,* translated Bazin's ontology into 'indexicality', a term derived from Peirce's semiotic theory, according to which the index is an existential bond between sign and referent (Wollen, 1998, p. 86). 'Ontology' and 'indexicality' have recently returned to the centre of the debate on the moving image, as they seem under threat of disappearance (see Nagib and

Mello, 2009). The reason is the introduction of digital technology, which allows for the creation of images without any referent in the outside world, as Miriam Hansen pointed out in her assessment of Kracauer's theory of redemptive realism (Hansen, 1997, p. vii ff.). Indeed, digital media do not work on the basis of photographic impression, but of pixels, that is, encoded 'picture elements' ('pixels') arranged on a grid for computer processing. As Rodowick explains:

> Because the digital arts are without substance and therefore not easily identified as objects, no medium-specific ontology can fix them in place. The digital arts render all expressions as identical since they are all ultimately reducible to the same computational notation. . . . Digital media are . . . simulations. (Rodowick, 2007, p. 10)

Rodowick goes on to say that 'what remains absent from the process of digital representation is what thinkers like André Bazin or Roland Barthes held fundamental to the photographic image: its causal force as a literal spatial and temporal molding' (Rodowick, 2007, p. 11). This, however, has not prevented filmmakers across the world from resorting to the digital for realistic ends, and once again here Bazin gains the upper hand for predicting that all technical innovations in the audiovisual media would ultimately benefit realism. Indeed, the digital has often enabled the shooting of films on locations and among populations which would otherwise be inaccessible to audiovisual reproduction, as eloquently illustrated by the Inuit film *Atanarjuat, the Fast Runner* (Zacharias Kunuk, 2001), analysed in Chapter 1.

This demonstrates that the digital can be applied to *resist,* as much as to elicit simulation, leaving it up to filmmakers to decide whether to privilege presentation or representation. And it revives the debate around realism and simulation embraced, for example, by Kracauer (1997, pp. 30ff.) which harks back to the very origins of film history and the opposition between Lumière's 'documentaries' and Méliès' 'fantasy films'. Resistance to simulation was also at the core of Bazin's preoccupations, when he championed the sequence shot and the depth of field as techniques that preserved the integrity of phenomenological time and space, as opposed to the artifice of expressionist cinema and emotional manipulation as yielded by Eisenstein's montage cinema. Stroheim, Murnau, Flaherty, Renoir and Welles were some of his heroes, with their preference for such techniques (Bazin, 1967, pp. 23ff.). By the same token, Bazin favoured presentational films such as Clouzot's *The Mystery of Picasso* (*Le Mystère Picasso,* 1956), which is exclusively constructed with 'the great painter in action' and consequently does not 'explain' Picasso, but 'shows' him (1997, p. 211).

My own view of realism often steers away from Bazin's rules and is not at all intended to privilege one mode of filmmaking over another: if I take issue with representational readings of films, I find representational films themselves as worthy an object of study as any other films. However, the hypothesis of this book also defines itself on the basis of cases in which simulation is averted, even if only to the benefit of the realism of the medium itself, including elements of Eisenstein's heritage as seen in films such as Glauber Rocha's *Land in Trance* (*Terra em transe,* 1967) and Mikhail Kalatozov's *I Am Cuba* (*Soy Cuba/Ya Kuba,* 1964), analysed in Chapter 3. Special emphasis is placed on examples picked from world new waves, such as the Japanese New Wave (Chapter 5), the Neuer deutscher Film (Chapter 2), the Brazilian Cinema Novo (Chapters 1 and 3) and, of course, the Nouvelle Vague (Chapter 1), including indigenous cinemas, such as those from the Sahel and the Arctic (Chapter 1), and other recent movements such as the New Brazilian Cinema (Chapter 4). But I also make room for some in-between loners, such as the couple Kazuo Hara and Sachiko Kobayashi (Chapter 6) and João César Monteiro (Chapter 7), who, although only marginally connected to new cinema movements, make waves in their own right.

In his book about realism in British Cinema, John Hill, quoting Raymond Williams, says that 'it is usually a revolt against previous conventions which characterizes a break towards realism in the arts' (Hill, 1986, p. 59). This is certainly the first reason for my electing new waves and new cinemas as a privileged field of research in this book. But there is a second, more important one, which is the presentational aspect of them. Indeed my keenest interest leans toward filmmakers who use the film medium as a means to produce, as well as reproduce reality. Theirs is an eminently physical, therefore expositional and exhibitionist cinema, which rejects a priori truths in order to make room for risk, chance, the historical contingent and the unpredictable real, regardless of whether they are popular or art, fiction or documentary, narrative or avant-garde films.

Presentational Ethics

My take on physical cinema, coupled with my questioning of the critic's detached objectivity and superior knowledge of the real, echoes in many ways the reactions against Cartesian traditions of body-mind dualism which have proliferated in film studies since the psychoanalytic turn of the 1970s. From the late 1980s, cognitivists such as Noël Carroll (1988) started to react against the Brecht-inspired opposition between illusionistic absorption and critical spectatorship inherent in psychoanalytic approaches to cinema. Apropos of Brecht and Brechtianism, Murray Smith dismissed 'the commonplace, with very ancient roots in Western culture, concerning the purportedly antagonistic relationship between reason and emotion' and 'the idea that undergoing empathy deadens our rational faculties' (Smith, 1996, p. 132). In the early 1990s, Deleuze's emphasis on sensory-motor modes of communication inspired critics such as Steven Shaviro to add the body to this conundrum, with a view to reinstating pleasure within spectatorial experience (Shaviro, 2006, pp. 12–15). This was followed by the celebration of the 'embodied spectator' in the 2000s, as most notably represented by Vivian Sobchack. Drawing on Merleau-Ponty's phenomenology, Sobchack proposed 'embodiment' as 'a radically material condition of human being that necessarily entails both the body and consciousness, objectivity and subjectivity, in an *irreducible ensemble*' (2004, p. 4). Along the same lines, Marks put forward the concept of 'haptic criticism' as a kind of physical fusion between film and viewer (2002, pp. xiii–xv). Even recent readings of Bazin, such as Philip Rosen's, highlight an intentionality within his phenomenology through which subjectivities behind the camera and in front of the screen are united through the 'obsession with realism' (Rosen, 2003, p. 43).

Efforts to break the boundaries between spectacle and spectatorship reached such heights, that Rancière ironically observed, with regard to the 'emancipated spectator':

> We do not have to transform spectators into actors, and ignoramuses into scholars. We have to recognize the knowledge at work in the ignoramus and the activity peculiar to the spectator. Every spectator is already an actor in her story; every actor, every man of action is the spectator of the same story. (Rancière, 2009, p. 17)

Rancière rightly questions whether it is not precisely the desire to abolish the distance that creates it: 'What makes it possible to pronounce the spectator seated in her place inactive, if not the previously posited radical opposition between the active and the passive?' (2009, p. 12). In order to move beyond spectatorship discussions which endlessly rehearse the active-passive binary, I propose to turn the focus onto the ways in which presentational cinema is indissolubly attached to realist modes of production and address, an aspect which in my view still requires further theorizing.

My proposal is to define realist modes of production and address, typical of new waves and new cinemas, as an 'ethics'. By this, I am certainly not referring to an 'ethics of representation', and even less to 'ethical' or 'unethical' films, which find in the passive spectators their 'victims' and in the critic, their 'judge'. It is also far from my intention to adhere to any Kantian ethics, which neatly separates empirical desires from the demands of morality and conditions right action to the a priori motive of duty. Indeed the films and filmmakers of my choice put forward a programme based on a unifying principle, through which they become at once the subject and object of their films, and, in so doing, condition morality and right action to the contingent real. Let me explain this by resorting to a much quoted phrase in film criticism, 'The tracking shot is a question of morals' (*Le travelling est une question de morale*), often attributed to Godard, but originally employed by Luc Moullet in a slightly different variant, 'Morality is a question of tracking shots' ('*La morale est affaire de travellings*', 1959, p. 14, see Chapter 1). The immediate attraction of this formulation resides in the way it attaches ethical value to the index as elicited by the continuous, uninterrupted camera movement across objective reality. Along the same lines, I would say that to choose reality instead of simulation is a moral question, but one which concerns casts and crews alone in their drive to merge with the phenomenological real, and this is why the stress on modes of production and address is here of the essence.

Needless to say, this view goes against the grain of the recent turn to ethics, which Rancière translates as 'an increasing tendency to submit politics and art to moral judgements about the validity of their principles and the consequences of their practices' (2009, p. 109). Such a tendency has been fully embraced by Cultural Studies (Zylinska, 2005), drawing mainly on Emmanuel Lévinas's defence of, and respect for, what he calls 'the infinite alterity of the other', but also on Lévinas's followers, notably Derrida, Irigaray and Spivak. Although belatedly, film studies followed this lead, producing a number of studies, such as Downing and Saxton's excellent book *Film and Ethics*, which makes clear from the outset that such an ethical turn 'is the encounter and the act of interrogating the self about its relationship to the other' (2010, p. 1). Spectatorial alterity also lies at the core of phenomenological approaches to cinematic ethics, such as Stadler's, who searches for 'ethical relevance' in the spectator's response to film narratives (2008, p. 3).

As far as ethics is concerned, however, I tend to agree with Lévinas's fiercest critic, Alain Badiou, for whom the idea of absolute alterity is nothing but 'the ethical name of God' (Badiou, 2002, p. 22), and amounts in the end to yet another form of dual thought. Following Badiou's terminology, what I call ethics about the films of my choice is their commitment to the truth of the unpredictable event. A basic faithfulness to the profilmic phenomenon, combined with the inherent honesty of the film medium, was indeed the main requirement of Bazin's realism, one which emerged from the experience of the disastrous consequences of Nazi-fascist lies. This was also Brecht's main concern, when he championed the unmasking of representational artifice as the only possible realist method. One could argue that Badiou's outright rejection of a universal 'other' and a priori truths disqualifies it as an ethical project. Badiou's ethics is however not averse to universals, and indeed recognizes the universality produced by a 'truth-procedure' (Hallward, 2002, p. xxvi), even though, according to him, 'there can be no ethics in general, but only an ethic of singular truths, and thus an ethic relative to a particular situation' (2002, p. lvi). Badiou's 'regime of truths' is governed by the notion of 'event': 'to be faithful to an event', he says, 'is to move within the situation that this event has supplemented, by *thinking* . . . the situation "according to" the event' (2002, p. 41).

Such notions of 'event' and 'situation' chime with my approach in many respects. In the first place, they acknowledge the precedence of presentation over representation in that the latter can only occur once all multiple singularities are presented at the same time within the situation (Badiou, 2006, p. 174), constituting a 'state' in the Marxist sense as well as in the common sense of 'status quo' (Hallward, 2002, p. ix). For its representational character, the situation is thus endowed with a normative element which does not hold any truths in itself. 'A truth', says Badiou, 'is solely constituted by rupturing with the order which supports it, never as an effect of that order', that is to say, by the emergence of the unpredictable event (2006, p. xii). The ethical subject, in its turn, is characterized by 'an active fidelity to the event of truth' (p. xiii). It thus bears an intentionality regulated by the uncertain and the unexpected, which creates the need for a choice, 'the same choice that divides . . . the courage of truths from nihilism' (Badiou, 2002, p. 35). The militant, utopian tone of such a statement reverberates through all the films in focus here. Beyond any particular political orientation they may embrace, they are all actively committed to the truth of the profilmic event. Oshima is a privileged example of someone who, in his New Wave days, rejected all repressive authority in the name of an 'active subjectivity' (*shutai*) inspired by Sartrean notions of responsibility, freedom of choice and bad faith relative to processes of victimization (see Chapters 5 and 6), all of which are akin to Badiou's thought. Above all, a fidelity to the contingent character of the 'event of truth', that is, to realism, is discernable across all films examined here, making them aesthetically and ethically comparable.

This book is thus structured on the basis of a set of prominent aesthetic features derived from a realist ethics which binds world films together across history and geography at their most creative peaks. Chapter 1, in Part I. Physical Cinema, focuses on the trope of the cinematic runner cutting across four typical new-cinema films: *Atanarjuat, the Fast Runner*, the first Inuit feature film; *Yaaba* (Idrissa Ouédraogo, 1989), a landmark in Sahel filmmaking; *God and the Devil in the Land of the Sun* (*Deus e o diabo na terra do sol*, Glauber Rocha, 1964), Brazil's Cinema Novo milestone; and *The 400 Blows* (*Les Quatre cents coups*, François Truffaut, 1959), the first Nouvelle Vague feature film. Stemming from entirely disparate historical moments, cultures and locations, these films arrive at a surprisingly similar presentational solution for key moments in the plot which elude verbal discourse, namely, the protagonists' protracted act of running on foot. Performed in reality, in vast wintry landscapes, burning deserts or Arctic sea ice, these races invariably take the upper hand over the diegesis and impose their own narrative, one related to the characters' recognizing, experiencing, demarcating and taking possession of a territory, and, in so doing, defining a people and its culture. Fictional, at times mythic as all these characters are, their act of running on foot gives material life to the virtual medium of film. At the same time, cast and crew testify to their total commitment to a moment of truth, their physical engagement with the profilmic event and their fidelity to what Rancière calls the 'honesty of the medium', in short, their ethics of realism.

Still under the theme of Physical Cinema, the focus shifts, in Chapter 2, to the work of Werner Herzog. In stark contrast to the films analysed in the previous chapter, which aim at producing a sense of continuity and belonging, Herzog's physical, or in his words 'athletic', approach to cinema seems to rely on an irretrievable loss of identity, a rupture between the human element and its environment through which the materiality of the former comes to the fore. Reality thus becomes synonymous with difference, a fact embodied by the legions of extraordinary beings who populate his entire oeuvre. In this chapter, I investigate the nature and validity of Herzog's claims to difference, the kind of realism deriving from his physical filmmaking and the ethics associated with both his presentational and representational modes of address. Starting from the director's body itself, omnipresent in his work in visual and/or aural form, I proceed to examine the physicality in Herzog's films in the light of their historical and aesthetic connections with New Wave movements, in particular the New German Cinema, the Nouvelle Vague and the Brazilian Cinema Novo.

Part II of the book is devoted to the examination of what I call The Reality of the Medium, encompassing filmic devices normally associated with 'anti-realism'. Chapter 3 focuses on Glauber Rocha's *Land in Trance* and Mikail Kalatozov's *I Am Cuba,* both of which address the theme of revolution by resorting to similar narrative techniques, including allegory, poetic language, synecdoche and personification. In my analysis, I dissociate realism from narrative mimesis, so as to describe the ways in which, in these films, the realist drive is transferred from the referent to the sign, that is, from the objective world to the medium itself, generating a 'realism of the medium'. I argue that these films testify to the survival of an ethics of the real, typical of new cinemas, even when a world in transformation eludes realistic representation.

Part II proceeds with the analysis, in Chapter 4, of *Delicate Crime* (*Crime delicado,* 2006). This film, a late output of the so-called Brazilian Film Revival initiated in the mid-1990s, offers fertile ground for the reframing of film theory in the 'the post-theory' era, as it undertakes a meticulous application and concomitant challenging of all the main principles defended by cinema's grand theory in the 1970s and 1980s. While subscribing through form and content to grand theory's pièce de résistance, the demise of narrative realism, it celebrates reality as captured through the cracks of representation. Disability and artistic creation seem to be complementary terms in a presentational regime in which the gaze construction veers toward exhibitionism rather than voyeurism, while the narrative exposes its own artifice by focusing on art (theatre and painting) at its making.

Part III, The Ethics of Desire, contains only one chapter entirely devoted to the analysis of *The Realm of the Senses* (*Ai no koriida,* Nagisa Oshima, 1976). The aim is to derive an unequivocal ethical stance from Oshima's choice to film live sex, which culminates in (simulated) death, an ethic that secures continuity between a filmmaker's innermost desires and the resulting film. The election of *The Realm of the*

Senses for the demonstration of this ethic is based on the fact that, as well as encapsulating a filmmaker and his team's commitment to truth, it brings to full fruition an ideal of a whole generation of filmmakers, as well as that of some of their predecessors, by exploring to their ultimate consequences cinema's indexical and presentational properties. In the same year of 1976, when Laura Mulvey published her famous article against spectatorial pleasure as elicited by American cinema, *The Realm of the Senses* proposed to radically incite visual as well as carnal pleasures, stretching to the limits the exhibitionist element Gunning observes in early erotic films. Indeed, in the film, scopophilia is encouraged to the point of pushing the passive voyeur, within and outside the fable, into actively and physically joining the erotic play. In many of his films, but particularly in this one, Oshima opened up the doors of Japan's intimacy in a clearly exhibitionistic show, making room for chance and the contingent, while at the same time attesting to the survival of an eroticism harking back to traditional arts, such as *shunga* (erotic prints) and kabuki theatre.

Part IV is devoted to what I call The Production of Reality in the cinema. I start by looking, in Chapter 6, at Kazuo Hara and Sachiko Kobayashi's films *Goodbye CP* (*Sayonara CP,* 1972), *Extreme Private Eros: Love Song 1974* (*Gokushiteki erosu: renka 1974,* 1974), *The Emperor's Naked Army Marches On* (*Yuki yukite shingun,* 1987) and *A Dedicated Life* (*Zenshin shosetsuka,* 1994). All these films have commonly been defined as 'documentaries' on the basis of their use of real characters and locations. However, they have extended the frontiers of the genre to hitherto unknown realms, by provoking the political and personal events in focus within the objective world, which at times include risks to the lives of cast and crew. In my view, these films testify to an auteurist realist project based on physicality pushed to the 'extreme' – as expressed in the title of the duo's second feature – as a means to go beyond realism as style and turn the act of filmmaking into producing, as well as reproducing, reality.

Still under the theme of The Production of Reality, the book closes by focusing, in Chapter 7, on the Portuguese director João César Monteiro, in particular on his so-called autobiographical films, including the João de Deus (or John of God) trilogy – *Recollections of the Yellow House* (*Recordações da casa amarela,* 1989), *God's Comedy* (*A comédia de Deus,* 1995) and *The Spousals of God* (*As bodas de Deus,* 1998) – and two self-starred films, *The Hips of J.W.* (*Le Bassin de J.W,* 1997) and *Come and Go* (*Vai e vem,* 2003), chosen for their ability to summarize most of the questions raised in the previous chapters. Like the Japanese duo examined in Chapter 6, Monteiro not only enacts but provokes the film events as much as possible in the objective world, enabling the examination of the term 'ethics' with reference to physical cinema, the autobiographical genre, auteur prerogatives and both phenomenological and medium realisms, thus defining its applicability within and beyond the realm of representation.

As the detailed analyses will hopefully demonstrate, in all the cases examined in this book, making films is making history, entailing change in the real life of casts and crews, and therefore producing an ethical reality.

Part I

Physical Cinema

Chapter 1

THE END OF THE OTHER

If truths exist, they are certainly indifferent to differences.
Alain Badiou

Running and cinema intersect at key moments in film history. At the birth of the Nouvelle Vague, at the height of Cinema Novo, in the first Inuit feature film, at the emergence of the Sahel cinema and other turning points cinematic runners reappear, played by real racing actors, experiencing with their own bodies and conquering hostile, harsh, even extreme environments. They are typical new cinema heroes, literally breaking new ground with their own feet and physical endurance whose limits they strive to transcend. The reason for their race varies in each case, they are legendary saviours, revolutionary rebels or ordinary fugitives. In all cases, however, their protracted act of running takes the upper hand over the diegesis and imposes its own narrative, one related to recognizing, experiencing, demarcating and taking possession of a territory, and, in so doing, defining a people and its culture. Fictional, at times mythic, as they all are, their run, enacted in reality, gives material life to the virtual medium of film and testifies to an ethics of realism.

In this chapter, I will look at four films in which races on foot, enacted in reality, give evidence of an actor's physical engagement with the cinematic event and define a film's foundational status. Spreading across four different continents and nearly half a century of film history, these examples, though a restricted sample of their kind, offer abundant elements for overarching conclusions. They are: *Atanarjuat, the Fast Runner* (Zacharias Kunuk, 2001), the first Inuit feature film; *Yaaba* (Idrissa Ouédraogo, 1989), the film that put the Mossi people of the Sahel on the world cinema map; *Black God, White Devil,* Brazil's Cinema Novo milestone, to which I will be referring through the literal translation of its original Portuguese title, *God and the Devil in the Land of the Sun* (*Deus e o diabo na terra do sol,* Glauber Rocha, 1964);[1] and *The 400 Blows* (*Les Quatre cents coups,* François Truffaut, 1959), the first Nouvelle Vague feature film. I will look at the runner on foot in these films as a cinematic trope which reveals a commitment to truth on the part of both crews and casts, telling us what peoples and cinemas across the globe have in common and how this commonality can generate original aesthetics in different places and times. Given their status as inaugural works of New Wave or New Cinema movements, they provide evidence to the cyclical reemergence of physical realism at world cinema's most creative peaks. More importantly, by resorting to the same trope, despite their stemming from the most different cultural, historical and geographical backgrounds, they offer physical belonging as an antidote to discourses of otherness, as the analysis below will hopefully demonstrate.

The celebration of god-like, mythical runners reaches historical heights with *Atanarjuat, the Fast Runner,* a film widely held as the founder of a new cinematic aesthetics springing directly from the Inuit people, their environment and culture. In the film's climactic scene, the protagonist Atanarjuat – meaning 'the fast runner', in Inuktitut – dashes for his life from treacherous rivals who have already killed his brother Aamarjuaq, 'the strong one'[2] (Fig. 1.1).

He suddenly finds himself trapped by a wide crack in the sea ice, but overcomes the obstacle with a superhuman jump and lands safely on the other side. This magic flight defines the protagonist's transitive role, one that enables him to connect natural and supernatural worlds

FIGURE 1.1 Running on ice: Natar Ungalaaq in *Atanarjuat, the Fast Runner*

and resolve long-lasting rifts in his community upon his return, as befits the figure of the mythical hero (Campbell, 2008, p. 170; see also Said, 2002). But the beauty of this legend only comes to the fore thanks to the cinematic accomplishment of it, which climaxes with actor Natar Ungalaak running stark naked and barefoot on the glacial landscape during more than seven minutes of edited stock.

Original though it is, *Atanarjuat* is certainly not the first film to resort to such extreme physical means in order to put a people and a land on the world cinema map. More than a decade earlier *Yaaba* had similarly dazzled the world by granting audiovisual expression and bodily presence to the Mossi people of Burkina Faso. Though heroism and myth are here scaled down to an innocent moral tale, the film opens significantly with its protagonist, the young boy Bila (Noufou Ouédraogo), shooting off barefoot on the hot, red surface of the Sahel savannah in pursuit of his girlfriend Nopoko (Roukietou Barry) (Fig. 1.2).

The running scene, which is replayed at the end of the film so as to indicate the completion of a cycle, has little consequence for the diegesis, functioning rather as an ornamental framing to the story. This notwithstanding, the visual and aural power of these child racers, who cross the rough landscape with no accompanying sound other than their own footsteps until they disappear on the far horizon, proved so great that it continued to reverberate through the director's later work. Fourteen years on, the same actors, now turned adults,

FIGURE 1.2 Running in the heat: Noufou Ouédraogo and Roukietou Barry in *Yaaba*

were still running together across the semi-desert landscape, in Ouédraogo's *Anger of the Gods* (*La Colère des dieux,* 2003), as if that was all they had been doing in the intervening years. In between, however, an important change had taken place. Bila, now turned into the warrior hero Salam, is endowed with supernatural powers and becomes the vessel of 'god's wrath', as indicated in the film title.

As such, it crosses the globe back in time to meet a film by Glauber Rocha, namely his Cinema Novo landmark *God and the Devil in the Land of the Sun,* whose first script was coincidentally called *The Wrath of God* (*A Ira de Deus*).[3] More significantly, this film features another emblematic desert runner, the rebellious cowherd Manuel, in the film's famous closing scene. After freeing himself from the forces of messianic religion and devilish banditry, Manuel dashes off in a desperate race over the dry backlands – the Brazilian *sertão* – which ultimately turns into the sea (Fig. 1.3).

He thus fulfils the film's revolutionary prophecy, expressed in the formula 'the *sertão* will become the sea, and the sea *sertão*', repeated both in the diegetic dialogue and in the *cordel*-style music that accompanies his dash.[4] Metaphysics, turned into political utopia, is again here inextricable from actor Geraldo Del Rey's real physical exertion as he covers long stretches of the desert's scorched, rugged surface under the blazing sun, in extended sequence shots.

FIGURE 1.3 Running in the desert: Geraldo Del Rey in *God and the Devil in the Land of the Sun*

Figure 1.4 Running in the wintry landscape: Jean-Pierre Léaud in *The 400 Blows*

Groundbreaking though it is, Manuel's race is a citation, and mythologizing, of an earlier cinematic runner, the adolescent Antoine Doinel in François Truffaut's *The 400 Blows* (*Les Quatre cents coups,* 1959). In the unforgettable closing scene of this Nouvelle Vague milestone, Doinel, incarnated with utter realism by Jean-Pierre Léaud, runs headlong toward the sea he has never seen. Though in a much milder environment than his followers, Léaud is also subjected to the strain of running uninterruptedly for several minutes across an inhospitable, wintry landscape (Fig. 1.4). Unlike Manuel, who disappears as the *sertão* is replaced by the sea through montage, Doinel actually reaches the sea he had never seen before. After briefly stepping into the water with his feet in socks and shoes, in a fleeting encounter with nature in an otherwise entirely urban film, he immediately recoils with a puzzled look fixed in what is perhaps the most famous freeze-frame in film history.[5] Social revolution, in the former, individual liberation, in the latter, make up the banners these films hold up for their cinematic followers, by means of physical commitment to the reality of the film event. In the sections that follow, I will first outline the theoretical underpinnings of my approach, then move on to the detailed analysis of each of these four films, with a view to identifying the ethical drive that animates their attachment to physical reality.

Physical Realism

My approach to physicality in the cinema may seem, at first sight, to echo the hype about 'the body' which has dominated film (and cultural) studies in the past two decades. If this may be the case in some respects, there is also a crucial difference. As the descriptions above already indicate, my focus is on modes of production and address, whereas body theories are predominantly concerned with modes of reception and spectatorship. While my interest lies in bodily enactment, body theories aim at reviving spectatorial pleasure, which, together with 'illusionistic absorption', had been banned in the name of critical spectatorship in the psychoanalytic era of the 1970s and early 1980s. A brief retrospect will help me substantiate my own approach.

As already alluded to in the introduction to this book, rebellion against normative spectatorship theories go back to the early 1990s, when critics turned to Foucault and Deleuze, the former for his sexual politics, the latter for his emphasis on sensory modes of communication, as a means to reinstate an 'embodied' spectator. This attitude is epitomized by Steven Shaviro's 1993 groundbreaking book, *The Cinematic Body,* which proposes to liberate the spectator from the 'psychoanalytic theorist's need for control' and 'phobic rejection' of 'a threatening pleasure' (Shaviro, 2006, pp. 12–15). In the 2000s, body theories received a further boost with the turn to 'haptics' and Merleau-Ponty's phenomenology. The most notable adept of the latter is Vivian Sobchack, whose highly influential writings attempt to bridge the divide between subjective and objective experiences of cinema by means of synthetic oxymorons, such as 'cinesthetic subject', 'embodied knowledge' and 'interobjectivity'. Her approach is also reactive to psychoanalysis and its defence of critical spectatorship, a criticism she extends to 'current fetishization of "the body"', because 'most theorists still don't quite know what to do with their unruly responsive flesh and sensorium' (2004, p. 59):

> Positing cinematic vision as merely a mode of objective symbolic representation, and reductively abstracting – 'disincarnating' – the spectator's subjective and full-bodied vision to posit it only as a 'distance sense', contemporary film theory has had major difficulties in comprehending how it is possible for human bodies to be, in fact, really 'touched' and 'moved' by the movies. (Sobchack, 2004, p. 59)

The explanation of how spectators can be 'touched' by the audiovisual media is precisely the point of Laura Marks's *Touch,* in which she puts forward the concept of 'haptic criticism'. Marks defines this mode of reception as 'mimetic', in another attempt to blur the boundary between subject and object. Rather than a 'disinterested, cool-headed assessment', haptic criticism 'presses up to the object and takes its shape' and thus 'warms up our cultural tendency to take a distance'

(2002, pp. xiii–xv). Sobchack and Marks's seductive language is generating a host of followers, such as Jennifer Barker, whose recent *Tactile Eye* is an unrelenting exercise in collapsing cinematic enactment and spectatorship into a single physical experience, as this statement exemplifies: 'Film and viewer co-constitute one another in the act of touching, skin to skin' (2009, p. 68). Another self-confessed Sobchack disciple, Jane Stadler, in her well-researched book on film and ethics, *Pulling Focus,* again rejects 'abstract paradigms such as psychoanalysis, structuralism and principle-based moral codes', proposing instead to focus on 'the qualitative nature of perception' and 'the evaluative practices inherent in spectatorship' (2008, p. 3).

These claims for sensory modes of spectatorship and assessment are useful insofar as they raise awareness of the dangers of artificial body-mind dualisms still prevailing in many branches of film studies. However, in their thrust to delegitimize all purely objective criticism, they often fall back into its reverse, that is, pure subjectivism through which the films themselves are almost entirely eclipsed. Take for instance these lines by Sobchack, describing how Jane Campion's *The Piano* (1993) 'moved me deeply, stirring my bodily senses and my sense of my body' and '"sensitized" the very surfaces of my skin – as well as its own – to touch' (2004, p. 61). For all the author's intellectual sophistication, does this not sound purely impressionistic? How many spectators feel the same way, and in any case what does this say about the film itself?

On the other hand, to refer to physicality as mode of production and address may sound like a conservative turn to foundational realist theories and vocabulary, such as Kracauer's, which states that cinema, as a photographic medium, is 'uniquely equipped to record and reveal physical reality' (1997, p. 28). Physical realism chimes even more obviously with Bazin's ontology, which determines that film, more than any other plastic arts, is destined to realism from birth as it enables a transfer of 'the reality from the thing to its reproduction' (1967, p. 14). The concept of index, or the material bond between sign and referent which translates Bazin's ontology into semiotic terms, will indeed be recurrent in this book. However, as much as Kracauer's redemptive realism and Bazin's ontology, indexicality relates to processes of recording, leaving open the ways in which the profilmic event is produced and dealt with by crew and cast. Here is where I believe there is still room for innovative theorizing, building precisely on such foundational realist theories, and Bazin in particular.

This does not mean, of course, to go back to artificial dualisms, but simply to privilege general interest over singular subjective experiences.

In a way, this study participates in what Elsaesser has called an 'ontological turn mark two', that is, an ontology which emerges from a 'post-epistemological' time and 'breaks with the Cartesian subject-object split, abandoning or redefining notions of subjectivity, consciousness, identity in the way these have hitherto been used and understood' (Elsaesser, 2009, p. 7). It continues, nevertheless, to be an ontology insofar as it cannot dispense with Bazin and recent scholarship on him. In an insightful essay on Bazin's phenomenology, Philip Rosen, for example, concedes that, for its emphasis on the primacy of the objective world over the subject, Bazin's realist theory has been 'treated as yet another activation of the classical subject-object dialectic familiar from the history of continental philosophy' (2003, p. 43). He however rejects this criticism by arguing that realism, for Bazin, is of value only insofar as it makes sense to a 'phenomenological cinematic subject': 'It is . . . the activity and desire of the subject – "our *obsession* with realism" – that makes indexicality the crucial aspect of the image for Bazin' (p. 49). Such an emphasis on the observing subject's intentionality allows us to draw a link between subjectivities at the opposite ends of the film spectrum, one at its production, the other at its reception, both unified by the desire for realism, which is embodied in the film itself: this, I believe, would set the critic free to passionately write about his or her object, without the need to describe the subjective physical symptoms of his or her passion.

The uses of Bazin's phenomenological realism seem indeed inexhaustible for both critics and practitioners, and it is not a coincidence that the filmmakers in focus here have made ample use, consciously or otherwise, of the Bazinian anti-montage formula of the long shot (deep focus) and the long take (sequence shot), aimed at preserving the spatiotemporal integrity of the film event. The dashes of both Doinel and Manuel were shot with cameras mounted on moving vehicles, in extended sequence shots that leave no doubts about the actors' bodily engagement and physical strain. Bila and Nopoko's race was shot in one extreme long shot with an Ozu-style static camera, equally aimed at preserving time and space ratio. *Atanarjuat* is a more complex case, as it was filmed with a digital camera allowing for extensive on-site and postproduction manipulation. The seven-minute footage of Atanarjuat's run is heavily edited and relies as much on long shots (both static and dynamic) as on close-ups of his face and feet. Its categorization as 'realist' thus necessitates further elaboration.

Querying the applicability of Bazin to *Atanarjuat*, White makes an interesting point: 'Almost every review of the film mentions this sequence [of the race], and it is not hard to see why. Although it is not edited with particularly long takes, the sequence does last for several minutes, and a sense of duration is pronounced' (White, 2005, p. 59). This sense of duration is however one, at least in principle, conveyed by trick – that is, montage – and would not respond to Bazin's realist demand of allegiance to phenomenological time and space. This notwithstanding, Kunuk himself remarks that digital technology was resorted to precisely for the sake of a realism which would be unattainable on celluloid, thereby justifying the use of close-ups, as opposed to depth of field:

> This digital technology is always there. You shoot it and then you watch it. You improve it right on the set. That [camerawork] is Norman Cohn's style. That's how he shoots, and it's better – it looks more real. When we have white-out – when the snow is white, the sky is white – that's going to be visually too 'hot', so you have to get close, and Norman knows all about that. (Chun, 2002, p. 21)

What is here at stake is not only the fact that the image can be 'improved' (manipulated) on the spot and in postproduction, but that it could not possibly have been made on that site and in those conditions (i.e., 'realistically') were it not for digital technology. There is, of course, a whole discussion on whether digital imaging could have any indexical value, given that it does not work on the basis of photographic impression, but of pixels for computer processing (Rodowick, 2007, pp. 10–11). This, however, has never prevented filmmakers across the world from resorting to the digital for realistic ends, also because, as Elsaesser notes, contemporary world cinema 'does not mourn the so-called loss of indexicality of the photographic image' (2009, p. 7), an element it seems to live without even when striving for realism. It is perhaps also worth remembering that Bazin himself had left a margin for realistic devices beyond the long-take-long-shot combination and always welcomed technical improvements which 'permit the conquest of the properties of the real' (Bazin, 2005, p. 30).

Although no one would doubt the authenticity of the locations and populations in all the four films in focus here, the fact remains that in *Atanarjuat* the digital brings into question the extent to which the scenes were enacted in reality. This is perhaps the reason why both the photographer Norman Cohn and the director Kunuk never miss an opportunity to confirm that they were indeed real. Making-of insets were used as background to the final credits in the film itself to show how the shooting of the climactic race was carried out with a camera mounted on an oversize sledge, pulled and pushed by crew members

Figure 1.5

Figures 1.5–1.6 *Atanarjuat,* final credits: 'making-of' insets of the naked run prove its authenticity

on foot on an ice surface where no motor vehicles would have had access, while Ungalaaq enacts his naked run. Real enactment, as seen in these insets, comes out as a moral stance for both crew and cast, which unites them under the same realist banner (Figs. 1.5 and 1.6). This is something which exudes from the film as a whole, but in particular from those nearly impossible tracking shots produced in the icy landscape.

Privileged for its ability to preserve spatiotemporal continuity, in a complementary manner to the long take and the long shot, the tracking shot (or the *travelling* as the French call it) is a common companion of cinematic runners, as they, in the protagonist roles, drag the camera through the territory of their actions. The tracking shot has been associated with realism since *Cahiers* critic Luc Moullet, at the dawn of the Nouvelle Vague, coined the famous phrase 'Morality is a question of tracking shots' ('*La morale est affaire de travellings*', 1959, p. 14), incessantly quoted thereafter and often attributed to Godard in one of its several variants, '*Le travelling est une question de morale*'. By this formula, first used with relation to the films of Samuel Fuller, Moullet intended to highlight a filmmaker's commitment to the objective world with all its unpredictable ambiguities, even if this compromised coherent storytelling:

> The spectacle of the physical world, the spectacle of the earth is his [Fuller's] best terrain of inspiration, and if he is attached to the human being, it is only insofar as this human being is attached to the earth. (Moullet, 1959, p. 15)

This link between a character/actor and a particular land is indeed what seems to supply Atanarjuat's race with proto-indexical value, as highlighted by the tracking shots.

In fact physicality, in all four films in focus here, is present at all levels, including the fictional plot. As befits the construction of the classical hero, on the level of the fable, all four protagonists have to endure injustice and general misunderstanding in order to achieve their honourable aims, including all sorts of physical trials. Atanarjuat has to win a punching-heads competition, before he is given the hand of Atuat, who had been initially promised to his rival, Uqi (Fig. 1.7). Bila is forced by his father, who controls him with a stick, to do squatting exercises with his arms crossed over his chest and hands pulling his own ears, as a punishment for his generosity towards the ostracized old woman Yaaba (Fig. 1.8). Doinel, in his turn, is submitted, in front of different audiences, to violent slaps in the face for negligible misdemeanours, and his life is marked throughout by physical discomfort, caused by cold, dirt and hunger (Fig. 1.9). Not to mention Manuel's trajectory of physical penances as a follower of the messianic leader Sebastião. All these acts, played out for the sake of fictional coherence, draw the viewer's attention to an actor's bodily existence as it slowly migrates from fiction to fact. This process can be observed in several passages akin to the running scenes, such as Manuel's climb of the hundreds of steps of Monte Santo on his knees, carrying a giant boulder on his head (Fig. 1.10). The blood that trickles down his head at

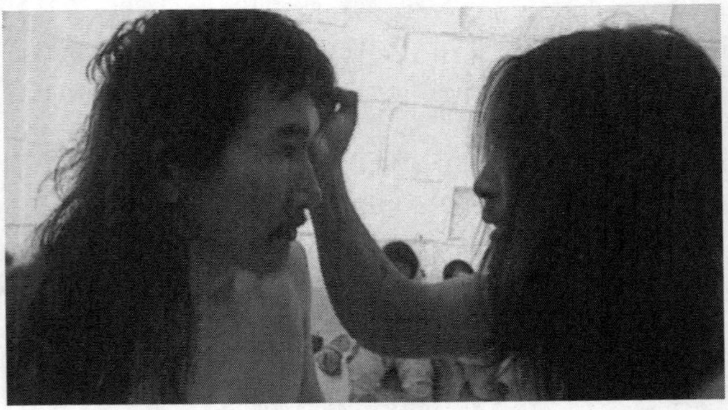

FIGURE 1.7 The punching-head competition: physical endurance in *Atanarjuat*

FIGURE 1.8 Physical punishment in *Yaaba*

the end of this feat looks, and is, real, a fact confirmed by testimonials of crew and cast (Magalhães and Bastos, n/d). Another case is Atanarjuat's final crash at the end of his superhuman race, when the actor Ungalaaq is photographed lying flat on the real ice, his naked body shaken by violent shivers as his character approaches death.

Such bodily engagement with fictional acts indicates a commitment on the part of the cast. The nature of this commitment cannot be simply described as a Stanislavskian naturalistic enactment through which an actor 'lives' the part as if in complete symbiosis with a character. Both Stanislavski's theatrical realism and its flipside, Brecht's anti-illusionism, were very much the subject of discussion at the time of *God and the Devil,* and Othon Bastos, in the role of the outlaw Corisco,

FIGURE 1.9 Physical punishment in *The 400 Blows*

FIGURE 1.10 Manuel's physical penances in *God and the Devil in the Land of the Sun*

shows extraordinary skills in resorting to and alternating both styles in his performance. However, naturalistic performance, in theatre, cannot but be restricted to psychological effect due to the spatial limits of the stage on which actions, objects and circumstances are forcibly suggested, rather than realized. As Stanislavski puts it:

> Of significance to us is: the reality of the inner life of a human spirit in a part and a belief in that reality. We are not concerned with the actual naturalistic existence of what surrounds us on the stage, the reality of the material world. (2003, p. 141)

The opposite happens in the cinematic cases under scrutiny here. In them, bodily commitment on the part of both crews and casts starts precisely with the belief in the reality of the material world, which goes in hand with a belief in cinema's unlimited power to convey this reality. Moved by this belief, crews and casts feel not only enabled, but morally obliged to express the truth, not any truth, but the truth about the land and the people the film is focusing on through a fictional plot. Rather than symbiosis with fictional characters, the actors' physical engagement with performance is thus as much an engagement with a real context as it is with a film about it. As a film event, physical acting relates to contingency, rather than narrative mimesis, with presentation of reality as it happens, rather than representation, and this is where commitment translates into an ethics.

The Missing Other

With their focus on former colonized peoples and, in one case, a marginalized character, the films in focus here would lend themselves easily to analyses of 'otherness'. Indeed, for some, physical filmmaking is tantamount to the experience of 'difference', as Marks puts it:

> What the work of art, the writing, and the world in which they exist have in common is not as valuable as the *differences* among them are. The world would cease to exist if this common language were found. (Marks, 2002, p. x)

She goes on to say that 'a look that acknowledges both the physicality and the unknowability of the other is an ethical look' (2002, p. xviii). This statement, harking back to Lévinasian ethics, fails, however, to explain how otherness would survive within a scheme of 'haptic criticism' in which the critic's look 'takes the shape' of its object. My ethical hypothesis, in fact, starts from an opposite premise, that of the extraordinary coincidence of tropes adopted across the most distant parts of the globe when it comes to foundational films and film movements. In his critique of Lévinas's ethics of the 'Altogether-Other', Badiou states that, in 'a system of thought that is both a-religious and genuinely contemporary with the truths of our time,' the real question is that of 'recognizing the Same'. He says:

> There is no God. Which also means: the One is not. The multiple 'without-one' – every multiple being in its turn nothing other than a multiple of multiples – is the law of being. The only stopping point is the void. . . . Infinite alterity is quite simply *what there is*. Any experience at all is the infinite deployment of infinite

> differences. Even the apparently reflexive experience of myself is by no means the intuition of a unity but a labyrinth of differentiations, and Rimbaud was certainly not wrong when he said: 'I am another.' There are as many differences, say, between a Chinese peasant and a young Norwegian professional as between myself and anybody at all, including myself. As many, but also, then, *neither more nor less.* (2002, p. 25)

This is the statement made by all the films in focus here, almost in the manner of a manifesto – and here again the importance of looking at films as mode of address, rather than 'haptic' (but othering) mode of reception, comes to the fore. In them, difference is simply what there is, and therefore 'otherness' in relation to a 'self' or 'same' makes no sense. The characters are anything but victims of alien forces. If there are any victims and villains, they all circulate within the unified cosmos in which fable and the real are conflated.

The world of *Atanarjuat* is entirely Inuit. In the length and breadth of the Arctic territory covered by him and the other nomadic characters in the film, there are not the remotest sign of peoples or any languages other than Inuktitut, not to mention representatives of former colonizers. Exactly the same happens in *Yaaba,* in which there are no traces of foreign presence in the vast Sahel landscape. The colonial look in particular is conspicuously absent. Even when the ostracized old woman of the title (*yaaba* meaning 'grandmother') crosses the large river in search of medicine for the gravely ill Nopoko, it is still the traditional Mossi world she encounters on the other bank, no cars, electricity poles, radios, TVs, in short, no traces of what is normally understood as 'Western civilization'. Rocha's *God and the Devil,* related as it is to Third Cinema and postcolonial movements, also eschews ideas of otherness, not least by following to the letter the then fashionable Gramscian idea of the organic intellectual, based on the equivalence of *homo faber* and *homo sapiens.* Accordingly, the film provides a sealed-off cosmos of a universal *sertão,* which 'has a dignity and a wholeness that depends on isolation and scarcity', as observed by Ismail Xavier (2000, p. 114). The word 'dignity' is fitting here, as the aim of preserving a cosmic integrity is precisely to avoid, for both the film and its makers, the degrading condition of victim. As for *The 400 Blows,* if the hero Doinel carries the mark of 'difference', this is typical of the romantic hero and thus opposed to postcolonial notions of subaltern difference, and in any case enacted in a corner of the globe customarily identified with that of the colonizer.

This is not to say that the same directors did not engage with representations of colonial and postcolonial difference in various stages of their careers, with Ouédraogo focusing on African diasporas in

France (*The Heart's Cry/Le Cri du coeur*, 1994); Rocha directly confronting the European white power in his African film, *Der Leone Has Sept Cabeças* (1970); and Kunuk including European explorers in his second Inuit feature-length film (*The Journals of Knud Rasmussen*, 2006). Exceptional though these films also are, they do not (and are not intended to) have the same foundational value as the ones this chapter is about. 'Our culture has never *really* been exposed from the inside', Kunuk has said (Chun, 2002, p. 6), and indeed *Atanarjuat* holds the primacy of the insider's point of view with relation to the Inuit culture, despite such honourable predecessors as Robert Flaherty's *Nanook of the North* (1922). Varga makes a fitting remark in this respect: 'The cinematic transformation of the legend makes use of southern-based systems of representation to reclaim culture as distinct from the experience of colonisation through which Inuit are produced as victims' (2006, p. 233). In other words, the film's major contribution relies precisely on the absence of the other. The Sahel landscape, its Mossi people and Moré language have been similarly established by *Yaaba*, in a way that finds no precedents; the case is the same with Rocha's *sertão* (backlands), its *cangaceiros* (outlaws) and messianic leaders, which, in a time of consolidation of national cinemas, became the real image of Brazil.

Atanarjuat, The Fast Runner

All films are multilayered by nature, thanks to the complexity of different media they involve, but *Atanarjuat* is outspokenly so. In order to assess how physical realism interacts with myth, fiction and ethnographic research, as well as with advanced digital technologies and experimental art forms in this film, the critic must undertake a veritable work of archaeological excavation so as to penetrate its condensed flesh.

The film, which was to become *Atanarjuat, the Fast Runner*, the worldwide acclaimed first Inuit feature-length fiction film, took six years to be completed, from 1995, when production commenced, to 2001, when it was first screened at the Cannes Film Festival, receiving the Caméra d'or award and going on to win six Genie Awards (Canadian Oscars), including Best Picture, among many other prizes. This protracted period of planning and preparation resulted in an exceedingly lengthy original of five and a half hours, which had to be reduced to 172 minutes (still way beyond the 100 minutes average of a feature film), and this is certainly among the factors contributing to the compactness of the ready product. But there are other, more important ones.

In fact, the film's origins could be traced much further back, in 1989, when Isuma Productions was founded, or even earlier, in 1985, when the New York video artist Norman Cohn first visited Igloolik to meet Zacharias Kunuk and Paul Apak Angilirk for possible collaboration. With them, Cohn formed the trio who would later be responsible, respectively, for the cinematography, direction and scriptwriting of *Atanarjuat*. What these and other Isuma members have done together over the course of more than two decades are, of course, self-sufficient pieces of work, most notably the video recreations of Inuit life in the 1930s and 1940s, *Gathering Place* (*Qaggiq*, 1989), *Going Inland* (*Nunaqpa*, 1991), *Fish Traps* (*Saputi*, 1993) and the TV series *Our Land* (*Nunavut*, 1994–5). But these can also be seen as separate elements of training that would later coalesce in *Atanarjuat*, insofar as they enabled extensive experience with various technologies to shoot in that particular area of the Arctic; recovering and describing Inuit traditions associated with hunting, eating, singing and shamanic rites; and developing original aesthetic forms ensuing from the previous two. In this sense, *Atanarjuat* is, in White's words, 'a kind of expansion on the sorts of issues raised in Kunuk's video work' (2007, p. 352).

The film's overstretched gestation was above all the result of an obsessive drive for authenticity, entailing meticulous research with a view to reconstructing to the smallest detail what Inuit life might have been between 500 and 1,500 years ago, the period when the legend of Atanarjuat is believed to have been formed (Angilirk, 2002, p. 7). This included the restoration of the ancient Inuktitut language and the production of clothing, tattooing and cooking utensils and tools with their original materials and methods. The compilation of the various versions of the legend required an equally punctilious work. The storyline skeleton was provided by four testimonials given in 1972, 1987, 1990 and 1991 by Michel Kupaaq, an Igloolik inhabitant born in the mid-1920s. These were further enriched by versions given by Kupaaq's younger brother, Hervé Paniaq (who also integrated the scriptwriting team); Émile Imaroitok; Guy Makkik; Elizabeth Nutarakittuq; and elders George Kappianaq and François Quassa (Angilirk, 2002, p. 199).

Scriptwriting was yet another painstaking process, including several stages of translation, transcription and adaptation to make the resulting text accessible to Igloolik actors and crew, as well as to English and

French speaking collaborators and producers. Inuktitut had originally no writing system. Present-day Inuit normally make use of a syllabic alphabet first developed by a Wesleyan missionary in the mid-nineteenth century and currently taught in schools (Saladin d'Anglure in Angilirk, 2002, p. 225). For this reason, the screenplay was simultaneously written in two different languages and writing systems, Inuktitut in its syllabic system, and English in Roman characters. This is how Norman Cohn retells the process:

> We [Paul Apak Angilirk, Zach Kunuk, Hervé Paniaq, Pauloosie Qulitalik as well as Cohn] discussed every scene, every gesture, every line of dialogue, and wrote two scripts at the same time, arguing and acting things out around the table. Apak wrote the scenes down on one laptop in the old Inuktitut font we got from the school, while I wrote the same scenes in English on our second laptop, from the same discussions. We had to do this. The actors would learn their characters and lines from the Inuktitut script, but we had to finance the film from the English script, since no one in the Canadian film industry could read Inuktitut or think like Inuit. (Cohn in Angilirk, 2002, p. 25)

Both versions are published side by side in Angilirk's edited book (2002), and it is not difficult to imagine the different cultural weights each of them carries along.

This quick overview of the preproduction process can give an idea of the overwhelming wealth of materials contained in the film, forcibly compressed in the editing process. This notwithstanding, on a very superficial level, the narrative seems to be relatively easy to follow. In an Inuit clan an old rivalry separates two families. Handsome Atanarjuat falls in love with and conquers the local beauty, Atuat, who had already been promised to Uqi, the strong son of chief Sauri. The rivalry between the two parties is enhanced by wicked Puja, Uqi's sister who is also infatuated with Atanarjuat and finally manages to become his second wife. Uqi and his gang, in a coup orchestrated by Puja, eventually attack Atanarnajuat's hunting camp, kills his brother Aamarjuaq who was sleeping next to him, while Atanarjuat manages to escape, naked and barefoot, on a formidable race across the sea ice. Rescued by Qulitalik, a shaman long estranged from his clan, Atanarjuat recovers his strength on a remote island. During his absence, however, Uqi rapes Atuat and threatens her and her son with starvation, unless she accepts to become his wife. He subsequently murders his own father Sauri, who opposes his taking Atuat by force, and becomes chief. His is however a short-lived glory, as Atanarjuat makes a triumphal return to take revenge and restore order.

Were it only for the elements highlighted in this synopsis – love, jealousy, chase, murder, rape and revenge – the film would fit perfectly into the thriller-genre category, and Kunuk is the first to acknowledge this:

> Atanarjuat wasn't the only legend we heard but it was one of the best – once you get that picture into your head of that naked man running for his life across the ice, his hair flying, you never forget it. It had everything in it for a fantastic movie . . . and, at the same time, buried in this ancient Inuit 'action thriller' were all these lessons we kids were supposed to learn. (Kunuk in Angilirk, 2002, p. 13)

A closer look, however, discloses a film that could not be further apart from generic classifications. A mass of encoded details resisting formulaic genres underlies its narrative surface which may, in a first instance, be attributed to the original footage having been cut down, in Kunuk's words, 'to where we couldn't cut it anymore' (Chun, 2002, p. 3). The fact remains that, rather than suppressing what is usually seen as 'dead time', it is dialogue and action scenes that are compressed to the point of incomprehensibility, while landscape shots, atmospheric insets, detailed images of daily activities with no immediate diegetic value are leisurely stretched.

The beginning of the film is a good example of this. The opening images are a snowy landscape unfolding as far as the eye can see. The opaque white sphere of the sun marks the centre of a fuzzy horizon involved in the blue hues of the dawn. In the distance, the figure of a man turns slowly and idly round, while dogs howl and roam aimlessly around him. Who is this man and what is he doing there? The viewer will probably never know, unless she or he has a prodigious memory able to retrospectively link him to Qulitalik, the estranged shaman who 20 years later (and played by a different actor) will save Atananarjuat from death, after his naked race on ice. In this beginning, atmosphere, not factual clarity, is what matters. Crosscut with the outdoor shots, we see the interior of an igloo replete with people of all ages; on the foreground two middle-aged men compare the patterns on their animal-skin clothes. The dialogue informs us that one of them is a foreign visitor. The other – but again the spectator will hardly be aware of this at first viewing – is Kumaglak, the father of the future chief Sauri. Back to the outside, a man (Qulitalik, whose identity has not yet been disclosed to the viewer) takes his time polishing a sledge, then, with his wife, piling up provisions on it, setting the dog team to it and bidding farewell to another woman (later revealed as his sister Panikpak, a shaman married to Kumaglak). Back in the igloo, the two middle-aged men are now naked from waist up, sitting on the floor and having their hands tied behind their backs and their necks tied to their toes. Time passes, as the wasting of the oil lamp indicates, a menacing growling is uttered by the stranger and suddenly Kumaglak falls to the side. He is dead and his walrus-teeth necklace is taken by his rival and put around the neck of Kumaglak's son, Sauri. At this stage, and probably even after seeing the whole film, it is virtually impossible for the viewer to guess that Sauri has betrayed his father by helping the stranger in the competition; and that Kumaglak preferred Tulimaq (Atananarjuat's father) to his own son, and for this reason Sauri, after becoming chief, will turn against Tulimaq and his descendants. All the viewer can be sure of, until here, is the extreme cold outside, the closeness and tension among the members of the clan in the igloo, the worried tattooed face of Kumaglak's wife, Panikpak, lit by the orange hues of the oil lamp, the haunting sounds of the dogs and the wind. What motivates the extended duration of these atmospheric details and the extreme compression of dialogue and action?

A crucial detail, of which again the viewer will not become aware of until much later in the film, may help us elucidate this question, namely that the exterior scenes, which *precede* the dispute taking place inside the igloo, actually happen *after* Kumaglak's death. Qulitalik is collecting his dogs and polishing his sledge *because* the stranger has won the competition and, as Kumaglak's brother-in-law, he now feels constrained to depart. This temporal zigzag, affecting the montage throughout the film, albeit encoded in atmospheric details with no apparent narrative scope, gives us the key to the film's editing style. Rather than the demands of a normal feature-length film, it is a non-chronological conception of time which is at stake here, quietly subverting the narrative progression on the film's surface.

Bazin, in his defence of realist cinema, often resorted to the Bergsonian notion of *durée,* or duration, to describe 'life time', or 'the simple continuing to be of a person to whom nothing in particular happens', as is the case in certain scenes of *Umberto D* (Vittorio De Sica, 1952), in which the rendering of a character's experience of time takes the upper hand over the narrative (Bazin, 2005, p. 76). This may be partially the case with the atmospheric scenes in *Atanarjuat,* but 'duration' has further and even more suitable resonances with them. As Deleuze explains, for Bergson 'past and present must be thought as two extreme degrees which coexist within duration, the former of which is defined for its state of distension and the latter, by its state of contraction' (Deleuze, 2002, p. 39). As a result, 'the present is only the more contracted degree of the past' (2002, p. 40). This seems entirely applicable to the contracted action and dialogue scenes, as opposed to the extended atmosphere descriptions in the film. For Bergson, moreover, duration is equivalent to memory, because it incorporates interior and exterior changes and 'prolongs the before into the after' (1968, p. 41). And indeed it is a glimpse into the realm of memory and remembrance we are being offered with *Atanarjuat*'s crosscutting montage. That this intertwines subjective and objective time experiences becomes clear, in the opening scenes described above, when we hear a voiceover commentary superimposed on Qulitak's departure scene and spilling over Kumaglak's competition with the stranger:

> We never knew what he was or why it happened. Evil came to us like death. It just happened and we had to live with it.

This voice, as we later learn, belongs to old Panikpak, recalling, 20 years on, the loss of her husband and the rift that divided her family thereafter. Simultaneity, an interpenetration of subjective and objective experiences as triggered by memory is what takes place here, along the lines of Bergson's definition: 'Simultaneity would be precisely the possibility of two or more events entering within a single, instantaneous perception' (Bergson, 1968, p. 43).

An even more startling chronological overlap occurs later in the film, when Atanarjuat, now a grown-up, is disputing Atuat's hand with Uqi. A punching-heads contest is organized between the two in a purpose-built igloo to accommodate a large audience, among them Atuat, sitting next to Panikpak, her faithful protector, and Puja, next to her father, chief Sauri. In preparation for the main fight, a lot of singing and other minor competitions take place, such as pulling-mouths between Amaqjuat and one of Uqi's companions, and throat singing between Atuat and Puja. These two competitions are apparently concomitant, as the sounds uttered by both the competing men and women are simultaneously heard. However, as the image cuts back and forth between the two couples, an attentive viewing reveals that both Atuat and Puja are quietly sitting in the background to the fighting men, making it impossible to tell exactly when their throat singing takes place.

Disjointed timelines and nonlinear narratives are usually associated with the modern in art, as a result of subjective perceptions of the real inflected by memory. Within modern literature, it is Marcel Proust, a Bergson contemporary and enthusiast, the most eloquent example of it, as he has based the entire seven volumes of his *In Search of Lost Time* on the development of the interference in the present of fleeting moments of remembrance, such as the taste of a madeleine. These, he writes, 'had the common quality of being felt simultaneously at the actual moment and at a distance in time . . . [They] imposed the past upon the present and made me hesitate as to which time I was existing in' (Proust, 1981, p. 904). In *Atanarjuat,* a similar flash of the past takes hold of Panikpak, who during the singing in preparation for Atanarjuat's fight with Uqi is jolted by the sudden memory of the precise moment her husband died, 20 years ago, and awoke her from a slumber; a shot of this very moment, lasting a fraction of a second, is duly interspersed to indicate the sudden grip of the past over the present with fatal consequences to the future.

Most interestingly, this modern sensibility presents astonishing similarities to the traditional Inuit way of understanding time, as conveyed in the film. Saladin d'Anglure notes that

> Inuit in general, and shamans in particular, would often change scale in their dreams, rituals or funny tales. This is one of the keys to understanding their symbolism. . . . This was likely how, in the film, Panikpak chose to give the name of her dead mother, Atuat, to the newborn girl who would later become Atanarjuat's wife. Then, when Atuat herself gave birth to a baby boy, Panikpak gave the child the name of her murdered husband, Kumaglak. (Angilirk, 2002, p. 213)

This is how, in *Atanarjuat,* 'time is regained,' to resort to Proust's famous expression, by means of characters who replace their dead, and in so doing keep their memory alive in the present. Scale and character correspondence is also the only way through which the story can be properly understood, once the bewildering swapping of young and old faces, performed by a corresponding actors' swap, is deciphered. The end of the film is enlightening in this respect. After Atanarjuat takes revenge on Uqi and his gang, stopping short of killing the three of them, an exorcism ritual takes place, led by shaman siblings Qulitalik and Panikpak. They invoke the evil stranger, Tuurngarjuaq, whose spirit reappears to be chased away forever. Through this, the spirit of dead Kumaglak is revived in his namesake, the infant child of Atuat and Atanarjuat, whose face in close-up is combined with the voice of the dead man as he asks his widowed wife to sing his song.

That all these characters live 'outside time', in Proust's words, is made clear by the lack of temporal markers in the film. Indeed, *Atanarjuat* eschews genre categories, above all, due to the impossibility of classifying it as either period or contemporary drama. History is a bulk of interacting events, with no before or after, while characters live in an eternal present. This effect is achieved through the enclosure of the diegesis within a sealed-up, uniform cosmos, in which there is no room for an 'other' bringing in the perspective from the outside. Even the evil spirit of a foreigner who causes a family to fall apart speaks the same language and abides by the same rules and habits as they do.

Most importantly, however, and what radically separates *Atanarjuat* from the period drama, is the fact that all characters are played by genuine Inuit people, who are familiar with the facts and habits described in the film, even if their lives differ greatly from these traditions nowadays. This cast, combined with the shooting on real locations, which are not only similar to those where the story once may have happened, but exactly those where the legend was collected, are the ones responsible for this process of presentification which Bazin once defined as inherent to realist cinema (2005, p. 78). And so it happens that a story, which supposedly occurred over a thousand years ago, looks like a documentary of Inuit life today.

In short, it is the film's *physicality* which drives it away from established genre categories. Brecht, in his epic theatre, recommended the transposition of the action to the past tense, so as to draw a line between an actor and the character played and, in so doing, call the attention to the reality of the former and fictitiousness of the latter (Brecht, 2001, p. 138). By bringing all action, however remote its actual location in time might have been, into the present tense, *Atanarjuat* is not producing illusion of reality, according to the generic norm, but merging past and present into a timeless physical real.

Here is where the actors' heroic feat, above that of the characters, comes into play. As I have hinted at in the introduction to this chapter, the runner on foot, with his physical engagement, develops a parallel narrative to the main storyline, which is concerned with describing a territory and taking possession of it. This constitutes Atanarjuat's mission in the film, as performed by the extraordinary Natar Ungalaaq, running like a naked god on a dazzlingly cruel landscape, falling repeatedly into its freezing puddles, rising again, jumping like a superman and finally crashing flat to near death on the ice. But it is also that of all other actors who physically engage with that particular landscape and its extreme conditions, not least Peter-Henry Arnatsiaq, in the role of Uqi, who also rolls semi-naked on the ice during his fight with Atanarjuat, and falls into endless ice puddles; and also Lucy Tulugarjuk (Puja) and Sylvia Ivalu (Atuat), both of whom have to pose naked on the snow, as Atanarjuat returns with a new dress for the latter and a punishment for the former. It is even unfair to single out individual actors: all of them have given their utmost commitment, including the anonymous crew behind the camera, to the production of this unique masterpiece. Their film is the true expression of activism: not representation of victims, but the empowerment of a people, who are sovereign over their land beyond time.

Yaaba

As we have seen, *Atanarjuat* is constructed on the basis of accumulation of details, overlapping temporalities and concentration of meaning, a work enabled by, and typical of, the digital era. In contrast *Yaaba* is based on distension, geometric unfolding of space and time, depuration and general economy of means. In a thoroughly uniform Mossi world, characters take their time to utter their simple lines with solemn clarity in front of a predominantly static camera, while the scenes unfold in rigid chronological order, allowing for no temporal blurring, not even dissolves. These aesthetic features derive, on the one hand, from stylistic options compatible with Bazinian realism, including the idea of cinema as a 'window on the world' and the primacy of the objective real over the observing subject. But they are equally due to the constraints imposed by a stringent budget and the use of 35mm celluloid, entailing bulky machinery and devices not practicable in a semi-desert region, away from urban utilities. Together, these factors gave birth to what has been referred to as *Yaaba*'s 'hieratic' mise-en-scène (Boughedir, 1995, p. 28), a style which has placed Ouédraogo, at least at this stage of his career, alongside ascetic filmmakers such as Bresson (de Baecque, 1990, p. 13), and I would add Ozu, whose cinema can offer enlightening clues to this film, as we will see.

Yaaba is indeed the work of a cinephile, reflecting all director Ouédraogo had learned in his extensive training as filmmaker at the now defunct Institut Africain d'Études Cinématographiques, in Ouagadougou, then in Kiev (former USSR) and finally at the Institut des Hautes Études Cinématographiques, the famous IDHEC, in Paris.

After several shorts and a first feature film shot on 16mm, *The Choice* (*Yam daabo,* 1986), he finally embarked, with *Yaaba,* on the 35mm format but not before surrounding himself with an international team of skilled specialists, starting with the Swiss executive producer Pierre-Alain Meier, who brought with him the director of photography Matthias Kälin, himself a film auteur, and the make-up artist Nathalie Tanner whose filmmaking pedigree includes her celebrated father, director Alain Tanner. From France, he invited the experienced sound engineer Jean-Paul Mugel, a frequent collaborator of the likes of Wim Wenders, Agnès Varda and Manoel de Oliveira, as well as his former teacher at IDHEC, the cameraman Jean Monsigny (see Cressole, 1998). To these were added some of the best cinematic talents in the sub-Saharan region, such as the Burkinabé film star Rasmane Ouédraogo, the Cameroonian experimental composer Francis Bebey and a host of unforgettable actors recruited among the inhabitants of Tougouzagué village, a few miles away from where the director was born. Burkina Faso also contributed significantly to the budget, thanks mainly to the intervention of Watamou Lamien, a governmental counsellor who had lent his support to many talented African filmmakers. Sadly, Lamien was killed in a car crash on his way to visit Ouédraogo on location (Cressole, 1998); *Yaaba* is deservedly dedicated to him. This strong team, coupled with the director's deep knowledge of the settings and people in focus, gives the film an overall sense of self-confidence and precision that has been the cause of much praise, but also suspicion.

Yaaba was lauded at Cannes, where it won the FIPRESCI prize, among other awards. Its moral tale, centred on the characters of an elderly woman and two children, also facilitated its worldwide distribution and exhibition, both on cinema screens and TV. This success encouraged Ouédrago to immediately throw himself into a second film in the same sober style, *Tilaï* (1990), this time a tragedy of mythic overtones, involving father-son betrayal, oedipal love and fratricide. *Tilaï* achieved even greater success at Cannes, where it received the Jury prize, going on to conquer the Étalon d'Yenenga, the main prize at FESPACO (the Pan-African Film Festival of Ouagadougou), thus consolidating Ouédraogo's reputation internationally. This notwithstanding, a considerable amount of time has been, and continues to be, wasted by critics, both from Africa and elsewhere, in discussions of whether *Yaaba* and *Tilaï* have been made for an audience vaguely defined as the 'Africans', or for an even more elusive 'West', the quintessential 'Other' which these critics insist differs radically from the former (see Diawara, 1992). Even a recent book on African cinema spends several pages with this unproductive debate, which invariably ends with the veiled reproach that both films, for their highly artistic endeavour, are not 'popular' enough for African audiences (Murphy & Williams, 2007, pp. 162ff.). In response to such prescriptive and ultimately sterilizing criticism, Ouédraogo reiterates in his interviews that:

> It's intellectuals who accuse my films of not being African. They forget that the technique is universal, even if we learn it in France. It is like science or medicine, we are entitled to them, they represent knowledge that belongs to the world and, therefore, to me as well. (Nagib, 1998, p. 118)

It is indeed clear from its opening images, the dash of the child protagonists Nopoko and Bila on the vast red Sahelian landscape, that *Yaaba* is a world film, one which creatively replays universal tropes in an environment never before shown on film with such realism. Ouédraogo locates the source of the original story, also written by him, in oral literature:

> [It is] a tale from my childhood, a form of nocturnal education we acquire in my birthplace between 7 and 10 years of age, just before we go to sleep, if we are fortunate enough to have a grandmother. (Baron, 1989)

The figure of this wise grandmother is represented in the film by Sana, the outcast old woman whom the boy Bila affectionately calls *yaaba* (grandmother). Despite its local origin, however, the developed story is essentially the work of a cinephile, which draws entirely on an earlier foundational realist film, *Pather Panchali* (Satyajit Ray, 1955), a decisive detail which seems to have passed unremarked by most. Ray's first film, and first instalment of his Apu trilogy, revolves around the character of an elderly, frail woman, Indir, a constant victim of bullying by her much younger sister-in-law in whose house she lives. Indir, however, draws secret help from her sister-in-law's little daughter, Durga, who steals fruit from a neighbouring orchard to feed her. A younger brother is born, Apu, who soon joins Durga in supporting their aunt, even after she is expelled from home. In *Yaaba,* too, it is a boy and a girl (although the boy is here the lead), the cousins Bila and Nopoko, who side with old Sana, against the prevailing mind in their village that she is a witch. Bila finds himself equally compelled to steal – a chicken, among other things – in order to feed her. The details indicating the elderly women's penury are sometimes identical in both films, such as the ragged shawl both Yaaba and Indir vainly try to mend. Also similar is the bond between both pairs of children, suggested through affectionate teasing, hide-and-seek games, and even fierce love tests, such as pretending to be drowned in a pond (Bila), disappearing in a rice field (Durga) or not waking up from sleep (Apu and Nopoko). In both cases, play escalates to serious illness. In *Pather Panchali,* after an escapade to watch a train passing by, the siblings are caught by monsoon rain leading to Durga's pneumonia and tragic death. In *Yaaba,* when Nopoko intervenes in defence of Bila in a fight with three other boys, she is cut by a rusty knife and nearly dies of tetanus. The experience of death is in fact the most important lesson the old woman teaches the children, and here Ouédraogo seizes the opportunity to quote Ray literally, by replaying the famous scene in which the siblings, in *Pather Panchali,* find their aunt sitting on the ground in an apparent slumber, her head lowered over her bent knees. Upon Durga's touching her, she falls to the side and the children realize with horror that she is dead. Sana also falls dead to the side, when Bila tries to wake her up from apparent sleep, sitting on the ground and head lowered over her bent knees.

Rather than lack of originality on the part of Ouédraogo, what this intertextuality demonstrates is the extent to which universal tropes and realism go in hand when it comes to exploring a new cinematic vein. Ray himself had voraciously resorted, for his first film, to Italian Neorealism and more importantly to Renoir, whose realist methods he had experienced in practice by assisting the French director during the shoot of *The River* (Jean Renoir, 1951) in India. Moreover, child protagonists, since Neorealism and *Germany Year Zero* (*Germania Anno Zero,* Roberto Rossellini, 1947), are historically associated with new realisms, as they perfectly mirror filmmakers' own learning processes as they chase for images never shown on screen. Bila and Nopoko, as much as Durga and Apu, are setting out to discover and take possession of a territory which is new to them as much as to the film spectator, and are thus the channel through which novelty migrates from the fable to the film aesthetics.

In *Yaaba,* this aspect is further emphasized by the actors' physical link to the real locations. The combination of these with their real inhabitants conveys a sense of naturalness and belonging which, in the words of Serge Daney apropos of Souleymane Cissé, 'operates, not an aestheticization of the world, but an immediate inscription of the body into the environment' (apud Barlet, 1996, p. 165). The resulting beauty, beyond its picture-postcard effect, derives from the *continuity* physicality produces between the body and its environment, as illustrated by

FIGURE 1.11 Sana's brown withered skin is one more shade of the red soil, in *Yaaba*

the extreme long shots of Sana's seminaked figure slowly crossing the vast, barren landscape, where her brown withered skin is just one more shade of the red soil (Fig. 1.11). Physical link, in *Yaaba,* is best represented by Bila's act of running on foot. In the majority of his appearances, Bila is indeed running, be it in his childish games, to escape his father's anger, to fetch help when Nopoko falls ill or in his regular visits to Sana. Bila's connective mobility enlightens the viewer both on the Sahel landscape and on the relation between the various geographical sites in the film: the market, the pond, the cemetery, the fields where cattle graze, Sana's half-ruined hut outside the village walls.

It has been noted that Bila's eagerness and curiosity toward the world stand for 'the values of modern Africa' (Ukadike, 1991, p. 56). Within the realm of the fable, the film is entirely atemporal, with no indications of premodern or modern phases of Africa. However, it is indeed the case that Bila's constant running in a straight line projects the film towards a better future. It is a teleological movement whose ultimate goal is social change – an aspect that has been closely analysed by Xavier with regards to Manuel's dash in *God and the Devil* (1999, p. 32), and I will return to this in due course. As such, his character embodies the fierce criticism of traditional ways that pervades the film as a whole, despite it being passionately rooted in the Mossi traditional culture. This criticism does not emerge from clashes with alien cultures (which are entirely absent in the film), but from the social problems inherent to this very community. Scene after scene demonstrates the nefarious consequences of prejudice, be it, for example, against an adulterous wife (Koudi), whose drunk husband (Noaga) has become impotent, or against the drunk himself. In their turn, marginal characters such as Sana and Noaga, are the ones endowed with progressive thought, thanks to their disengagement from society and its rules. The main message Sana has for her apprentice Bila is that people 'have their own reasons', leading him to forgive the unfaithful Koudi and make friends with Noaga.

The advantages of Bila's enlightened views are fully demonstrated in the episode of Nopoko's illness. The motherless girl is being tended by her aunt, Bila's mother. Efforts are made by the village male population to find treatment for her. A magical healer is hired who demands the sacrifice of several animals, all to no avail. Bila however resorts to his mentor Sana, who goes to fetch the herbalist Taryam, living on the other side of the river. Taryam's entry into the village is barred by Bila's father, but his more sensible mother sends the boy after Taryam again, and he returns with the medicine which finally saves Nopoko from death. Winners and losers are thus clearly defined, with women proving to be wiser than their bossy, traditionalist husbands, and science prevailing over superstition. A happy ending is finally achieved that duly satisfies the requirements of the moral tale.

One may, however, ask where realism would be found in all this. Not in the fable, of course, but in the *presentational* quality of its narrative style, which exposes, beyond the demands of the fable, the reality of the actors and the scene. *Yaaba*'s presentational mode of address can be best understood through what constitutes its most outspoken cinephile aspect, that is, its affinities with Ozu. Among the choices implied in what Alain Bergala refers to as 'the Ozu system' is, in the first place, Ozu's famous rejection of all camera movements, except on very rare occasions. But Bergala draws the attention to another, more subtle detail, which is that the stationary camera often starts to roll before any characters appear in front of it and continues to roll after they are gone, which effects the sense that 'the enunciation precedes the enounced' (Bergala, 1980). This precedence, continues Bergala, is certainly the rule in all films, but is normally erased in order to preserve the spectator's illusion that the filmed preceded the filming. In *Yaaba,* too, the camera is predominantly static, moving only very occasionally in slow pans or short tracking shots. This Ouédraogo ascribes to the impossibility of installing cranes on that location as well as to budgetary constraints, which allowed for a limited length of tracks. However, it does not explain the fact that empty bits of static shots, before and after the appearance of characters, are not edited out. This exclusively stylistic choice, reminiscent of Ozu, causes a short delay that indicates to the viewer how that particular scene was made, a piece of information which is usually excluded in the montage. It is a gap in the action that reveals how the characters, as it were, step up to the 'stage' and 'present' themselves. This effect is further intensified by another presentational device relating to the gaze construction, which Bergala also points out about Ozu:

> The Ozu gaze, 'undecided' between a direct look at the camera and an entirely fictional gaze, sets the spectator into a singular position: . . . that of a spectator who is not truly centred (as operator) nor entirely excluded from the fictional gaze construction (that is, forced out of their spectatorial position through direct address). (Bergala, 1980)

Now let us look at *Yaaba*. Here too the scenes are often arranged so as to place the gaze in an intermediary position. A typical example is this: after a dialogue has taken place and the talking parties are gone, a third character stays behind, turns slightly toward the camera, stopping just short of meeting the spectator's gaze, then utters a comment on what has just happened. This arrangement produces a spectator inside the scene who is situated on the borderline between voyeurism and active observation. It is a figure who 'presents' the scene to the viewer in a way which would not differ greatly from the performance of a *griot* storyteller, present in so many African films, or even from a *benshi* explicator from the Japanese silent-movie era, whose heritage Ozu also carries in his films.

Murphy & Williams have noted, in *Yaaba,* the recurrence of close-ups of smiling faces, which they attribute to Ouédraogo's penchant for comedy (2007, p. 160). It may be so, but the role of these faces is more complex in that they incorporate passive and active spectatorship within the diegesis. The intentionality of this device can be observed in the prevalence of triadic compositions, in which two characters conversing in the foreground are observed by a third in the background. This, of course, requires the use of long shots, and here is where Ouédraogo moves away from Ozu and his attachment to shot-reverse shot montage, and sends us back to Bazin's realism based on space-time continuity. The insertion of a judgemental figure within the scene is actually a very distinctive, auteurist feature in *Yaaba,* in which it is employed as a structuring device of the film as a whole. Even when no verbal comments are uttered, this diegetic spectator will be there to shake their head and smile to express their opinion to an audience within the film or even to the film viewer alone. The smiling faces of Bila, his mother and Sana are fitting illustrations of this procedure (Figs. 1.12–1.14).

Figure 1.12

Figure 1.13

Figures 1.12–1.14 Judgmental figures within the scene: smiling faces in *Yaaba*

In a variation of the triadic composition, the voyeur remains invisible to both the characters in the film and the film viewer until the end of a dialogue, when he/she emerges from behind a wall or bush with a smiling face (denoting ruse, rather than humour) to utter a comment. The typical illustration here is the figure of an elderly man with no function in the film other than to surface from time to time from behind a wall or bush, laugh at someone's lovemaking and say 'That's life' (Fig. 1.15). A last variation will show a dialogue between two characters; once the dialogue is finished and one of the parties is gone, the remaining party turns towards the camera and utters a comment. This happens, for example, between Bila and Nopoko, when they are on their way to fetch water from the pond; Bila sees a cow with calf and stops to get a little milk for Sana; Nopoko, however, decides to carry on and, at this moment, Bila turns and actually looks directly at the camera to laugh at Nopoko's 'cowardice', a moment at which the fourth wall is effectively broken (Fig. 1.16).

Both the enunciative camera placement and the spectator within the scene are *presentational* devices, calling the attention not only to the arbitrariness of fiction, but to their own reality, that is to say, the reality of the medium. They bring the awareness, on the one hand, of a Foucaultian society of surveillance, where envy, intrigue and betrayal are rife, thus preventing the formation of any romantic nostalgia for traditional ways; on the other, they place the spectator within this same network of invigilation that spreads beyond cultural boundaries. Borders are effectively crossed in the fable by Sana, who takes the boat across the large river in search of Taryam and the healing power of his

FIGURE 1.15 The spectator/voyeur within the scene, in *Yaaba*

FIGURE 1.16 Breaking the fourth wall, in *Yaaba*

herbal science. Hers is a search for a better world, which is not defined by difference or otherness, but simply improved humanity. The same happens on the level of the film medium, in which border-crossing cinephilia is put to the service of a new realism.

GOD AND THE DEVIL IN THE LAND OF THE SUN (BLACK GOD, WHITE DEVIL)

This foundational Cinema Novo film owes much of its renown to the way it provided cinema with the sound and image of Brazil's national identity. Everything it shows, people, landscape, music, language, culture and history, seems to be endowed with the power to reveal a deeper, 'more real' Brazil, a country which had remained unknown to film audiences at home and abroad until then. Clear though this effect may seem to be, it is no less a puzzle insofar as all techniques employed to achieve it, including acting, shooting, editing and mixing, are usually associated with anti-realism. Rocha once stated about this film that 'It is a fable. The characters are not realist: realist is the author's attitude towards them' (Viany, 1965, p. 128). In this section, I will focus on this 'realist attitude' as an ethical stance that places presentational truth above representational mimesis, a method that determines, on the one hand, the exposure of the inner workings of fiction, and, on the other, the bodily engagement of crew and cast with real locations, regardless of the extreme conditions they may present. My hypothesis is that this enables revelatory realism to interact with anti-realism, so as to produce the emblem of a nation. At the same time, it causes the nation to expand over its geographical boundaries and become the stage for the enactment of universal tropes.

In order to grasp the 'national-identity effect' in *God and the Devil*, one must in the first place confront an aporia, which is the fact that the country 'Brazil' does not exist in the film. There is certainly a 'land of the sun', as announced in the title, which is incessantly photographed, referred to in the dialogue, commented upon in the lyrics of songs and suggested by the instrumental music track. However, this land is not called Brazil, but *sertão*. 'Manuel and Rosa lived in the *sertão/* Labouring the land with their own hands',[6] says the song which introduces the protagonist couple at the beginning of the film, emphasizing the characters' physical link with their *sertão* homeland. What exactly is *sertão* and what does it mean in the film? This untranslatable term, so current in Brazil both in its singular and plural forms, *sertões*, but as complex to conceptualize in Portuguese as it is in any other language, has been the theme of voluminous literature. In geographical terms, the *sertão* can refer to the *caatinga* or semi-desert shrubland of the northeast, including the hinterlands of the states of Bahia, Alagoas, Sergipe, Pernambuco, Paraíba, Rio Grande do Norte, Ceará and Piauí; but it can also denote the *cerrado* or tropical savannah of Minas Gerais, in the southeast; or even the lush swampy area of Goiás and Mato Grosso, in the country's centre-west. In the face of such varying territories and landscapes, stretching over more than 1 million square kilometres, it would be perhaps simpler to define the *sertão* negatively, by what it is not, that is to say, the coastal area of Brazil.

Sylvie Debs, in her book *Cinéma et litérature au Brésil: Les Myths du Sertão: emergence d'une identité nationale*, undertakes an extensive survey of the various meanings of the word, from its uncertain etymology to its fluid geographical boundaries, coming to a collection of fixed elements:

> A land that is rustic, isolated, wild, poor, interior, scarcely inhabited, located in the northeast, arid, pastoral, whose population is conservative. (2002, p. 115)

Such a categorization reflects a political point of view insofar as it limits the *sertão* to the semi-desert northeast, hence to poverty, deprivation and oppression. This is certainly also the case in *God and the Devil*, in which the semi-desert *sertão* is at the origin of peasant rebellion, religious messianism and social banditry. These, in fact, demarcate the tripartite thesis-like structure of the film narrative. In the first part, cowherd Manuel rebels and murders his rancher boss, who denies him his due pay because some of the cattle under his responsibility have died in the drought. He is chased up by two of the rancher's sidekicks, whom he also kills, but not before they kill his mother. This launches the film's second part: having become a fugitive, Manuel, dragging his hesitant wife along with him, decides to follow the religious leader Sebastião, that is to say, the 'path of god'. He becomes a fervent believer, abiding unconditionally by his leader, even when this involves human sacrifice, until the day when Sebastião's community is massacred by Antônio das Mortes, a professional killer at the service of ranchers and the church. Part three starts here, with Manuel and Rosa now taking the opposite path, that is, that of 'the devil', or social banditry, by joining the gang of the last *cangaceiro* leader, or *sertão* outlaw, Corisco. But again Antônio das Mortes is on the watch and soon succeeds in exterminating Corisco and his gang, letting only Manuel and Rosa escape alive. The final scene provides a synthetic closure to this thesis schema. Both Sebastião and his negative double, Corisco, had proposed a solution in the form of cosmic reversion, by prophesying that 'the *sertão* will become the sea, and the sea *sertão*'. Antônio das Mortes, however, offers a more pragmatic, though no less enigmatic way out by predicting that: 'One day there will be a greater war in this *sertão* . . . A great war, without the blindness of god and the devil' (cf. Rocha, 1985, p. 279). The end of the film enacts the sum of these prophecies, as Manuel and Rosa lunge on a race across the desert land, while an extradiegetic choir repeats that 'the *sertão* will become the sea, and the sea *sertão*' and that 'the land belongs to man, not to god or the devil'. Rosa falls over and stays behind, while Manuel carries on running until the final image of the sea, superimposed by the montage, brings the film to a close.

Both the figures of messianic preachers and *cangaceiros* are typical of the arid hinterlands of the Brazilian northeast and a favourite subject of oral literature of that region, most notably the *cordel* literature, or narrative poems, illustrated by woodblock prints and contained in leaflets, which are sold in street markets and other places across the northeastern states. Despite being distributed in printed form, *cordel* preserves its oral character, since it is intended to be read or sung out loud by the author, the seller, or the purchaser before a semiliterate audience. Tales of *cangaceiros* and miracle workers are considered the most exclusively Brazilian addition to this literature, whose origins go back to the Portuguese leaflets and manuscripts which, since the end of the sixteenth century, travelled the length and breadth of the northeast hinterlands. Rocha famously drew on the *cordel* content and poetic form to write the lyrics of the songs, which introduce characters and scenes in the film, in a presentational manner not dissimilar to the woodblock prints' illustrative function in the *cordel*. Within the diegetic world, a corresponding figure of a fairground blind singer, Cego Júlio (Blind Júlio), with a guitar hanging on his back, takes up the role of connecting characters and carrying the narrative forward, thus complementing the structuring function of the extradiegetic *cordel* music.

As for the location of Monte Santo, or 'holy mount', where Sebastião and his followers gather, the references are primarily historical. The mount was one of the sites occupied by the legendary Antônio Conselheiro and his followers, at the end of the nineteenth century. A messianic leader of anti-republican, millenarian convictions, Conselheiro commanded the greatest peasant rebellion in Brazilian history, the war of Canudos, which ended with the massacre of the rebels by military troops in 1897. In the film, the events involving Sebastião and his followers on Monte Santo are obviously based on the history of Canudos, and an advised audience will not fail to recognize their primary source: Euclides da Cunha's canonical book *Os sertões,* first published in 1902 and admirably translated into English by Samuel Putnam as *Rebellion in the Backlands,* in 1944. Cunha's book records the war in epic style and minute detail, including the prophecy registered in an apocryphal notebook, found among the debris of the war, that 'the *sertão* will turn into seacoast and the seacoast into *sertão*' (Cunha, 1995, p. 193). As I have observed elsewhere (Nagib, 2007, chapter 1), the replacement of the promised 'seacoast' with 'sea' provided the film with its most powerful audiovisual motif, which has also become the most recurrent utopian trope in Brazilian cinema ever since.

This notwithstanding, *God and the Devil* is far from a faithful rendering of Cunha's book, or even of the Canudos war. The messianic leader of the film incorporates features of Antônio Conselheiro as much as of other figures, such as José Lourenço, who led a revolt in Caldeirão de Santa Cruz do Deserto, in the state of Ceará, in the 1920s; and, more importantly, of another Sebastião, the leader of the Pedra Bonita sect in Pernambuco, which also ended in a bloodbath in 1838 (Viany, 1965, p. 126). The Pernambucan Sebastião is a character in the novel *Pedra Bonita,* by José Lins do Rego, from which Rocha drew a number of episodes, including the sacrifice of a child with whose 'innocent blood' Sebastião, in the film, hopes to 'cleanse Rosa's soul'. With this, the frontiers of the *sertão,* in *God and the Devil,* extend further north to

Pernambuco and Ceará, and retroact in time to encompass the early nineteenth century.

The truth is that the *sertão* in the film is a vertiginous conflation of disparate places and periods, starting from the fact that the *cangaceiro* Corisco, in real life, was killed in 1940, and therefore could have never been a contemporary of either the real Conselheiro or Sebastião. Moreover, Rocha's *sertão* stretches down south, and closer to the present day, when it comes to another canonical book among its sources, Guimarães Rosa's novel *Grande sertões: veredas* (translated into English as *The Devil to Pay in the Backlands*). In Rosa's novel, the *sertão* is not at all located in the northeast, but in the hinterlands of Minas Gerais, in the Brazilian southeast, presenting different vegetation, topography and human characteristics from those of the northeast. Although *God and the Devil* has very little in common with Guimarães Rosa's storyline, except for a vague resonance of its northeastern *cangaceiros* with their corresponding Minas Gerais *jagunços,* it overlaps with the novel entirely as regards the conception of *sertão* as a totalizing objective as well as subjective cosmos, with no fixed territory or period. Proverbial phrases, such as 'the *sertão* is everywhere' and 'the *sertão* lacks a lock', as found in *The Devil to Pay in the Backlands,* could be read as subtitles to *God and the Devil* from its legendary opening image, a long aerial sequence shot of the arid backlands stretching as far as the eye can see. From the top of Monte Santo, Sebastião announces: 'We will stay for a year on Monte Santo waiting for a rain of gold. Then we will go to an island in the middle of the sea and let the fire from hell burn once for all this Republic of disgrace'. But soon after he acknowledges that 'The island does not exist, we carry it inside our soul' (cf. Rocha, 1985, pp. 267–8), confirming, as in Guimarães Rosa's novel, that the *sertão* is the overriding rule on Earth – and it is indeed endless dry land that the camera captures from the top of Monte Santo.

Encompassing inner and outer worlds, the cosmic *sertão* leaves no room for clear-cut oppositional binaries, on the contrary, it is the locale par excellence of fusion and confusion: god and the devil, as representatives of good and evil, are equivalent and interchangeable. As Arrigucci Jr notes about *The Devil to Pay,* the book is structured upon 'the inversion of positions, mixtures and reversibilities, from the sexual to the metaphysical, from the moral to the political planes, with all their resulting complications' (1995, p. 449). The same applies to *God and the Devil,* in which standardized concepts of 'difference' with relation to race and gender, for example, give way to characters in permanent transmutation. They are alternately good and bad, murderers and saviours, hetero and bisexuals, and race is a category that simply does not exist among a multicoloured and multifaceted demographics, within which Corisco, known in real life as the 'Blond Devil', sports long dark-brown hair. This is where the translation into English of the film title as 'Black God, White Devil' becomes thoroughly inappropriate, as it introduces a predetermined racial element which escapes the film's structuring principle. 'Black' Sebastião is not opposed to 'white' Corisco, but compares with him in every respect, as both aspire to make justice through murder and looting, both subscribe to the apocalyptical *sertão*-sea prophecy and both find their end in the hands of Antônio das Mortes. Love and hate are inextricable feelings, which imprison characters in a complex chain of jealousy. Manuel devotes himself so completely to Sebastião, that Rosa feels estranged and ends up killing the latter 'out of jealousy', as Cego Júlio explains the murder to Antônio das Mortes. Corisco and Dadá, in their turn, are entirely devoted to Lampião (or Virgulino Ferreira da Silva, the most legendary *cangaceiro* of all times, in real life) and Maria Bonita, who have just been murdered by the police. Corisco, however, resents Dadá's protracted mourning of Maria Bonita, though he also remains attached to Lampião to the point of 'incorporating' him and speaking alternately with Lampião's and his own voice – to Dadá's annoyance. This relationship later results in an altercation between Manuel and Corisco, the former defending Sebastião, the latter, Lampião, until both agree that their idols were 'great, but could also become small'. This mixed view of the world is consistent not only with Guimarães Rosa's erudite, philosophical writing, but also with *cordel* literature, as eloquently illustrated by these verses, describing Lampião in the leaflet *The True Story of Lampião and Maria Bonita* (*A verdadeira história de Lampião e Maria Bonita*):

> *He had all the qualities*
> *That a person can have*
> *He was a nurse and a midwife*
> *False, coward and brave*
> *Weak like an old nag*
> *Sly as a serpent.*[7]
> (Cavalcanti Proença, 1986, p. 376)

The implicit homosexual attraction between Manuel and Sebastião, Dadá and Maria Bonita, Corisco and Lampião becomes overt in the case of Dadá and Rosa. The two women become immediately enthralled with each other and deliver themselves to a mutual tactile exploration of their skins and facial features; they even simulate a wedding between them with the wreath of a bride Corisco has just raped. But Rosa's mutating sexuality continues to evolve. Instead of hating Manuel's second leader, as she had done to Sebastião, she feels irresistibly attracted to Corisco. When Manuel rebels against Corisco's method of making justice through bloodshed, she thrashes him with his cartridge-belt (an act which mirrors Manuel's previous beating her up, under Sebastião's orders), and later engages with Corisco in the only and remarkable lovemaking scene in the film.

Arrigucci Jr. approaches the mixed forms and contents of *The Devil to Pay* to the Baroque, the figures of Faust and the double, as well as to Thomas Mann's *Dr Faustus* and the modern novel in general (1995, p. 450). The mode of address utilized in the film also follows in many ways the modernist formula as developed by Guimarães Rosa. Messianic leaders and *cangaceiros* are seen through the lenses of both high literature and popular *cordel*, the former offering its tragic, operatic pathos, the latter its presentational, down-to-earth tone, through which the enunciation, in the form of an extradiegetic narrative singer, precedes the enounced (in a similar procedure described about *Yaaba,* in the preceding section). Villa-Lobos's modernist musical project suited to perfection Rocha's system of equivalences, with his series of 'Bachianas Brasileiras' which combine Bach's polyphony with Brazilian folklore. Villa-Lobos's music was employed throughout the film, in alternation with *cordel* singing, as a means to reinforce the correspondence between high and low cultures. Indeed, the 'Bachianas' are based on similarities identified by Villa-Lobos between Bach and certain Brazilian musical forms, such as the arioso and the sentimental inflections of the Brazilian *modinha.* For this reason, each movement of the 'Bachianas' has two titles, one in classical terms (prelude, aria, toccata, etc.), and another in Portuguese (*modinha, choro, ponteio,* etc.). The grandiose opening of the vast *sertão,* at the beginning, for example, is accompanied by the second movement of 'Bachianas Brasileiras n°2', which has the double title of 'Aria' and 'Canto da nossa terra' ('Song of Our Land').

The construction *en abîme* of endlessly mirroring characters in *God and the Devil* results in Manuel's desperate ethical quest, which Sérgio Augusto has compared to the sixteenth-century character Goetz, in Sartre's play *Lucifer and the Lord* (Viany, 1965, p. 191), who strives to do absolute good and absolute evil, so as to match god and the devil in their almighty equivalence. The negation of otherness is thus defined as the basic situation and the major philosophical and political challenge in the film.

The *sertão*-sea formula, rather than a solution to the eternal recurrence of the same, offers the characters yet another signifier of imprisonment in infinitude and enigma. The 'seacoast' of the prophecy reproduced by Cunha would still make a certain sense in terms of teleology, if understood as the wealthy Brazilian littoral as opposed to the poor northeastern *sertão*; but the image of the sea in itself has no meaning other than the unknown. For this reason, the *sertão,* on the representational level, is not Brazil or any other country, but simply the only existing, inexplicable world. Accordingly, its human element cannot be merely defined as the 'Brazilian', and not even the *sertanejo* (the *sertão* man), in the racial sense Cunha attributed to it. Racial theories of Cunha's time made sense on the basis of comparison with, and difference from, a European paradigm, as Ortiz explains:

> Being a Brazilian means to live in a country geographically different from Europe and inhabited by a different race from the European. . . . [In] Euclides da Cunha's book about Canudos . . . the northeastener is only strong insofar as he is inserted into an environment which is averse to the flourishing of the European civilization. (Ortiz, 1998, p. 18)

The exclusion of oppositional binaries, as much as the concepts of 'otherness' and 'difference', makes Rocha's project incompatible with any preestablished political agenda, and in this sense *God and the Devil* has very little in common with what is normally understood under the rubric of political cinema. As Xavier reminds us, Manuel's final race in the desert 'does not imply any "model of action" typical of political films with pedagogical concerns. It does not define a specific perspective; it merely evokes the possibility of perspectives' (1999, p. 33). While dealing with popular culture and myths with a seriousness and dignity it had never enjoyed in Brazilian art cinema, Rocha is at the same time extremely critical of the beliefs it endorses. 'The preacher says that "the *sertão* will become sea, and the sea *sertão*" with a sense which is alienated, mystical, chaotic, metaphysical and all the rest of it, with all the complications derived from bigotry', he says (Viany, 1965, p. 127).

> The question of what the prophecy means is secondary. For me, the problem resides in how the prophecy is interpreted. There is, for example, another prophecy by Antônio Conselheiro: in year 2000, there will be many hats and only one head. It is another prophecy you can interpret in many ways. What you should not forget is that Antônio Conselheiro was a nutcase. (Viany, 1965, p. 129)

Accordingly, Rocha uses the idea of the sea as a 'symbol', to which he attaches a 'revolutionary sense' (1965, p. 127). More significantly, he mixes Sebastião's prophetic/nonsensical speeches with Marxist phrases so as to extract the revolutionary potential of the religious discourse and, conversely, to highlight the purely utopian, quasi-religious content of Marxist slogans. Here is a telling extract of one of Sebastião's speeches:

> Those who wish to reach salvation will stay here with me from now on until the day when a sign from God will appear on the Sun. One hundred angels will descend with their fire spears to announce the day of departure and show us the way through the paths of the *sertão*! And the *sertão* will become sea, and the sea will become *sertão*! Man cannot be the slave of man! Man must leave the lands which do not belong to him and search for the green lands of heaven. (cf. Rocha, 1985, p. 266)

It is clear that this mystical, 'chaotic' *sertão,* with no defined territorial borders or time frame, cannot be the one which conveys the strong sense of national identity I referred to at the beginning of this section. National identity, which the film unquestionably renders, must then stem from elsewhere, and here is where my hypothesis of physical realism comes into play. Rather than the stage of history, the *sertão* in *God and the Devil* is a laboratory where film crew and cast experience with their own bodies the conditions of a land that gave birth to such messianic movements on the one hand, and social banditry on the other. Accounting for the film's sensory realism there is, of course, in the first place, Rocha's own life experience from being born in Vitória da Conquista, in a region of Bahia he also refers to as *sertão,* though a long way south of the area of Canudos and Monte Santo. Figures such as the professional killer Antônio das Mortes, with his characteristic long cape, which so impressed the likes of Fassbinder and Scorsese, stem from his childhood memories. As well as being surrounded by other *sertão* experts, such as documentarian Paulo Gil Soares and film director Walter Lima Jr, he had also met and interviewed old survivors of the Canudos rebellion, blind storytellers and even the actual killer of Corisco, Major Rufino, still alive in those days. But it is the way all actors and the camera itself engage with the extreme conditions of the chosen locations that gives the viewer the piercing sense of reality, a reality that could be located nowhere else but in Brazil. Physicality is best exemplified in the film by the act of carrying a huge boulder on one's head up the steps of Monte Santo. Euclides da Cunha had already magnificently identified human suffering at the origin of those same steps, constructed in the early nineteenth century under the orders of the missionary Apollonio de Todi, for whom the mount was reminiscent of the Calvary of Jerusalem:

> Today, whoever climbs the long *via sacra,* some two miles in extent, along which at intervals are twenty-five stone chapels, housing the Stations of the Cross, will be able to form an idea of the constant, unremitting labor that was expended in the erection of this site. Supported by concealed walls, paved in some places while elsewhere the bed of living rock has been carved into steps, in other places sloping upward, this white quartzite roadway, where the litanies of Lenten processions resounded more than a century ago, and over which legions of penitents have passed, is a marvel of rude and bold engineering skill. (Cunha, 1995, p. 163)

The human suffering imbedded in those steps over the centuries was reinforced by testimonials heard by Rocha in the research period preceding the shooting of the film, such as this by old Ioiô, referring to the arrival of Antônio Conselheiro to his village: 'The people took to following him, some singing to their *bentinhos* [amulets], others with boulders on their heads, helping him repair the steps and build up the chapels' (Viany, 1965, p. 11). One of the extras in the film, a woman chosen from among the villagers of Monte Santo, is repeatedly seen in the film serenely sitting with a cobble stone on her head. It is however the ascent of Monte Santo by actor Geraldo Del Rey, in the role of Manuel, on his knees and carrying a huge boulder on his head, the most graphic, lived-in experience of the *sertão* ever shown in film. In a sequence lasting for an unnerving five minutes of handheld camera footage, with no sound other than his groans, Manuel repeatedly drops the boulder on the ground and struggles to bring it up onto his head again, until he reaches the top of the mountain with (real) blood trickling down his face, to the hysterical cheers of the crowd.

Del Rey's acting style is ascribed to Stanislavski's naturalistic school by both Rocha (Viany, 1965, p. 131) and Othon Bastos (Bax, 2005, p. 97), the latter, the extraordinary actor who embodies Corisco through a Brechtian approach. There is however very little naturalism in his and all other cast members' acting style. Theatricality prevails throughout, in Rosa's solemn gestures when piling manioc, Manuel's overtly fake murder of the rancher with the blade of his machete turned upwards, or Sebastião's clearly false slapping of Manuel's face without actually touching him. The clearing in the *sertão* where Corisco performs his reincarnation of Lampião has even the shape of a theatre stage, on which actors' movements are restricted to its borders. It is therefore not in representational acting, but in presentational enactment where realism resides. By looking straight at the camera and varying his intonation and pitch to play alternately Corisco and Lampião, Bastos is calling attention to the reality of the actor, rather than that of the character, very much in accordance with Brecht's precepts. In so doing, however, he is not breaking illusionism, as Brecht envisaged, as much as highlighting the reality of the environment, the dry earth and the scorching sun under which the cast is constrained to perform. The camerawork, or 'participant photography', as director of photography Valdemar Lima calls it, is entirely geared toward reinforcing this reality and integrating the human element into the landscape (Viany, 1965, p. 17):

> We swallowed a great deal of dust on the trans-northeastern highway. We climbed one hundred times the steps of Monte Santo. We killed rattle-snakes and *jararacas* [another venomous serpent]. We ate *mocó de macambira* [a kind of bread made of *macambira* bromelia leaves], in our *sertão* experiences. We walked kilometres on foot carrying our equipment in our arms, on our backs and on our heads. We crossed areas of *mandacaru* and *xique-xique* cactuses, *macambira* and *favela* plants . . . We struggled, suffered, saw, heard and made a film. (Viany, 1965, p. 21)

Statements such as these have no value of evidence, of course, but are enlightening when checked against the actual results. Lima's 'participant' camera, in fact, behaves with an agency and assertiveness comparable to that of the characters – or actors. Mostly handheld, it circles

FIGURE 1.17 Othon Bastos, playing alternately Corisco and dead Lampião, calls attention to the reality of the actor, in *God and the Devil in the Land of the Sun*

around the characters as if questioning them from all angles, it shakes when climbing steps or confronting action, it extracts the meaning of objects by describing their shapes, for example, by following the length of a spear blade up to its sharp end, or the horizontal and vertical branches of a cross to reinforce the meaning of human sacrifice commanded by religious thought. It turns in the opposite direction around gyrating Corisco and Rosa in each other's arms, to the operatic singing of the first movement of 'Bachianas Brasileiras n° 5', nearly materializing the couple's trancelike state.

On the other hand, 'participant photography' resonates with the Gramscian concept of the 'organic intellectual', very much in fashion in those days of political euphoria in which socialist revolution seemed so close at hand (it was a military coup that took place instead, in the same year when *God and the Devil* was launched). But rather than with political upheavals, it is with the mystical and incongruent beliefs of messianic preachers and *cangaceiros* that the camera physically engages with, performing a circular ballet that finds no resolution until Manuel's utopian dash at the end. The camera's circular movement combines with the prevailing triangular disposition of the characters, allowing for one interrogative figure to promenade between two confronting characters, as if to blur any clear sense of opposition.

Figure 1.18

Figure 1.19

Figures 1.18–1.20 A state of confusion and dilemma is created by the camerawork and characters' disposition at the phenomenological stage of shooting: triadic compositions in *God and the Devil in the Land of the Sun*

Examples abound: Manuel between his wife and mother; Antônio das Mortes between the priest and the rancher; the sacrificial baby between Manuel and Sebastião; Corisco between Manuel and Cego Júlio and many, many other cases. Shot-reverse shot montage is not an option in this mixed world, where oppositions can never be clearly defined. Rather than tricking at the editing table, it is at the phenomenological stage of shooting where this state of confusion and dilemma is created primarily by the camerawork.

The *sertão* is lastly the laboratory for experimentation for Rocha's extremely erudite cinephilia. Here, naturalistic representation is entirely overlooked, when it comes to experimenting with Bazinian sequence shots, Godard's jump cuts and asynchronic sound mixing, Eisenstein's vertical montage and Ford's ballad-style Westerns, not to mention the Brazilian *cangaço* genre, which Rocha wanted to critically revisit and remodel. Even here contrasting citations are put together only to be immediately neutralized, for example, through the placing of elliptical, fast-edited action scenes, alongside extremely protracted interior monologues, a process Xavier referred to as the alternation of rarefaction and excess, scarcity and saturation (1999, pp. 35–7).

All tools were valid as virtuoso exercise, so long as they were reinvented anew through direct experience of the physical environment. This is what Manuel's race at the end of the film signifies. Not only an obvious citation of the celebrated ending of *The 400 Blows,* and not the final encounter with the sea, which only the spectator, but not the character, can see. But the painful, bodily experience and recognition of a harsh, cruel soil, under an unrelenting sun, which happens to be unmistakably located in Brazil.

The 400 Blows

This film classic is at the origin of all the main ideas developed in this chapter: an ethics of realism manifested in tropes whose originality derives from their being reenacted in physical reality. At the same time it is the film in which these concepts are most subtly concealed, as compared to the other cases examined here. The innovative power of *The 400 Blows* is unquestionable from the simple fact that it inaugurated the French Nouvelle Vague, which radically changed the way films were done worldwide and continues to reverberate in world cinema up to this day. However, this innovation was carried out by the film without causing any sense of rebellion. The reason may lie precisely in this term 'classic' I purposely employed to suggest the film's seamless narrative construction, through which all physicality is absorbed into the naturalness of the fable. Most techniques employed – the balance between the episodes, the smooth dissolves between shots and scenes, the suave background music, the nuanced psychological description of the characters, the beauty of the images – are meant to seal all possible cracks on the narrative surface and keep any dissonant interferences of the phenomenological world at bay. And yet critics never fail to succumb to the film's overwhelming sense of 'realism' and 'authenticity', as its main qualities have consistently been described. I concur with this view and will therefore devote this section to an attempt at unravelling the indexical quality of *The 400 Blows* from its tightly woven fictional mesh.

As Don Allen points out, Truffaut 'had never wanted to revolutionize the French cinema, [but] merely to return to the "good" traditions of the Thirties, represented by Vigo and particularly Renoir' (1985, p. 36). This kind of 'conservative' attitude is easily identifiable and includes extensive borrowings from the American cinema, and Hitchcock in particular, as regards point of view construction on the basis of an individual hero, linear storytelling, sutured montage and the creation of suspense. Cinephile citations, which abound in the film, are never there to break the narrative flow (as is invariably the case with Godard), but, on the contrary, to enhance its efficacy. There is no sense of aesthetic rupture and no grounds for scandal in the chosen storyline, an innocent tale of coming of age. It is in fact so hard to pin down how the film reconnects with 'the reality of its time', as Gillain has put it (1991, p. 5), that critics have opted en masse to believe that *The 400 Blows* is nothing but Truffaut's own life story, sprinkled with improvised additions by the adolescent actor Jean-Pierre Léaud. This is understandable with regard to a filmmaker who writes as eloquently and convincingly as he films, and who was the brain behind the *politique des auteurs,* of which *The 400 Blows* was meant to be the most literal cinematic translation. As everything else in the film, authorial signature is discretely, though efficiently, inscribed into the diegesis, Hitchcock style. The obvious illustration here is the famous scene in the fairground, in which Truffaut stands next to Doinel inside a gyrating rotor machine, filmed in such a way as to reproduce the mechanism of the praxinoscope, a predecessor of the cinematographe. The physical experience of the centrifugal force, which plasters participants against the rotor wall, unites character, actor and auteur in a cleverly devised fusion of film fable and real life. Such stylistic exercises alone, however, would hardly suffice to fuel the autobiographic legend around *The 400 Blows.* The culprit is again Truffaut himself, who has always volunteered detailed accounts of his life, and his childhood in particular, at every opportunity. Here, in effect, resides the scandal no one can find in the film: in the *real* illegitimate child Truffaut had been, who never met his natural father, was rejected by his mother and stepfather, then sent to a reformatory and finally allowed to flourish as an artist thanks to his substitute father, the legendary film critic André Bazin. With the exception of the events relating to Bazin, mentioned only in the form of a posthumous homage in the dedication, all the other facts are recounted in the film.

The 'myth Truffaut' triggered by *The 400 Blows* has since never ceased to grow, fed as it has been by the voluminous written documents and epistolary exchange he produced in his lifetime, unveiling among other things an acrimonious correspondence with his stepfather, as well as his parents' divorce allegedly caused by the revelation of his mother's adultery contained in the film (see de Bacque and Toubiana, 1996). Truffaut was also famously a 'man who loved women', as one of his film titles goes, and this detail coupled with his love for the red-light district of Pigalle, from his Parisian childhood, have continued to spice up his public profile to this day. Regardless of the sensational appeal it undoubtedly has, however, the articulate analysis of Truffaut's life and films has resulted in superb studies, such as Gillain (1988, 1991, 1991b), de Bacque and Toubiana (1996), Allen (1985), Cahoreau (1989), Malanga (1996), Butterfly (2004), Holmes and Ingram (1997), not to mention Truffaut's wonderful writings themselves (1975), and I will be constantly resorting to them in this analysis. My argument is not against biographical approaches, but simply that Truffaut's autobiographical style cannot account for the spectatorial experience of realism in *The 400 Blows* – or indeed in any other of his films. The question is, as Doniol-Valcroze has put it already at the launch of the film in 1959,

> not to know if his hero Antoine is he [Truffaut] or not. What matters is that Antoine exists with surprising truth, and this continuous over-authenticity which fascinates us during the entire projection does not exclude humour, or fantasy, or poetry, or the dramatic quality of the cinematic narrative and the power of its progression. (apud Butterfly, 2004, p. 39)

It might be, as Butterfly suggests, that 'the "I" of François Truffaut is more universal than singular, more archetypal than subjective' (2004, p. 39). Being, however, *outside* the filmic reality, despite his fleeting auteurist apparitions, the autobiographical author cannot provide any indexical value to the characters or the story. Representational realism, revolving around verisimilitude rather than the reality of the film event, would be likewise unfit to provide this link, as critics have often, but mistakenly, remarked. Don Allen, for example, has attributed the 'authenticity' of Antoine's portrait to the 'quasi-documentary style of the camerawork' (1985, p. 36). He says: 'The restrained, unemotional treatment has the effect of inducing spontaneous sympathy in the spectator and a feeling of collective responsibility, even guilt' (p. 36). This is however misleading, as the term 'spontaneous sympathy' sends us back to narrative identification processes and vraisemblance, rather than the production of material truth. Moreover, uncommitted camerawork, as we know, is hardly fit to elicit 'spontaneous sympathy', much less 'guilt', but is more often employed to incite critical, distanced spectatorship. In any case, the fact remains that the camera in *The 400 Blows* is not at all uncommitted, but a consummate accomplice of Antoine Doinel, in an entirely character-driven plot construction, in which the protagonist's point of view prevails over all others. Documentary style is, however, verifiable in another interesting way, that of uncovering the material existence of characters and objects, in such a way as to reinforce the truth of the fable. The rotor scene is again an example here, as it highlights characters overwhelmed by the sensations experienced in reality by their own bodies as actors, who are moreover shot by a camera which is itself at times placed inside the machine and experiencing the centrifugal force along with them. Let us call it the camera's 'tactilism', which goes on a par with the characters' overdeveloped sense of touch, this in turn subtly interwoven with the sub-theme of physical exertion and bodily punishment within the plot.

Let us start with the opening tracking shots of the film, along the streets of Paris, showing from different angles, at a distance, the Eiffel Tower, all the while brushing on some notable sites, such as the Palais de Chaillot where the Cinémathèque Française used to be located, until it finally meets the tower proper and shows it from the inside, before driving away from it again. This is an entirely extradiegetic opening, in principle serving merely as a background to the initial credits with no narrative function other than to specify the settings of the story as Paris – which would place this film immediately within the realist tradition of a Rossellini, for example, who famously made his characters emerge out of real cityscapes, such as Rome and Berlin. Thanks to an interview with Truffaut, collected by Gillain (1998, pp. 96ff.), we know that this sequence was originally planned to be part of the story. Antoine and his classmate René, having skipped school, would take a taxi to visit the Tower, but the driver, an Algerian who has just begun at the job, would constantly lose his way and revolve around the tower several times before finally reaching it. This idea was in the end abandoned, the point-of-view shots of the boys were never shot and the Eiffel Tower footage was used as background to the credits instead. Gillain aligns this opening with the final encounter with the sea, saying that: 'The introduction and the conclusion of *The 400 Blows* are organized around images of quest and reunion with a mythic object: the Eiffel Tower and the sea' (1991, p. 97). I would say that these two framing sequences of the film are comparable for one more reason: the demythologizing of both the tower and the sea through tactilism. Indeed, on a closer approach, they turn out to be nothing other than a heavy iron cage – under which the name of the director François Truffaut is significantly inscribed, or 'imprisoned' – in the former case, and sheer cold water into which Antoine briefly immerses his shod feet before recoiling, in the latter. Both the camera, in the former, and the character, in the latter, lose interest in their mythical

FIGURE 1.21

FIGURES 1.21–1.22 Confronting material reality: the Eiffel tower as an iron cage and the sea as sheer cold water in *The 400 Blows*

objects of desire and immediately turn away from them upon touch and close inspection. Urban and natural environments are before anything else material reality and offer no escape from a society represented throughout the film by the metaphor of the cage.

I am entering again a well-trodden terrain, about which a great deal of excellent criticism has been written, so I will restrict myself to some specific aspects of the prison theme in the film, starting with art viewed as an escape from the material world. Antoine Doinel, in the film, carries the mark of *difference* and this difference is conceived in the form of artistic drive. The rendering of Antoine is the typical 'portrait of the artist as a young man', as James Joyce called his autobiographical novel, depicting a romantic, rebellious character at the dawn of modernism. Likewise, Antoine cannot resist his creative impulse, which invariably leads to punishment and repression by society around him. We are introduced to the protagonist at school, where during a class of French a calendar illustrated with the figure of a pin-up is circulating and lands on his desk. Unlike his classmates, who are satisfied with surreptitiously looking at the image, Antoine feels compelled to interfere, by drawing a moustache on the female figure. This has been read as a preemptive aggression to a hostile mother figure later to appear in the film (Gillain, 1991, p.74), but it is nonetheless a creative impulse that distinguishes him from the others and entails an isolated punishment. The metaphor of prison makes its first appearance in the form of a tight corner behind the blackboard, where the teacher orders Antoine to stand while the class continues. There again he cannot resist his artistic drive and secretly inscribes a poem on the wall:

Ici souffrit le pauvre Antoine Doinel
Puni injustement par Petite Feuille
Pour une pin-up tombée du ciel
Entre nous ça sera dent pour dent, oeil pour oeil

The translation used in the English subtitles is somewhat adapted for the sake of rhyme: 'Here suffered Antoine Doinel unfairly/Punished by a prof for a pin-up clad barely/So it's now forsooth, eye for eye, tooth for tooth!' A typical romantic hero comes out of these verses: an innocent, poor soul, who can see the world better than anybody else, is unjustly picked up and punished for a collective wrong. Discovered again, Antoine is accused by the teacher Petite Feuille of trying to be a 'new Juvenal', who cannot even differentiate between an Alexandrine and a decasyllable. Physical punishment follows once again: Antoine is ordered to clean up the mess on the wall and, as homework, to conjugate in all tenses of the indicative, conditional and subjunctive modes the phrase 'I dirty the classroom wall and misuse French versification' – which triggers the hilarious voiceover of Antoine's thought amplified through a haunting echo: '*Que je dégradasse les murs de la classe*', containing another poetic rhyme.

The teacher's crass misunderstanding of the precocious genius he has in his classroom is obviously derived from a point of view construction centred on Antoine that governs the film as a whole. And this is just the first of a long series of flights of genius on the part of Antoine, which will be curtailed by his school, family and society in general in the form of physical punishment and confinement. At home, he is prevented from doing his homework by an abusive mother, who sends him on untimely errands. As a result, he is advised by his friend René to skip school, and this is when he accidentally sees his mother in the arms of a lover. Back in school the next day, and without a note of excuse because his stepfather had arrived the night before precisely when he was about to forge one, he lies to the teacher that he missed school because his mother had died. Once the truth is revealed, punishment is not slow to arrive, this time in the form of violent slaps in the face by his stepfather, in front of his entire class.

Another attempt at creative writing is made through a pact between Antoine and his mother, when she promises him money in exchange for a good mark in his French essay. Antoine then delves into the study of Balzac's *La Recherche de l'absolu,* and memorizes it to the point of reproducing a section of it literally in his essay. As a result, he receives a zero for his essay, of course, however the point of view construction is again so manipulative in favour of the romantic hero, that the spectator is led to believe that he is once more the victim of gross injustice. A last manifestation of Antoine's obsession with writing comes in the form of his stealing a typewriter from his stepfather's office. All goes wrong again, and this time the punishment is the cruellest. He is sent to jail at first and then to a juvenile delinquency centre. There, the routine of physical punishment will resume, including another violent slap in the face in front of all the inmates during lunch time, until Antoine's final escape towards the sea.

In the realm of the fable, Antoine is constantly being confronted with a world which denies him the right to individuality and original creativity. This denial comes regularly through the corporeal experience of the real, in the form of shock, especially remarkable in the unannounced, loud slaps in the face. This is how his romantic imagination is regularly forced back down to an earth destitute of metaphysical aura.

In Benjaminian terms, he is constantly being pulled down from the realm of *Erlebnis* – something lived through – to that of *Erfahrung*, or the experience in the flesh. Benjamin says about Baudelaire that 'he indicated the price for which the sensation of the modern age may be had: the disintegration of the aura in the experience of shock' (1999, p. 190). For Baudelaire, shock was produced by the confrontation between the indifferent crowds and the detached *flâneur* perambulating in the streets of modern Paris. Antoine's romantic wanderings through the streets of Paris are not exactly confronted with an indifferent crowd, but with the facticity of an indifferent, material world. Thus, his experiences of escape yield no better results than those of imprisonment. Instead, they mean sleeping rough in the cold winter, filling his empty stomach with milk hastily drunk from a stolen bottle, washing his dirty face with the frozen water of a street fountain, in short, being in permanent discomfort.

All this is in accordance with normative representational realism, in that, as Grodal puts it, it coincides with negative rather than positive experience: 'This is perhaps based on the assumption that "pain" is more real than "pleasure", thus evoking more genuine behaviour', continues Grodal (2002, p. 87). Margulies also associates realism to 'bodily discomfort' (2003, p. 5), and no doubt discomfort is stressed in the film as the very condition of Antoine's life. He is himself a dirty boy who is once granted a bath in a basin in his kitchen, but only because his mother wants to buy his silence about her lover. He messes his hands with coal, when filling up the stove, and wipes them in the house curtain. He is in charge of the disgusting rubbish bin in the house, and all other details about his daily routine are equally uninviting. However, yet again, it would be misleading to indentify this as the way through which the sense of authenticity is produced. Truffaut himself made no secret of his intention of attenuating any visual roughness deriving from poverty and dirt in the film plot:

> The settings of my film are sad and sordid, and I was afraid of rendering an unpleasant atmosphere. Thanks to the scope format, I obtained a stylization effect, which could account for a larger reality. (Gillain, 1988, p. 96)

More importantly, the scope format allowed for longer shots and fewer cuts. This brings us back to a typical Bazinian realism of the medium: long takes and long shots, coupled with the rejection of all studio facilities, including the scenes in Antoine's flat, all of them shot in a real one-bedroom flat in Paris, and the quasi-documentary footage of

Paris itself. In order to truly account for the realism of *The 400 Blows,* however, it is indispensable to consider the experience of shock, the power of the material real clashing against the film's pervading romantic imagination with its ruthless indifference, as wonderfully exemplified by the cold waves of the sea soaking Antoine's feet at the end of the film.

In fact the entire camerawork, montage, acting and plot construction gear toward this moment of physical truth. Antoine manages to escape the reformatory by finding a gap in the fence during a football match, in one of the many deriding scenes about sport activities in the film (other examples are the gym teacher being progressively abandoned by his pupils who follow him in queue in the streets of Paris and Antoine's stepfather's overblown passion for car rallies). As he loses his pursuer, there follows a long tracking-shot of c. two minutes of Antoine running alongside a country road. Music here is suspended and the only sounds are of his footsteps and occasional birds. All attentions are turned to Antoine or, more precisely, to Jean-Pierre Léaud exercising his body in the long run. For a moment, representation, so carefully maintained during the entire film, is lifted to reveal not only the person of an actor but his act of performing for a film. Rather than the desperate dash enacted by Geraldo Del Rey at the end of *God and the Devil in the Land of the Sun,* with his arms turning around and feet stumbling on the rugged surface, Léaud runs like a professional runner, as if he were entirely aware of the distance to be covered and keeping an according pace to save his breath, his arms duly folded and moving in harmony with his body. This is not the representation of an escape, but the presentation of a running actor which then smoothly mixes, through a dissolve, with the Seine estuary over which the camera pans to recapture Antoine, as he briefly pauses under a high tree, in a contemplative pose entirely redolent of the romantic hero as found, for example, in the painting of Caspar David Friedrich. Another long tracking-shot follows him as he descends the steps toward the beach, runs to the sea, dips his feet into the water and then turns back to the camera. The film finishes here, with a frozen close-up of his face. This ending has a predecessor, already indicated by Truffaut himself and commented upon by critics such as Allen (1985, p. 44). It is Vigo's *L'Atalante* (1933), in a scene toward the end, when Jean, desperate to see the image of his stranded wife reflected in the water, runs along the beach at the Havre, nears the sea, but then retraces his steps, rejecting what seems to be the possibility of a suicide. As for the sea in *The 400 Blows,* death is also a meaning considered by Malanga (1996,

FIGURE 1.23 Antoine Doinel as a romantic hero, in *The 400 Blows*

p. 253), who draws on Daney and his idea of photographic stasis as representative of the death drive in this and other films (1993, p. 38). The return to the motherly womb is another popular interpretation of Antoine's race toward the sea, and Gillain reminds us of the pun *mer-mère* (sea and mother) overused by critics apropos of this ending (1991, p. 98). Instead, I propose a more matter-of-fact view, the mere facticity of water, matching that of the iron cage of the Eiffel Tower at the beginning of the film, that is to say, the clash of physical experience against the heroic aura, modernism against romanticism, which is at the end congealed without solution.

Chapter 2

THE IMMATERIAL DIFFERENCE: WERNER HERZOG REVISITED

From close-up, no one is normal.
Caetano Veloso

This chapter will examine the work of Werner Herzog, a fascinating instance of physical filmmaking that differs considerably – at least in principle – from the ones analysed in Chapter 1. In these, physicality is resorted to as a means to establish a material link between cast/crew, the profilmic event and the resulting film, so as to generate a sense of belonging and identity. In contrast, Herzog's physical approach to cinema seems to rely on an irretrievable loss of identity, a rupture between the human element and its environment through which the materiality of the former comes to the fore. Reality thus becomes synonymous with *difference,* a fact embodied by the legions of extraordinary beings who populate his entire output.

In the sections that follow, I will investigate the nature and validity of Herzog's claims to difference, the kind of realism deriving from his physical filmmaking and the ethics associated with his mode of address within and beyond the realm of representation. Starting from the director's body itself, I will proceed to the examination of physicality in his oeuvre in the light of its historical and aesthetic connections with the New German Cinema, the Nouvelle Vague and the Brazilian Cinema Novo.

The Excessive Body

There is hardly a greater champion of physical cinema in the world than Werner Herzog. A physical, or, in Herzog's preferred expression, 'athletic' approach to cinema has been the cause of his entire career, now spanning more than four decades of uninterrupted filmmaking. At the same time, characterizing physicality in Herzog's films is anything but a simple operation. Not only because there is a general perception that, as Gilles Deleuze put it, Herzog 'is the most metaphysical of film directors' (2005, p. 189) – and I will return to this in due course – but because physicality in his films can only be properly apprehended once a major obstacle is abstracted from them: the director's body itself. The complexity of this task can be measured by both the number of films he has directed so far – nearly 60 since his first short, *Herakles,* of 1962 – and the ubiquity of his visual and/or aural presence in the majority of them. Authorial presence takes place in Herzog's films in a variety of ways: through the director's intradiegetic bodily appearances as the film narrator; through his extradiegetic voiceover commentaries; through apocryphal or (mostly adapted) quotations in the form of titles applied to the films, whose tone and contents leave no doubt as to their source being, once again, the director himself; or pointed cameo appearances.

Authorial assertion and physical presence is a common device, in particular in modern cinema, where it is used as a means to call the spectator's attention to the reality of the cinematic apparatus and the tricks of representation, examples ranging from Woody Allen to Jean-Luc Godard,[1] from Takeshi Kitano to Michael Moore. The double figure of the actor-director has provided filmmakers since Erich von Stroheim with an effective means to attach indexical value to fiction, and I will look more closely into this question in Chapter 7, apropos of João César Monteiro. As for directorial voiceovers, a notorious example closer to Herzog's cultural background and New German Cinema origins can be found in the figure of Alexander Kluge, whose peculiarly smooth background voice narration constitutes a hallmark of his films. These two apparently antagonistic filmmakers, standing at the opposite poles of 'physical' and 'intellectual' filmmaking within the New German Cinema spectrum, have in fact further interesting contact points which will be examined in the next section. The documentary genre is particularly prone to the self-referential mode, as it often requires a filmmaker's direct involvement in the facts in focus, reaching extremes with the I-movie and the 'private documentary' forms, in which directors merge with their subjects to the point of becoming indistinguishable from them, as I will discuss in Chapter 6 with reference to Kazuo Hara and Sachiko Kobayashi. In all these cases, authorial presence is meant to question a director's position of authority and make them as vulnerable as the other actors before the camera. Not so in Herzog's case.

His voice in spoken or written form, often accompanied by his visual appearance, is invariably that of the conventional omniscient narrator, detached from the historical world and endowed with the power to determine the film's unified perspective and meaning. This can be observed from his earliest works, such as *The Flying Doctors of East Africa* (*Die fliegenden Ärzte aus Ostafrika,* 1969) through to the recent *Grizzly Man* (2005), in which the director reserves for himself the last word on his subjects. Mystical, mostly apocalyptical prophecies and divine invocations are common features of both written and spoken commentaries, in particular in his fiction films, such as *Fitzcarraldo* (1982), *The Enigma of Kaspar Hauser* (*Jeder für sich und Gott gegen Alle,* 1974)and *Heart of Glass* (*Herz aus Glas,* 1976), even when the director's voice is momentarily replaced by that of an extradiegetic professional speaker (*Signs of Life/Lebenszeichen,* 1967) or of an intradiegetic first-person narrator (the priest Gaspar de Carvajal, in *Aguirre, the Wrath of God/ Aguirre, der Zorn Gottes,* 1972). These embodied or disembodied voices constantly remind us of god's incomplete work of creation, his wrath against his creatures, the evils of society and the inevitable doom of all titanic rebels.

This literally resonates with what is otherwise metaphorically described as the 'voice-of-god' or 'voice-of-authority' typical of the expository mode in the documentary genre, as defined by Bill Nichols (2001, pp. 105ff.). Nichols includes in this category both visible and invisible speakers, as well as explanatory titles, all of which are inherent to Herzog's narrative repertoire. Traditionally, however, the voice-of-god is that of a professionally trained speaker, with no authorial input, so as to confirm its neutrality and objectivity with relation to the facts in focus. Herzog also resorted to this kind of professional narrative voice in his early films, such as *Signs of Life* and *The Unprecedented Defence of the Fortress Deutschkreuz* (*Die beispiellose Verteidigung der Festung Deutschkreuz,* 1967). But his highly subjective discourse was hardly suitable to a neutral reading, and even risked involuntary humour, a case in point being the end of *Signs of Life,* when an uninterested speaker reads off-frame grandiloquent lines of inscrutable philosophy. This danger was certainly perceived by Herzog himself, who subsequently tried a kind of self-questioning and self-parodic multiple voiceovers in *Fata Morgana* (1970; more on this film in the next section). This was an interesting experiment, which however had no follow-ups, as he decided thereafter to take up the narrative voice himself, a role he has performed in the conservative voice-of-god/voice-of-authority style ever since, even when he must speak in his heavily accented English, a trait which over the years has become integral to his public persona. This he justifies by saying:

> In my 'documentaries' you will often hear my voice. One reason for this is that I would rather audiences who do not understand German listen to *my* voice in English rather than hear me in German and read the subtitles. I think the result is a stronger connection to what I originally intended for the film. I have also never liked the polished and inflected voices of those overly trained actors. (Cronin, 2002, p. 55)

Various interesting points can be drawn from this statement. In the first place, the director seems to believe – or fear – that the diegetic audiovisual universe of his films might not be sufficient to convey his 'original intentions', hence the need to add his explanatory voice. That this voice is also aimed at reasserting the director's authority over the meaning of his films is something Herzog has made exhaustively clear throughout his career. Another point to remark is Herzog's drive to make himself instantly recognizable to audiences, through his particular voice and accent, as an *actor* who is actually *better* than those professionally trained. This is what, in my view, characterizes his persona as a *competitor* to his films, rather than part of them, and this is why I deem it possible and indeed necessary to separate the two.

In all, Herzog's attitude seems to be in frank contradiction with his claim that 'he is his films', as expressed in the title of a documentary about him, *I Am My Films: A Portrait of Werner Herzog* (*Was ich bin, sind meine Filme,* Erwin Keusch and Christian Weisenborn, 1979). Not so much in the sense of a split auteur figure, divided between the abstraction of words and the density of images, as once observed by Corrigan (1986, p. 6), but in the director's unrelenting efforts to outdo his films to the point of turning them into mere accessories in the construction of the legend around his person. In fact, his urge to control the perception and reception of his films goes far beyond his intrafilmic voices. Despite his pose as an artisan and manual worker, averse to intellectual reflection and oral expression, Herzog has proved in all these decades an extremely eloquent writer and speaker, through a voluminous literature about and around his films, alongside copious interviews and public talks he is always keen to volunteer all over the world. With the release of most of his oeuvre on DVD, in boxes, cases and discs duly illustrated with photographs of the director himself alongside or even in lieu of images of his films, one is additionally presented with Herzog's voice providing critical commentary about his own product in the extras, a role normally performed by third parties, such as film experts, crew or cast members. The self-mythologizing, victimizing and heroicizing machinery set in motion with rare competence by this hard-working and highly organized filmmaker leaves so little room for independent criticism that one wonders why so many of us still bother to write about him – or rather, if at all possible, about his films. The reason can only be that Herzog is *not* his films, and that these are at the same time more and less than the director wants us to believe.

Herzog, as a person, is a media phenomenon, whose writings and opinions hardly ever surpass the level of self-help literature or New-Age esotericism. His vocabulary is extraordinarily limited and purposely vague when describing his own filmic imagery, with undisguised self-infatuation, as 'strange', 'eerie', 'mysterious', 'stylized', 'primordial', 'archetypical'. His theory about his own spontaneous generation, 'as if film history had never existed' (Pflaum, 1979, p. 59), and that 'cinema is not the art of scholars, but of illiterates' (Greenberg, 1976, p. 174) cannot be taken at face value by any serious criticism. This however allows me to explore the main theme of this chapter, concerning difference as synonym for material reality.

An undeniable trump of Herzog's oeuvre as a whole, difference has become for him the subject of unrelenting commercial exploration. More than that: by disengaging himself from history and film history, he has fashioned himself to the international media as the 'embodiment' of difference. However, as is the case with all artworks, Herzog's films are solidly grounded in history, film history and the director's and his collaborators' cultural backgrounds, and for this reason are much more than a mere collection of 'eerie' visions and landscapes. Herzog's oeuvre, and his early work in particular, are invaluable eyewitnesses of both social and scientific interest, of man-provoked destruction, death and decay (*Fata Morgana, La Soufrière,* 1977), of human-animal kinship (*Heart of Glass, The Enigma of Kaspar Hauser, Stroszek,* 1976), of man's (male's, as Herzog's films are hardly ever about women) irrational thirst for power (*Herakles, Aguirre, Heart of Glass, Echoes from a Sombre Empire/Echos aus einem düsteren Reich,* 1990), of how the debris and detritus of capitalist society extend their tentacles to the farthest corners of the globe (*Encounters at the End of the World,* 2007). Most strikingly, Herzog's documentary approach (even when fictional) to ethnic, disabled and other minorities has drawn worldwide attention to their personal plights and political causes (*Land of Silence and Darkness/Land des Schweigens und der Dunkelheit,* 1971; *Where the Green Ants Dream/Wo die grünen Ameisen träumen,* 1984; *Wodaabe: Herdsmen of the Sun/Wodaabe: die Hirten der Sonne,* 1989). Herzog's keen perception of the physical world and his typically new-wave drive to unveil hidden aspects of reality have placed him at the forefront of international trends that would take years or even decades to develop, not least his 'athletic' relation to artistic production, which was in advance by around a decade of the ethos of healthy eating, exercising, drug-free living and environmental respect. The music produced by the Popol Vuh ensemble, led by Florian Fricke, Herzog's personal friend and collaborator, is also a clear predecessor of the atmospheric New Age music which would take some 15 years to become trendy, after the groundbreaking launch of the Popol Vuh sound in *Aguirre.* Above all, with his tireless search across the world for 'transparent images', Herzog has anticipated the severed sensory links with the world of a late-capitalist, globe-trotting society, eternally searching for difference through indiscriminate tourism, only to find more of the same: identity everywhere.

However, Herzog's physical cinema can only operate on the basis of a presentational mode, in the sense of what Rancière defines as an 'aesthetic regime of art', which, according to him, affirms the 'absolute power of style'. For Rancière, a work of art conceived under this regime, 'would bear no traces of the author's intervention and display instead only the absolute indifference and passivity of things with neither will nor meaning' (2001, p. 117). It is precisely in the indifference of things, the sheer, opaque materiality of death which pervades Herzog's oeuvre as a whole, where physicality is presented as an irreducible element. This physical element, however, remains stubbornly resistant to representation, hence Herzog's misadventures with mainstream cinema and Hollywood, into which he periodically tries to introduce his 'athletic' methods with no convincing results so far. Examples are *Cobra Verde* (1987), *Rescue Dawn* (2006) and above all *Fitzcarraldo,* Herzog's most complete fiasco to this day, but also his greatest box-office success, thanks to the media event it became with the sensational narrative, cleverly woven by the director, of the disasters surrounding its production and his heroic acts in overcoming them – and I will return to this film in the last section. Since then the *Fitzcarraldo* legend has continued to grow, with Herzog constantly publishing and talking about it, and in so doing refuelling its marketability.

That *Fitzcarraldo* constitutes a dividing line within Herzog's work had already been keenly perceived by Noël Carroll, who wrote, close to the time when the film was launched:

> [I]n vouching for something ineffable – in pointing it out and symbolizing it distinctly – Herzog makes those dimensions and properties of experience that he champions more and more effable. . . . In recent works like *Fitzcarraldo,* Herzog's approach is becoming predictable, a repetition of mannerisms from earlier films – e.g., South American exoticism, an impossible vision, the worship of the ineffable power of music, a physically dangerous feat, Kinski, etc. The extraordinary is reduced to the formulaic; the mysterious becomes routinized; the ineffable hackneyed. (1998, pp. 298–9)

I would add to this the ethical issue at stake when physicality must be staged. It is one thing to locate, with a ferociously critical eye, the signs of purposeless destruction in a landscape; it is another to *cause* this destruction for the sake of a purposeless film, as was the case in *Fitzcarraldo,* with the tearing down of the Amazon jungle and the endangering of many lives, including those of the native Indians, a few of whom actually died. All this for the sake of a less than sympathetic protagonist, who 'dreams' of bringing opera into the jungle, a feat which, by the way, had already been achieved by someone else, not just in reality, but also within the film fable, with the Manaus Opera House. This Herzog calls 'the conquest of the useless', as the title of his lengthy *Fitzcarraldo* diaries goes (2004), in which the victim and hero is Herzog himself rather than the Indians and the jungle. As Corrigan had once warned, 'Herzog's most dangerous and vulnerable position may be in extending his fiction of self and film into one of the most ethically reprehensible dimensions of commercial filmmaking' (1986, p. 13).

This being said, there has hardly ever been a more ethical approach to race, ethnicity, mental and physical disability, poverty and marginality in general than in Herzog's films. In a way entirely different from Hara and Kobayashi's participative challenging of their marginal characters (see Chapter 6), but with similar results, in Herzog's films characters are given room to express themselves beyond stereotypical understandings of (their) difference. Their exceptional nature does not arise from comparison against the norm, but from their highlighting of the distortions contained in prevailing models of normality, and examples will be presented below. The results of Herzog's approach to difference have been compared to the subjective deformation of the objective world typical of expressionism (see Prager, 2007, pp. 56ff.), as well as to the romantic view of misunderstood geniuses living in abnormal bodies and/or minds. I would attribute them in equal measure to an ethics of realism that entirely depends on characters and situations found in the objective world as a given, and therefore resistant to representation. To a great extent, this is what determines their success in some films – *Stroszek,* in my view, is Herzog's best achieved social criticism, and perhaps Herzog's best film altogether, which entirely dispenses with his habitual metaphysical musings and 'visionary' landscapes – and failure in others, Kinski's performance in *Cobra Verde* and *Fitzcarraldo* being the obvious examples of involuntary self-parody resulting from excessive representation.

One could thus say that, as a filmmaker, Herzog thinks with his body; as a thinker, however, he remains hopelessly hostage to the insufficient power of his verbal discourse, which limits and often works against the most original and innovative properties of his own films. Hence perhaps his resentment against intellectuals, and academia in particular, expressed in statements such as this:

> Academic thought is a serious disease, this kind of vivisection, of assassination they carry out on something which is alive and beautiful. (Nagib, 1991, p. 250)

As Prager points out, 'Herzog casts a long shadow over most attempts at interpretation and critique' (2007, p. 2). However, the oral commentaries he provides his films with, as well as the subsidiary literature produced by him around them, have no function other than to add an intellectual, reflexive layer to the factual events in focus. If these two layers remain tenaciously separate and conflictive, this is due to Herzog's own lack of understanding of his interferences, as well as to his uncontrollable fear that images and sounds will not be able to speak for themselves. This friction has been recently spotted with sharp precision by Jeong and Andrew apropos of *Grizzly Man.* Commenting on Treadwell's own film among the bears within Herzog's film, the authors note that: 'Treadwell's video is the authentic cinematic kernel, the uncontrollable outside, lodged inside the film, a trace of the Real which Herzog tries vainly to envelop in his well-formed film language' (Jeong and Andrew, 2008, p. 8). They conclude by saying that: 'Through the yawning gap opened up between the two irreconcilable languages in *Grizzly Man,* the spectator/auditor glimpses the Real and recognizes it as death itself' (p. 11). My interest in this chapter is likewise to look into the gap between the language of physical experience and Herzog's voice-of-god so as to retrieve the indexical trace – or the absolute materiality of death.

It was typical of the new waves of the 1960s – and Herzog appeared during that period – that directors needed to be enshrined to make themselves noticed. At the height of the *politique des auteurs,* in the mid-1950s, Truffaut used to say that there are no good or bad films, but only good or bad directors. 'What matters in a good filmmaker's career', he famously stated, 'is that it reflects a director's thought, from the beginning of his career to his maturity. Each one of his films marks a stage of his thoughts, and it does not matter at all if the film is a success or a failure' (Truffaut, 1988, p. 73). However, Truffaut's protector André Bazin was highly sceptical of this formula, reminding his disciples at the *Cahiers* that mediocre directors could very well make great films, and geniuses sometimes extinguish after a first masterpiece. 'God, as Sartre has already pointed out, is not an artist!' joked Bazin (1985, p. 252). Following Bazin's cue, I suggest that, if we are to look at Herzog as an artist, we need to start by stripping the authority from his voice-of-god, contextualize and historicize his films, and only then attempt to understand their actual material. In the sections below, I will look at a choice of Herzog's films which connects him through realist devices to other new cinemas and directors, in particular Alexander Kluge, François Truffaut and Glauber Rocha. This will hopefully help us evaluate his position within, and contribution to, film history, as well as the extent to which his films subscribe to an ethics of realism.

Literal Difference

Herzog belongs to a generation born during World War II, and this horrific experience could not but be present in his work. However, there are no more than three films directly addressing this subject in his entire production so far: *Signs of Life, Little Dieter Needs to Fly* (1997) and *Invincible* (2000), and even in these, as Prager rightly observes, a means is always found to draw the focus away from political and historical questions (2007, p. 143). On the other hand, Herzog's work as a whole is littered with signs of death, all of which are directly or indirectly related to wars of one kind or another. It would be wrong, of course, to read all these signs as relating to one single war or event, nonetheless the horror emanating from Herzog's stories and characters and their rebellion against an inevitable and catastrophic defeat, as seen in *Signs of Life, Aguirre, Woyzeck, Nosferatu* and *Cobra Verde,* the relentless screaming heard by Kaspar Hauser, the eminent doom announced in *Fata Morgana, Lessons of Darkness* and so many other films, would they not suggest a single cause (or trauma) behind them? Herzog relishes saying that he 'articulates our collective dreams', but do we all have such apocalyptical dreams? Do they not instead derive from a particular experience of catastrophe, which affected the world as a whole, but one nation in particular, that of the filmmaker, as its main cause and final casualty?

Because Herzog is so reluctant to acknowledge any preexisting reasons or historical grounding for his filmmaking, his comments are rarely enlightening on this subject. I will therefore resort at some length to another German filmmaker, Alexander Kluge, whom Corrigan once defined as 'the most articulate filmmaker in Germany' (1983, p. 96), and who, unlike Herzog, has always been all too keen to talk about war, history and filmmaking. It may sound inappropriate to compare a cerebral artist such as Kluge to a self-defined instinctive filmmaker such as Herzog. However, as we will see, the contact points between the two are too significant to be overlooked, when it comes to questions of realism.

Born in 1932, Kluge is known as the mastermind of the Oberhausen Manifesto, which kick-started the cinematic renaissance in Germany in 1962. He is 10 years older than Herzog, who is himself a predecessor of his other New German Cinema colleagues, such as Wenders and Fassbinder. However, Kluge is contemporary to Herzog in his beginning as a filmmaker, after having started as a prolific writer, taking as a starting point for both activities the experience of the Third Reich and World War II. Kluge calls the years immediately after 1945 the *abarischer Punkt*, or, in an approximate translation, çentre of gravity of his work (apud Roberts, 1983, p. 80), drawing on a concept in Physics which determines the point where the attraction forces between two masses (or planets) balance one another. This is significant, for Kluge, insofar as it defines the World War II experience as a moment in German history that inflected both its past and future in equal measures, requiring a corresponding artistic approach able to encompass a backward and forward perspective into history. This defines his realist method, which is based not on rounded narratives, but on situations that work as the centre of gravity for further real or imagined events in the past and future.

Kluge's first incursion into cinema is *Brutality in Stone* (*Brutalität in Stein,* 1960), a short film conceived in partnership with experimental filmmaker Peter Schamoni, who would also collaborate with Herzog in the short film *Precautions against Fanatics* (*Massnahmen gegen Fanatiker,* 1969). *Brutality in Stone* is an analysis of Nazi architecture in Munich through a montage of aggressive corners and sections of monumental columns, walls, steps and halls. The combination of symmetrical shapes to convey abstract concepts – in this case, the notions of power, brutality and destruction – is strongly reminiscent of Eisenstein's vertical montage, a lasting influence on Kluge, who will regularly resort to excerpts of films by Russian constructivists, including Vertov and Dovzhenko, in his subsequent films. This petrified monumentality is then intercut with an interview with a former concentration-camp commander, who coolly describes the workings of gas chambers in mass executions.

Herzog's early cinematic style resonates entirely with this structuring mode, as illustrated by his first short *Herakles,* made less than two years after *Brutality in Stone.* Relying basically on editing effects, *Herakles* obeys a similar principle of visual rhyme, inherent to Eisenstein's vertical montage, with close-ups of the contracting muscles of exercising bodybuilders, which are then crosscut with horrific archival images of an accident during a car race at Le Mans, in which dozens of bystanders were killed. As in Kluge, will to power is directly associated, through montage, with human carnage.

It is however only in his next short, *Porträt einer Bewährung* (1964), that Kluge starts to collaborate with the film editor Beate Mainka-Jellinghaus, from then on his constant partner in the making of his essentially montage cinema. Mainka-Jellinghaus becomes so central to Kluge's work that her name appears as 'co-director' (or co-author) of some of his films, including the feature *Miscellaneous News* (*Vermischten Nachrichten,* 1986). Not to be overlooked, of course, is the fact that Mainka-Jellinghaus, having impressed him with her work for Kluge (Cronin, p. 276), also became Herzog's faithful editor from his first feature, *Signs of Life* (1967). Montage in the work of both directors becomes so crucial because it involves a 'learning process' of reality (as Kluge defines it in one of his books of the 1970s, *Learning Processes with a Deadly Outcome,* English edition 1996) after brutal and irrational destruction. It is a destruction that affected not only lives and property, but also, and principally, the connection between thought, language and the material world. As much as Herzog's house in Munich, Kluge's in Halberstadt was bombed in 1945, an experience which for the latter meant that

> the homely (*heimatliche*) world of family and the province, the world of historical continuity, all of a sudden became, in a catastrophic way, uncanny (*unheimlich*), imaginary. (Roberts, 1983, 78)

Montage will thus offer both directors the opportunity to reestablish the link between human perception and concrete reality. In order to fulfil this programme, Kluge resorts to his realist method, conceived as a 'counter-programme' to the deductive method, based on 'laws, rules and values imposed from above', through which 'reality is *represented*' (Kluge, 1975, p. 201). Instead, he proposes a 'radical, authentic observation' whose results seem 'absolutely alien, "unseen", to average realism' (1975, p. 209). This resonates with Herzog in many ways, most notably in his permanent search for primacy, that is, images and sounds that were never seen or heard before. Peculiar to these images and sounds is their resistance to encoding into language, that is, their purely presentational quality.

Herzog's rebellion against language has been observed by many, including Prager (2007, pp. 4ff.), who resorts to Heidegger's idea of a poetic realm beyond the word as a possible interpretive tool for non-verbal characters such as the cave-child Kaspar Hauser. Closer to Herzog, it is however Kluge's radical realism that sheds a better light on this matter, as it starts precisely by questioning language. From Marx he borrows the idea that our five senses are a product of world history and that capitalist society imposes upon them the sensuality of possession through which they are muted (Gregor, 1976, p. 166). Kluge is therefore interested in the first place in the 'sensuality of the have-nots'. To this he adds the Adornian idea that 'truth is only what does not fit into this world' (Kluge apud Roberts, 1983, p. 294), turning his focus upon those excluded from the capitalist productive system – women in the first place – as the ones capable of perceiving reality, precisely because they are located outside of it and are thus able, in Kluge's vocabulary, to 'protest'. Protest, for Kluge, derives from a process of 'literalization', that is, the liberation of words from metaphors and conventional meanings. His characters literally 'dig' the earth in search of 'concrete' meanings for things – and what some of them, such as the character played by Hannelore Hoger in *The Power of Emotion* (*Die Macht der Gefühle,* 1983),[2] stumble over are buried bombs from World War II, that is, not the concept of war, but war in its materiality. Kluge's camera never captures the surface of events, but looks behind them, invading the backstage of operas and fashion shows to unveil the workings of gyrating stages, the contents of props, the fabric of actors' costumes and so on. In *The Power of Emotion,* Alexandra Kluge (Kluge's sister and a constant actor in his films) asks an opera singer how he can perform with a 'spark of hope' on his face in the first act, when he knows, after 84 performances, that the story will have a terrible ending. In the same film, the idea that 'feelings burn', and that opera is the 'powerhouse of feelings', conjures up the images of a fire at the Berlin Opera House; this leads to a firefighter looking inside the cup used in the opera *Parsifal* in search of the meaning of the Holy Grail – only to find cobwebs in it. Does this not remind us of passages of Herzog's films, for example, the Indian who throws out the Bible because he cannot hear the voice of god in it, in *Aguirre*? Or the tribal man, in Kenya, who does not recognize the drawing of an eye on a poster, because there are no eyes as huge as that in his community, in *The Flying Doctors of East Africa*? Not to mention the thesis-like approach to Kaspar Hauser, who, with his aversion to logic and abstract thinking, refuses, for example, to believe that a tower, which he ceases to see once he turns away from it, is bigger than a room inside this tower, which envelops him entirely. The fact that these characters are all 'outsiders' to the capitalist productive chain endows them, as in Kluge, with the power to perceive the world in its literality. They are therefore realists.

Dependent as it is on direct experience, Kluge's montage cinema cannot rely on ready-made stories. Instead, it evolves by means of an associative procedure focusing on 'situations', which presuppose a pre- and a post-history, in keeping with the associative mechanism of the brain:

> I see something in the present which reminds me – otherwise I would not be able to perceive it at all – of something earlier in the past, a representation of fortune or misfortune, and through this I can perceive the present and decide about the future. All associations take place through this triple movement, because our perception always needs a ground which is not located in the present. (Gregor, 1976, p. 167)

An example of this procedure can be found in *The Assault of the Present on the Rest of Time* (*Der Angriff der Gegenwart auf die übrige Zeit*, 1985), in which images of scrap metal are associated with those of a dinosaur egg found in China, as well as to contemporary artworks, which will only acquire value once they become old. Kluge's multimedia approach to the cinema, once referred to by Miriam Hansen as 'disciplinary promiscuity' (1996, p. xi), is an essential part of this associative process, which makes an image or sound in the present give way to all sorts of other images and sounds, extracted from history books, fairy tales, painting, other films, music, theatre, literature and opera. Kluge's usual voiceover commentary is nothing but one more medium retelling a situation, which in turn triggers its pre- and post-histories through a series of concurring media.

Rather than purely formal exercises in automatic writing, Kluge's cinema is made of obsessive attempts to understand catastrophic political events through unprejudiced means, hence the recurrence in his films of bombings, massacres, fires and floods of massive proportions, which naturally connect to human feelings, emotions and fantasies. An example regards the way the act of flying is linked to the circus, in *Artists Under the Big Top: Perplexed* (*Artisten in der Zirkuskuppel: ratlos*, 1968), which Kluge explains as follows:

> In the first place, to fly is a permanent metaphor in a circus tent. Secondly, the open sky: the fact that humans want to fly is the strongest expression of their desire for omnipotence. In the third place, there is fantasy, through which I give a hint to the viewers that they may associate freely, they can fly with their thoughts at will, without worrying about logic. (Gregor, 1976, p. 167)

Metaphors of flying and the circus are also recurrent in Herzog's work, though not necessarily interconnected. Airplanes and the act of flying are a focus from as early as *The Flying Doctors of East Africa* (1969) through to *Little Dieter Needs to Fly* (1997), including, of course, the flying ski-jumper Steiner, in *The Great Ecstasy of Woodcarver Steiner* (*Die grosse Ekstase des Bildschnitzers Steiner*, 1974); and circus-related scenes appear from *Signs of Life* to *Invincible*, including the memorable *Kaspar Hauser* circus, which displays an array of recurrent Herzogian characters and motifs. Needless to say, flying and airplanes also mean war and death, as Kluge shows us in *Learning Processes,* in which this idea is illustrated with a picture of the wreckage of a German airplane in Stalingrad, in one of Hitler's last war efforts (Kluge, 1973, p. 269). This picture is uncannily reminiscent of airplane wreckage in Herzog's *Fata Morgana* (Figs. 2.1 and 2.2) – and it is now time we devote some attention to this extraordinary film, as it is the one in which Kluge's associative method and multimedia style, that is to say, his particular understanding of realism, is most strongly reflected.

Fata Morgana marks the climax of Herzog's engagement with experimental filmmaking, under the influence of the American Underground films and German non-narrative cinema. The film is described by Herzog as an exception in his filmography, as it did not emerge from a coherent script, but from the editing room (Cronin, 2002, p. 274), although he did have some ideas for a science fiction film which were discarded during the shoot. This is indeed essentially a montage film, in which the contribution by Mainka-Jenllinghaus acquires paramount importance. Shot mainly in the Sahara desert (Algeria and Niger) and the Sahel savannahs (Burkina Faso and Mali), the film also incorporates location shots in Munich, Kenya, Tanzania, Ivory Coast and Lanzarote (Canary Islands). Nothing connects the landscapes, objects

Figure 2.1

Figures 2.1–2.2 Signs of war: airplane wreckages in Kluge and in *Fata Morgana*

and characters captured on these different locations, as they do not form part of a coherent narrative. The tripartite division of the film, marked by the intertitles 'Creation', 'Paradise' and 'The Golden Age', are as ineffective to the formation of a story as Kluge's misleading intertitles. The film events do not even constitute a situation, in Kluge's sense, as situations contain in themselves micro-narratives calling for further development. They are not exactly abstract either, although they often overflow the borders of the figurative, as in the aerial shots of migrating birds and vast lakes mirroring the sky. But living beings and objects have all been so radically decontextualized, that their original meaning has gone astray. Mirage – or Fata Morgana, as per the film title – indicates precisely that: a process of refraction entailing the vision of events that have taken place in another space and/or time and lost their meaning to the present. Many mirage images appear in the film, in the form of a moving point on the far horizon which could have been motor vehicles, animals or birds, but which remain resistant to cognition in the present.

This is thus a film about severed links, due to undisclosed reasons. However, they invite the viewer to follow the clues offered by the association of the images among themselves, with music and with voiceover commentary, that is to say, through montage. The beginning of the film suggests some sort of narrative line, as an elderly female voiceover (that of German film historian Lotte Eisner) reads from the Popol Vuh myth of the Quiché, of Guatemala, describing the emptiness of the world before creation. The first sequences of images correspond, to a certain extent, to this description, as they result from endless tracking shots through desert landscapes of sand dunes and mountains, interspersed with indistinct mirages, all of which are utterly devoid of life of any sort. As narration progresses to describe the creation of plants, animals and finally human beings, the imagery progresses too, but in the opposite direction. The landscapes slowly start to populate themselves with unidentified debris, fire chimneys of oil refineries, power plants, tanks and weaponry rotting away behind barbed wire, and then shacks and ragged children wandering amongst rubbish, stray dogs, and then animal carcasses strewn on the sand, filmed with unnerving insistence, even the corpses of a cow with a calf nestled between its legs are filmed in macabre detail. This is followed by the image of a car turned over onto its roof, making room for a row of car carcasses, serving as housing to a population of a long-stretching slum. The removal of direct sound, replaced by disparate music tracks of Handel, Mozart, Couperin, Blind Faith and Leonard Cohen, make all these images seem level with each other. And so the beauty of the landscape slowly discloses its innards of filth and death. Creation is reversed to destruction. Living beings exist, but they all carry the sign of death, the indifference toward the onlooker represented by their thoroughly unemotional gaze straight at the camera. They are in all aspects comparable to the animals which several of them hold in their hands and as indifferent to the camera as they are. The boy with his fox, the scientist with his lizard, the diver with his tortoise, they are not just out of place and context, but out of a coded language to signify them (Figs. 2.3–2.5). They are pre- and post-creation beings, whose present has been turned into a void.

It should tell us something that all the characters who speak to the camera – with one single exception of a blind Malian, whose speech is offered no translating subtitles – are German expatriates. Among them,

Figure 2.3

Figure 2.4

FIGURES 2.3–2.5 Characters and animals out of a coded language to signify them, in *Fata Morgana*

suggestive examples are the man who reads out loud, stuttering and expressionless, a disintegrating letter received from his family back home in Germany 16 years before; and the white German teacher with a group of black children, feet stuck deep into the swampy soil, who automatically repeat after her: '*Der Blitzkrieg ist Wahnsinn*' ('blitzkrieg is insanity'). Was it 'blitzkrieg' that projected these uprooted characters so far away from home? Whatever the case, the film's montage is extremely effective in creating a sense of rupture whose cause remains unseen and unspoken, but is all the more perceptible in its conspicuous absence. Herzog is certainly not embracing Marxism as Kluge is, and the poetic text that forms the voiceover commentary in the film's latter parts is very much in the introspective, fantasy style of the *neue Subjektivität* (new subjectivity) then in vogue as a reaction precisely against politically engaged literature. But the connection of war with destructive capitalism could not be clearer, through the focus on humans and animals as debris of civilization and signs of death, the most telling motif being that of the airplane. This is in fact the obsessive opening of the film, in which an aircraft lands at an airport eight times in a row, each of them in a hazier setting. A few minutes later we are confronted with the disastrous result of this trip: the wrecked airplane in the desert, whose rotten machinery discloses its complete indifference to an implacable camera.

Herzog, at this stage, was clearly experimenting with mental processes of perception and cognition of reality, away from, but comparable to, drug-induced altered states. As he himself recalls, 'when [*Fata Morgana*] was finally released it was a big success with young people who had taken various drugs and was seen as one of the first European art-house psychedelic films, which of course it has no connection with at all' (Cronin, 2002, p. 46). Kluge and Mainka-Jellinghaus offered him a powerful tool to that end, by means of a realist method based on mental association processes and radical observation. In particular, the voiceover commentary as an additional narrative layer, in dialogue and often contradiction with the images, and therefore with no power of authority, is a Kluge-inspired device, which is abandoned in subsequent films, as Herzog takes up himself the role of a traditional commentator.

Other elements however would suggest further relations, such as to surrealism, in which experiments with dislocation of objects from the sphere of the functional and normal were also carried out – in automatic writing, for example – so as to reveal the 'reality' of mental functioning prior to rationality (Grant, 2005, p. 75), and I will come back to this in the next section. Thanks to its formal structure, *Fata Morgana* is the film through which Herzog comes closest to modern cinema, in the sense described by Deleuze, who, together with Bazin, locates the turning point between classical and modern cinema in World War II. This is how he defines 'opsigns' and 'sonsigns', or purely optical and sound situations, such as those encountered in *Fata Morgana*:

> A purely optical and sound situation . . . makes us grasp, it is supposed to make us grasp something intolerable and unbearable. Not a brutality as nervous aggression, an exaggerated violence which can always be extracted from the sensory-motor relations in the action image. Nor is it a matter of scenes of terror, although there are sometimes corpses and blood. It is a matter of something too powerful, or too unjust, but sometimes also too beautiful, and which henceforth outstrips our sensory-motor capacities. (Deleuze, 2005, p. 17)

Fata Morgana's visual and aural imagery contains this terrifying beauty, this indifference of death redolent of an unspeakable war.

Interestingly, Herzog gave the title of *Signs of Life* to his very first feature film, and the first to directly address the subject of World War II. In it, though battles are thoroughly absent, signs of death are rife, lurking in the archaeological ruins, mute human and animal countenances, and the still-life landscape of the Greek island of Kos. One of the German soldiers stationed there runs amok among these signs of utter indifference of nature and things, in a form of rebellion which is reminiscent of the 'protest' against 'average realism' undertaken by Kluge's outsider characters. In the short *Last Words* (*Letzte Worte,* 1968), also shot in Greece in the same period, a mass grave is uncovered on a small island from which a man, turned mute, is rescued. This film is nothing but a sketch of the inarticulate horror in the face of death, a theme that will resurface in a number of other Herzog films. This brusque rupture between words and things, signifiers and signified (see Elsaesser in Corrigan, 1986, p. 150), Kluge tells us, finds its root at the *abarischer Punkt* of a war after which reality had to be relearned.

Physical Difference

Alongside a Kluge-style realist method, surrealist tendencies make an early appearance in Herzog's cinema as an essential component of his physical filmmaking. As a means to understand this other facet of Herzog's physical realism, I will resort to further comparative approaches, with a view to contextualizing his work within New Wave trends beyond national boundaries.

In *The 400 Blows,* an object of encrypted symbolism crops up within an otherwise thoroughly realistic narrative, offering a most curious and enlightening insight into Herzog's *Fata Morgana* and another film he shot practically at the same time, *Even Dwarfs Started Small* (*Auch Zwerge haben klein angefangen,* 1969). I am referring to the pair of goggles worn by Mauricet, a classmate of the protagonist Antoine Doinel (Fig. 2.6).[3] Little has been written about this unexpected accessory, meant for swimming, but proudly sported by Mauricet during school time. Gillain connects it to the act of stealing, a theme which pervades the film from the moment René accuses Mauricet of having bought

Figure 2.6 Encrypted symbolism: the pair of goggles in *The 400 Blows*

the goggles with stolen cash (1991, p. 77). As for the character of Mauricet, Gillain defines him politically, as the 'collaborationist', as opposed to René, the representative of 'resistance' (p. 63), Mauricet being the one who squeals to Antoine's stepfather on his classmate's

Figure 2.7

Figure 2.8

Figures 2.7–2.9 The massacre of the goggles, in *The 400 Blows*

playing truant. But the question remains: why swimming goggles? No clue is sufficiently developed in the narrative to justify the recurrence of this mysterious object, which is even presented in two different colours, black and white. The violent reaction it triggers is however crucial to the narrative, as for once it gives the pupils the chance to collectively express their discontent with the repressive teaching methods utilized in their school. This is how this is staged: while Mauricet – who seems to be not only wealthier, but also more studious than his classmates – is reciting a poem in class, his goggles are snatched from under his desk, repeatedly pierced with pencil blows by Antoine and René, and run through the other pupils who empty an ink container into them before returning them to their thoroughly dismayed owner (Figs. 2.7–2.9).

It is common knowledge that Truffaut was under the spell of Jean Vigo's anarcho-surrealist boarding-school masterpiece *Zero for Conduct* (*Zéro de conduite,* 1933) when he shot *The 400 Blows.* However, hardly any surrealist procedures can be found in his film, except perhaps for these goggles, which, with typical surrealist humour, are torn from their primary function so as to reveal their material reality. In any case, this does not prevent this decontextualized object from being entirely absorbed into the cause-effect chain of a perfectly sutured montage. A thoroughly different effect is however produced when these goggles migrate into the two Herzog films mentioned above, *Fata Morgana* and *Even Dwarfs Started Small.* In *Fata Morgana,* goggles proliferate on the faces of different characters in the middle of deserts and other settings, in which they are partially or completely displaced, and always disconnected from, and actually obtrusive to, the narrative flow. Goggles are worn by a biologist who studies the behaviour of desert lizards such as the one he holds up to the camera as he speaks; by one of the children repeating 'blitzkrieg is insanity' on the command of the white German teacher; and most disturbingly by a drummer who performs in duo with a middle-aged pianist who looks like a housewife. In all these cases, the goggles prevent eye contact between characters and the camera (thus the viewer), adding to the illegibility of the scenes in question (Figs. 2.10 and 2.11). They are thus presented as the kind of uprooted characters analysed above as remainders of an unspeakable destruction which has stolen from them their nexus with the world and even their ability of coherent speech, as illustrated by the drummer whose singing through a distorting microphone is entirely incomprehensible.

Figure 2.10

Figures 2.10–2.11 Goggles prevent eye contact between characters and the viewer, adding to the illegibility of the scenes, in *Fata Morgana.*

Goggles appear again in *Even Dwarfs Started Small,* covering the eyes of a couple of blind dwarfs, the twin sisters Azúcar and Chicklets (Fig. 2.12). This film about rebel dwarfs in an educational institution bears comparison to *The 400 Blows* in interesting ways. In Truffaut's

FIGURE 2.12 Goggles adorn blind twin sisters in *Even Dwarfs Started Small*

film, the school is equivalent to a prison insofar as Antoine moves from the former to the latter to encounter the same levels of brutality, as exemplified by the violent slaps in the face he receives in both places. The photographic session at his admission to the reformatory gives him a taste of this violence, as the photographer manipulates his head as if it were an inanimate object and makes him hold up a sign containing his identity number. Something similar happens in *Even Dwarfs Started Small,* which, after the opening credits, moves on to a photographic session of the dwarf Hombre, whose participation in the rebellion will be told in flashback. As with Antoine, Hombre is ordered to hold a sign with his identity number to the camera (Figs. 2.13–2.17). More significantly, both Antoine and Hombre are subsequently interrogated by off-screen individuals. Antoine's interrogation is famously carried out by a female voiceover for which Truffaut allegedly never managed to find a face. Hombre, in his turn, is questioned by a male voice that is actually the only one seemingly coming from a 'normal' person, in a film in which all visible characters are dwarfs, including the institution's educator and even the lady in the car who accidentally stops by to ask for directions. This off-screen voice of authority thus locates any existing 'normality' in another, metaphysical realm, as opposed to the physical world of the dwarfs, in which difference is the norm.

Figure 2.13

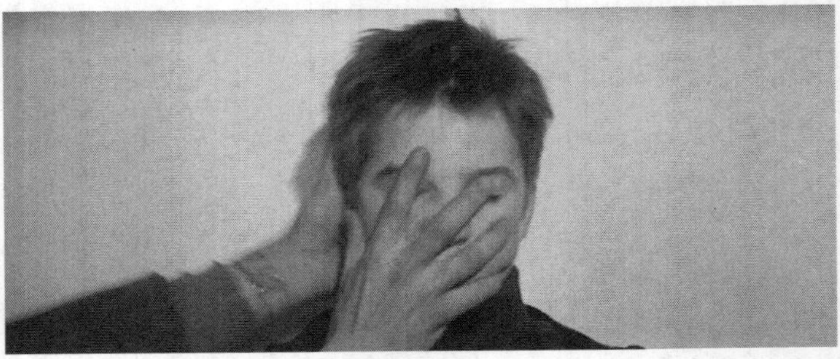

Figure 2.14

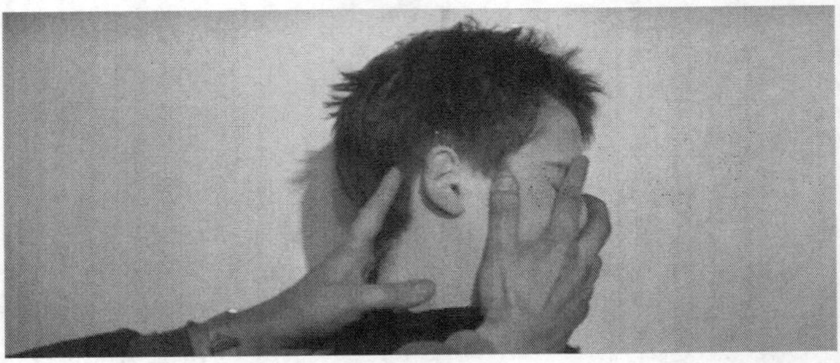

Figure 2.15

FIGURE 2.16

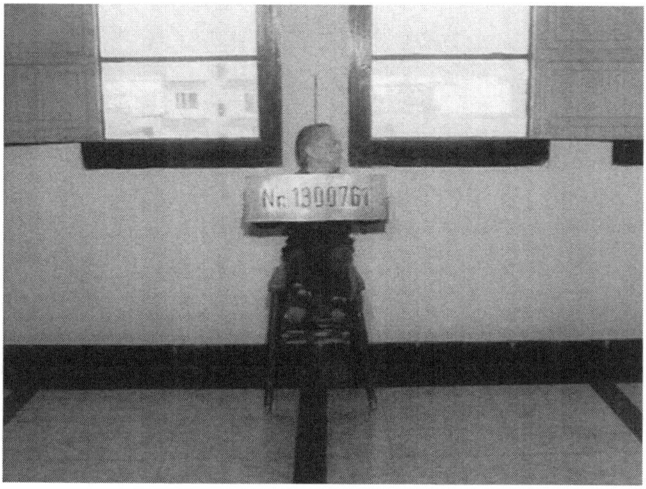

FIGURES 2.13–2.17 Photographic session in *The 400 Blows* and *Even Dwarfs Started Small*

The similarities between the two films stop here, as there are no collective rebellions in *The 400 Blows* except in the form of an innocuous massacre of a pair of goggles, while *Even Dwarfs* is the site of an almost unbearably detailed physical enacting of a nonsensical, self-destructive uprising. According to the interrogator's voiceover at the beginning of the film, the rebellious dwarfs had been left behind for bad behaviour on a collective outing with the institution's director. This causes an explosion of anger against the institution and its rules which leaves no objects, trees, flowerpots or animals intact in the building. Nothing in Truffaut's suave storytelling style can even remotely compare to this; however, a number of further clues to Herzog's surrealist tendencies can be drawn from Truffaut's forefather, Jean Vigo. Suffice it to remember that in *Zero for Conduct* the principal of the boarding school in which a rebellion of the boarders takes place is a dwarf played by the veteran actor Delphin. As in *Even Dwarfs,* surrealist dislocation here means glaring disproportion between the dwarfs' Lilliputian size and the huge dimensions of all objects around them. This causes some hilarious moments in *Zero for Conduct,* for example, when the principal struggles to rest his hat on a high mantelpiece, or when he looks in a mirror and checks himself against the image of his tall subordinate instead of his own. In *Even Dwarfs,* the irritating tension created by the sadistic and often disgusting acts committed by the dwarfs are also somewhat alleviated by a few humorous moments drawing on disproportion, such as the 'marriage' between Hombre and Pobrecita which cannot be consummated because Hombre is too short to climb up the bed.

But Herzog's film is not at all to do with humour, but rather with an uncontrollable drive to cruelty, meant to highlight the unbearable materiality of difference. And here we touch the work of another surrealist, Luis Buñuel, most notably his film about poor children in Mexico City, *The Forgotten Ones* (*Los olvidados,* 1950), which Herzog highlights as his favourite within Buñuel's work (Nagib, 1991, p. 246). This film was seen by both critics and the director himself as his renaissance after a long silence, which aligns him to the pattern of early career filmmakers (including Vigo, Truffaut and Herzog) who devote their initial works to children with whom they share a process of learning about the world. What brings *The Forgotten Ones* close to *Even Dwarfs* is the imaginative freedom with which the story is handled, regardless of any moral patterns this may contravene. At its launch, the film was execrated by left and right alike, and indeed Buñuel is merciless with his characters, and so is Herzog – at least in *Even Dwarfs* –, which means that for both directors poverty or disability is not a reason for victimization. A horrifying proof of this is offered in *The Forgotten Ones* through the character of a blind singer, who performs at a market to the sound of his own combined instruments. The man is followed by a group of thuggish kids, who attack him with stones, break his instruments and steal his money, while the blind man brandishes his cane aimlessly around him. Lying on the ground after the assault, the man stares ahead unaware that a chicken is staring back at him. Later, however, the blind man proves no better than his assailants, as he exploits an abandoned boy and tries to rape a girl who regularly brings him milk.

What happens with the blind twins in *Even Dwarfs* resonates remarkably with this, with the aggravating detail that sadistic representation is replaced with presentational, real sadism. The blind twins are constantly bullied by the other dwarfs and wave their canes around them without ever hitting their target. But this does not mean that they have any better principles than their tormentors, as they relish mounting on the real-life corpse of a sow killed by the other dwarfs from which the piglets continue to suck. The chicken parallel, a Herzog favourite, is also offered in its most macabre version in the images of a cannibal chicken pecking at a dead mouse and, more revoltingly, at another chicken, whose protracted killing is patiently detailed by the camera. That the blind twins are not only wearing goggles, but also swimming caps, in an arid location with no signs of sea or swimming-pools, singles them out through a supplementary sign of difference within a world of physical difference. Indeed, the twins are the only ones who do not participate in the rebellion orchestrated by the other dwarfs. Are they 'collaborationists' just like Mauricet, in *The 400 Blows*? In any case, they are blind, which could justify the goggles as corresponding to the dark sunglasses often worn by blind people, in which case this would also resonate with Buñuel. Commenting on *Belle de Jour* (Luis Buñuel, 1967), Evans identifies the dark sunglasses sported by the protagonist Séverine as a sign of authority as well as of bourgeois blindness (1995, p. 156). Buñuel was a fetishist, and objects in his films are always turned into sexual fetishes of one kind or another, including sunglasses, canes, chickens and birds in general. It is therefore easy to see how surrealist displacement would serve him in the creation and multiplication of genital substitutes which are governed by no politics other than desire. *Even Dwarfs* is also to do with the explosion of repressed sexuality, an exception in Herzog's work, in which eroticism hardly plays any role. This can be inferred from the interrogator's voiceover at the beginning, which relates that the dwarfs have engaged in gang-rape of the cook Marcela, although in the flashback sex is a much milder event, only suggested in the innocent bedroom scene in which the groom fails to perform and resigns to leafing through the giant porn magazines found in the educator's bedroom.

The goggles remain, however, unrelated to all this. An outspoken sign of difference, they are nevertheless entirely arbitrary, and could be placed on the face of anyone, even an undistinguished black kid among other black kids in an African setting, as seen in *Fata Morgana*. This wandering sign of difference is there to indicate the displacement, not only of dwarfs or blind people, but of the entire human race, and is therefore an allegory, as everything else in *Even Dwarfs*. Bazin highlights in *The Forgotten Ones* a truth which 'transcends morality and sociology: it is a metaphysical reality, the cruelty of the human condition' (Bazin, 1982, p. 54). Herzog is also trying to send a message about the displacement of human beings as a whole in a world marked by the indifference of death. The fact that dwarfs are adults in children's bodies results in their encapsulating and cancelling out the roles of villains and heroes, perpetrators and victims. They thus constitute a totality reaching beyond their individual existence. This is why, despite their despicable acts, unbearable high-pitched voices and laughter, sadism against animals of all sorts and outright stupidity in destroying their own environment, the dwarfs do not become detestable to the viewer (even if the film may do), because there is no suggestion that they are an abject other; on the contrary, they are simply the norm. Of course, the viewer may disagree – as I do – with the nihilist and rather conservative idea that humans revolve around themselves without ever making progress, as symbolized by the truck turning around itself in the courtyard of the educational institution; or that humans are animals just like the cannibal chicken, and a monkey can therefore replace Jesus Christ on a cross carried by the dwarfs at the end (a scene, incidentally, which is strongly reminiscent of the inspector tied to an upright bed, in *Zero for Conduct*); or that humans live in a prison of their own making, like the dwarfs, who rather than escaping through the paved road at their door, prefer to climb the lava cliffs which are too high for them and force them to return (reminding us again of Buñuel and the party prisoners in *The Exterminating Angel/El angel exterminador*, 1962).[4] But there is certainly more to it.

Prager links the allegorical style in the film to the expressionist deformation that opposed the racial ideals of Nazi German (2007, p. 57), and the fact that all dwarfs, despite their fictitious Spanish names, are native German speakers, resonates with this assessment. On the other hand, difference, in other Herzog films, is often related to artistic gift. *Stroszek*'s protagonist, Bruno, a childish mind imprisoned in a half-developed adult body, is a street singer and plays multiple instruments like the blind man in *The Forgotten Ones*. Kaspar Hauser, another child-adult, also likes to express himself through music. In the short *Last Words,* a wonderful shot capturing the protagonist's hands playing the lyre and going down to show the high-heel shoe on his disabled leg, establishes a direct link between art and disability. The difficulty in all these cases, however, is to find the normality against which difference is necessarily defined, and the virtues of art recognized. Virtually all Herzog's characters, from protagonists to unimportant extras, have something odd about them, as if all of them carried a pair of goggles in their pocket. Look at the Americans who lead the German Bruno to suicide, in *Stroszek*: a mechanic who extracts one of his few remaining teeth with a pair of pliers from his garage; a fat Indian living out of the beer cans he releases with kicks on the coin machine; a broker wearing a huge pair of spectacles as strange as goggles. They are all a bunch of 'freaks', as per the title of Tod Browning's 1932 film Herzog likes so much. It is the mirror that drives one mad, that is: the impossibility of difference. This is the horror that the dwarfs are shouting out to us: their inevitable belonging to the masses, the herds that so horrified Nietzsche and deserve nothing except utter indifference from nature. Against these ignominious herds, Nietzsche had conceived the superman, and this is also the path Herzog follows in another strand of his fiction filmmaking. In the next section, I will examine his adventures in the land of giants and the implications this entails to his realist drive and physical method of filmmaking.

Representational Difference

From the early 1970s, Herzog's films grow. Not only do they become outspokenly narrative and fictional, but their characters expand in size and meaning. The anti-humanism emanating from a humanity equated to animals and the inanimate world, as observed by Elsaesser (Corrigan, 1986, p. 150), is now replaced by aspiring super-humans. Cast-away, small-scale rebels, such as the soldier Stroszek in *Signs of Life* or the dwarfs in *Even Dwarfs Started Small,* give way to prophets of the apocalypse and New-World conquistadors endowed with cosmic vision, as in *Aguirre, the Wrath of God* and *Heart of Glass.* 'Dwarfs' continue to make their appearance, but they have also grown to become romantic heroes endowed with artistic gift, such as the protagonists of *The Enigma of Kaspar Hauser* and *Stroszek,* both performed by the eternal child

Bruno S. Increasingly, bodily difference incarnated by real cast-away and disabled characters, gives way to representational difference played out by professional actors, as epitomized by the figure of Klaus Kinski, who came to symbolize a significant portion of Herzog's output. Herzog has always made, and continues to make, all possible efforts to keep alive the legend that Kinski, unfortunately deceased in 1991, was as mad in real life as he is in his Herzogian roles, with the obvious intention of maintaining a continuum of the reality of difference across his oeuvre.

The change is however undeniable and entirely natural, as the director and his collaborators learned more about their métier, absorbed new influences and matured. What is distinctive in Herzog's case is the way in which his evolution toward narrativity, heroic storytelling and ultimately commercial cinema coincides with a turn to South American themes and locations. As I will argue in this section, the decisive event in this development seems to have been his becoming acquainted with the works of Brazilian Cinema Novo and, in particular, Glauber Rocha, entailing a focus shift from an ethics of realism to an ethos of power.

From the early 1960s, Cinema Novo films started to collect aficionados and emulators across Europe. According to one of the founders of the movement, Paulo César Saraceni, a network of exchange was in place as early as 1961, connecting São Paulo, Rio de Janeiro, Rome and Paris, through which the first Cinema Novo films, directed by Joaquim Pedro de Andrade, Gustavo Dahl, Glauber Rocha and Saraceni himself circulated (Saraceni, 1993, p. 102). In Italy, these early works were readily accepted at film festivals, garnering enthusiastic supporters among critics and filmmakers, such as Gianni Amico, Father Arpa, Pier-Paolo Pasolini and Bernardo Bertolucci. In 1961, the short *Cat Skin* (*Couro de gato,* Joaquim Pedro de Andrade, 1960) won the first prize in Oberhausen, where a year later the foundational manifesto of the New German Cinema would be launched; and in 1962 Rocha's first feature, *The Turning Wind* (*Barravento,* 1961), was consecrated in Karlovy Vary, the forum par excellence of political cinema in those days. The inaugural masterpieces by Glauber Rocha and Nelson Pereira dos Santos, respectively *God and the Devil in the Land of the Sun*[5] and *Barren Lives* (*Vidas Secas,* 1963), were then acclaimed in Cannes, and Cinema Novo went on to earn dedicated critics at the *Cahiers du Cinéma* (most notably Sylvie Pierre) and admiring filmmakers including Godard, who later invited Rocha to play the 'prophet' of political cinema, in his 1969 film *East Wind* (*Le Vent d'Est*). But it was in Germany where Cinema Novo was most warmly received among the new generation of filmmakers. First presented as a movement in 1966, at the Berlin Film Festival, in a show organized by Latin Americanist Peter B. Schumann, Cinema Novo continued to be disseminated through ever-growing retrospectives at festivals, cineclubs and, most importantly, on television. From 1967, Brazilian films were repeatedly shown on most public and regional channels, covering virtually the entire Cinema Novo production in its varying phases before and after the 1964 military coup.[6] The impact of these Brazilian films, alongside other Latin American productions, became visible in German cinema from the late 1960s. Peer Raaben, the composer of the scores for a number of Fassbinder films, once described to me in an interview[7] how the two of them had watched with fascination the Cinema Novo films and drawn on them for images and sounds. Raaben highlighted the importance, for his own compositions, of his becoming acquainted with Brazilian composers Villa-Lobos and Marlos Nobre, whose music is utilized by Glauber Rocha respectively in *God and the Devil* and *Antônio das Mortes* (*O Dragão da Maldade contra o Santo Guerreiro,* 1969). This latter film is indeed paid an explicit homage in the title of Fassbinder's *Rio das Mortes* (1970), a self-reflexive comedy parodying Hawks and Huston westerns as much as the Latin American fever and focusing on idle youths who plan a trip to Peru in search of a hidden Inca treasure. More significantly, *Antônio das Mortes* lends its title character to another Fassbinder film, *The Niklashausen Journey* (*Die Niklshauser Fart,* co-written and directed by Michael Fengler, 1970) through which the political role of filmmakers is discussed. The Latin American fashion was so widespread in that period, that many German filmmakers, such as Peter Lilienthal, Werner Schroeter, Peter Fleischmann and, not least, Werner Herzog, went to South America to shoot their films. Cross-fertilizations of all sorts took place in the process, a case in point being that of Fleischmann, who became close to many Brazilian filmmakers and critics, and invited the Cinema Novo cinematographer, Dib Lutfi, to photograph his *The Disaster* (*Das Unheil,* 1970) in Germany. Another prominent New German Cinema filmmaker, Volker Schlöndorff, claims to have drawn on Carlos Diegues's *The Heirs* (*Os herdeiros,* 1969) for his *The Tin Drum* (*Die Blechtrommel,* 1979) (Nagib, 1991b), and even a film student in those days, Wim Wenders, paid his homage to Rocha's *Land in Trance* (*Terra em transe,* 1967)[8] by quoting the protracted death of the film's hero, Paulo Martins, in his experimental film *Same Player Shoots Again* (1968).

Werner Herzog however is undoubtedly the filmmaker who most consistently and productively engaged with Cinema Novo. He is the first to acknowledge this relation, even attributing the original title of his *The Enigma of Kaspar Hauser,* 'Every Man for Himself and God against All' (*Jeder für sich und Gott gegen alle*), to a phrase he heard in Joaquim Pedro de Andrade's *Macunaíma* (1969).[9] Relations with *Macunaíma* are also visible elsewhere, for example, in *Fitzcarraldo,* which features the extraordinary actor Grande Otelo in a minor (and rather undignified) role of a clownish railroad warden. Otelo, one of Brazil's all-time greatest actors, is the memorable performer of *Macunaíma*'s title role, the 'characterless hero' of Mario de Andrade's seminal novel, who arrives in the world already in the body of an adult in Andrade's film. He thus personifies the kind of child-adult allegory dear to Herzog's fictional imaginary. Herzog used many other Cinema Novo actors in his Latin American films, most famously the Mozambican-Brazilian director Ruy Guerra, who plays Don Pedro de Ursúa in *Aguirre.* José Lewgoy, another Brazilian celebrity who embodied the populist leader Vieira in Glauber Rocha's *Land in Trance,* was also cast for important roles in *Fitzcarraldo* (the rubber baron Don Aquilino) and *Cobra Verde* (the sugar rancher Don Octavio Coutinho). The Brazilian presence in the cast of these films is further enhanced, for example, with the minor role as the porter of the Manaus Opera House played by Milton Nascimento, one of Brazil's most important composers and singers, whose music in Ruy Guerra's *The Gods and the Dead* (*Os deuses e os mortos,* Ruy Guerra, 1970) is certain to have impressed Herzog. Ruy Polanah, who appeared in Carlos Diegues's *Ganga Zumba* (*Ganga Zumba, rei dos Palmares,* 1963) and Ruy Guerra's *The Guns* and again *The Gods and the Dead,* is another of Herzog's predilections who features in *Fitzcarraldo.* These are however only the superficial signs of much stronger affinities underpinning form and contents of Herzog's films from *Aguirre* onwards.

Before we delve into Herzog's specific case, let us have a brief look at the kind of attractions Cinema Novo might have presented to the New German Cinema. Ismail Xavier ascribes Cinema Novo's impact abroad to the fact that it 'gave political meaning to the demands for authenticity typical of the European art cinema, combining those demands with the careful observation of reality' (Xavier, 1997, p. 4). It is indeed the case that, in its first utopian phase, Cinema Novo was defined by a turn to the materiality of poverty as found in the rural hinterlands of the Brazilian northeast, called *sertão.*[10] This secured a strong realist backing to the modernist aesthetics it was voraciously borrowing from Brecht, Eisenstein, Buñuel, Visconti, Pasolini and Godard, among others. Cinema Novo's three initial masterpieces, Rocha's *God and the Devil,* Pereira dos Santos's *Barren Lives* and Ruy

Guerra's *The Guns* (*Os fuzis*), all released between 1963 and 1964, are firmly grounded in this formula. However, social realism alone would not account for the international impact of this production, if we just consider that two decades earlier, Italian Neorealism had inaugurated modern cinema (as Bazin and Deleuze would have it) by offering precisely this: revelatory images of real poverty. Cinema Novo's most innovative contribution is probably to do with dimensions: the monumentality of its dry landscapes, the power of messianic religion over the destitute masses, the enormity of hunger, a word which lies at the core of Glauber Rocha's aesthetic thought, as famously expressed in his manifesto 'An Esthetic of Hunger' (1995). Thus, whilst lending itself to modern and self-questioning forms of storytelling, Cinema Novo opened up to metaphysical issues and supra-rational, trance-like states of mind which until then had lacked cinematic expression.

Baroque excess and characters in trance accrue and predominate in Cinema Novo's production after the 1964 military coup, which sees the demise of the socialist project and throws middle-class filmmakers, together with their screen alter egos, into an ethical crisis in the face of class struggle, as seen in *Land in Trance, Hunger for Love* (*Fome de amor,* Nelson Pereira dos Santos, 1965), *Antônio das Mortes, The Heirs, Gods and the Dead* and many other films. In a remarkable analysis, first published in 1967, Jean-Claude Bernardet had already noted the first signs of this crisis germinating in Cinema Novo's utopian phase, most notably in the figure of the hitman Antônio das Mortes, as he first appears in Rocha's *God and the Devil*:

> Economically dependent on the ruling classes, [this middle class] attempts to adopt the perspective of the people. But because it lacks a perspective of its own, it fails to constitute a real class, becoming instead atomized. Antônio das Mortes has the bad conscience Marx talks about. And this bad conscience is no other than Glauber Rocha's own, or mine, or that of us all, or better yet, of each of us. It seems to me that this is why Antônio das Mortes has such a seductive power, and this is why he is so resistant to interpretation. To interpret Antônio is to analyse ourselves. (Bernardet, 2007, p. 99)

In 1969, Antônio das Mortes reappears as the title role of *Antônio das Mortes,* which won the best director award in Cannes for Glauber Rocha and became his greatest success and most influential film abroad. In this film, the middle-class ethical dilemma finds expression in the figure of a regretful Antônio das Mortes, who, after having killed any number of *cangaceiros* and messianic leaders, as seen in *God and the Devil,* returns to face a *cangaceiro* straggler, but falls for a saintly woman and eventually takes the side of the poor he had been hired to crush; more significantly, he symbolically exhorts the enlightened classes to take up arms, by throwing a gun into the hands of a school teacher.

This situation resonated remarkably with events in Germany, then witnessing the ascension of the Red Army guerrilla movement (RAF), whose members were mainly recruited from the intellectual, progressive middle classes. As a result, citations of *Antônio das Mortes* proliferate in German cinema in the early 1970s, starting with Fassbinder's *The Niklashausen Journey,* in which a character called Antonio, sporting Antônio das Mortes's long dark cape, wide-brimmed hat, flashy-coloured scarf and rifle, is questioned by Fassbinder himself as to the role of the middle classes in the revolution (Figs. 2.18 and 2.19). Imbued with typical Brechtian pedagogy, the director wants to know who makes a revolution, who benefits from it and how a handful of four or five leaders, who do not even constitute a party, can decide for 'the people'. Answers to these questions are sought in a very Rocha-like way by means of historical allegories conflating past and present, and thus the film goes back to 1476, when a religious rebellion, led by the shepherd Hans Böhm, of Niklashausen, ended disastrously with its leader burned alive at the stake in Würzburg. Though Fassbinder would never engage directly with the left-wing utopianism prevailing in his time, Rocha's *Antônio das Mortes* inspired him to direct, in Elsaesser's words, his 'most explicit look at both the rhetoric and the sentiment behind radical activism and ultra-left militancy' with a film situated 'on the contact points between peasant mysticism and agit-prop theatre, the cult of Virgin Mary and revolutionary messianism' (1996, pp. 27–8). Elsaesser goes on to define *The Niklashausen Journey* as part of a batch of 'anti-Heimat films', including *The Poor Folk of Kombach* (*Der plötzliche Reichtum der armen Leute von Kombach,* Volker Schöndorff, 1971), *Mathias Kneissl* (Reinhard Hauff, 1970), *Jaider, the Lonely Runner* (*Jaider, der einsame Jäger,* Volker Vogeler, 1970), *Servus Bavaria* (*Servus Bayern,* Herbert Achternbusch, 1977) and, more relevant to my analysis, Werner Herzog's *Heart of Glass* (1976). That most of these films were shot in the 1970s, by directors who were self-confessedly impressed with Glauber Rocha and the Cinema Novo, is a clear sign of how historical allegory served their purpose to address the national question in their own countries.

Interestingly, *Aguirre, the Wrath of God,* the film which immediately follows Herzog's contact with Brazilian production, and even more so *Fitzcarraldo* have been called by the same Elsaesser 'Heimat films in the jungle' (1993, p. 130). But it is *Heart of Glass* that is more revealing of

Figure 2.18

Figures 2.18–2.19 Antônio das Mortes in Rocha's *Antônio das Mortes* and Antonio in Fassbinders's *The Niklashausen Journey*

this productive encounter and of Herzog's focus shift toward questions of power, messianism and the enactment of trance with real characters and locations. This film has been condemned by those quite rightly worried about evidence of 'an instrumentalism that would increasingly become more apparent both on- and off-screen' in Herzog's films, as

Rentschler put it (Corrigan, 1986, p. 160). At issue here is the fact that Herzog allegedly hypnotized most of the cast in the film, something which Rentschler connects to

> that infamous heritage under discussion in Siegfried Kracauer's *From Caligari to Hitler,* the procession of fictional mesmerists . . . which presaged the ascent of totalitarian leadership over a spellbound nation. Weimar films in fact display a marked predilection for hypnosis and hypnoid states, suggesting an affinity between these phenomena and the gripping potential of the cinematic medium itself. (Corrigan, 1986, p. 160)

Clear though these relations might be, once again it is imperative to separate the director from his films in order to properly comprehend the latter. That the cast was under hypnosis is something that Herzog asserts or rather boasts about, but many members of the cast themselves would deny it, as did, for example, Stephan Gütler, who plays the important role of a glass industrialist. When pressed, Herzog himself acknowledges that several cast members were not hypnotized, including the noted actor Josef Bierbichler, who plays the main character Hias and precisely the one who, in the film, is endowed with visionary and prophetic powers, as well as the real-life glass-factory workers and others. Whoever is familiar with the constructedness of Herzog's discourse about himself should at least cast some doubts on his actual power to hypnotize whoever it is, not to mention his intentions to hypnotize the audience with the film's opening sequence focusing on the torrent of a waterfall, which is perfectly innocuous even to the most suggestible child. No one would really believe, as Herzog's acolyte Alan Greenberg seems to do, that, when Herzog projected *Fata Morgana* to an audience under hypnosis, 'a housewife . . . clasped her hands to her breast as if in prayer' and 'a young man from Iran strained wide-eyed, leaning forward, trying to get inside' (Greenberg, 1976, p. 22) – a statement that moreover manages to be sexist and racist at the same time. On the other hand, it is not uncommon that directors will resort, through mere acting exercises, to emptying actors of their own personalities and even of their acting skills, so as to obtain from them a sort of mechanical delivery, as Ozu and Bresson, for example, have done. This is very much the kind of effect aimed for in *Heart of Glass*, with its paused, impersonal deliveries, as if actors were puppets or vehicles for someone else's voice. As a result, it becomes a slow film, one which requires attention and intellectual engagement, and not at all the kind of cathartic identification elicited by popular action cinema. For this reason, I believe, Rentschler misses the point when he applies to this film Metz's idea of the entranced viewer of illusionistic cinema (Corrigan, 1986, p. 164).

So let us for a moment forget what Herzog wants us to think about the film and try to investigate what it actually is. The central character, Mühlhias (shortened to Hias in the film), is a legendary figure of a wandering prophet, who allegedly lived in the Bavarian forests in the late eighteenth century. In the film he prophesies the doom of a whole population living around a ruby-glass factory, whose formula has been lost with the death of the last keeper of its secret. The young industrialist, living alone with his demented father, also goes insane with the approaching end of his empire and tries through violent means to retrieve the lost formula. Herzog added an opening and ending to the original Achternbusch script, so as to enhance the emphasis on the character of Hias and his apocalyptical prophecies. This also gave him the opportunity to insert some of his typical authorial titles, following the thoroughly unrelated final episode of the men living on an isolated island, who doubt that the earth is flat and venture into the sea: 'It may have seemed like a sign of hope that the birds followed them out into the vastness of the sea'. Rentschler highlights Achternbusch's discontent with these changes, through which Hias was removed from the film's main action and reduced to walking around 'in a coat taken from Orff's idea of peasant theatre' (Corrigan, 1986, p. 163). It may be that Herzog was inspired by Orff, but what really strikes you about Hias's coat is its similarity to Antônio das Mortes's cape. In fact this Bavarian prophet is strongly reminiscent of Antônio das Mortes, as well as of other Rocha characters, not least the preacher Sebastião, in *God and the Devil* (Fig. 2.20). Admittedly, the kind of religious

FIGURE 2.20 Hias's cape in *Heart of Glass* is reminiscent of Antônio das Mortes's

discourse pervading both *Heart of Glass* and *God and the Devil* goes back to European medieval traditions, which results, for example, in the industrialist's promise to 'carry a millstone to Trier' if the ruby-glass formula is found, in *Heart of Glass*, mirroring the image of Manuel carrying a heavy boulder up the steps of the Holy Mount, in *God and the Devil* (see Chapter 1 for an analysis of this scene).

As for Hias's position as a distant observer of an imminent catastrophe, as if detached from the diegesis, this defines him as a character entirely in the league of Antônio das Mortes, even if the kind of distancing effects employed in Herzog's narrative are not Brechtian in the same way that they are in Rocha and also Fassbinder. Just like Antônio das Mortes, Hias plays the role of the mediator within the master-slave dialectics of a class society, looking straight at the camera as if talking directly to the spectator. Placed outside his own prophecies of social doom, he conveys an external point of view akin to that of the filmmaker, as suggested by Bernardet apropos of *Antônio das Mortes*. It is however in the physical enactment of the trance (regardless whether through hypnosis or not) of a whole population gone insane under the rule of a mad tyrant that *Heart of Glass* most resembles Rocha's works. The demented industrialist's father, played by Wilhelm Friedrich, who refuses to leave his armchair, even resembles physically the celebrated actor Jofre Soares, the blind landowner who has also lost his wits in *Antônio das Mortes*.

One must also note that through some kind of uncanny coincidence Rocha and Herzog were resorting to very similar motifs already at a time when they could not possibly have known of one another's work.[11] Incomprehensible singing through voice distortion as seen in the scenes with the pianist and drummer or the religious procession in *Fata Morgana*, or the girlish voice screaming a song in the opening of *Even Dwarfs*, find a striking parallel with the high-pitch female voices singing an African-Brazilian, trance-inducing repetitive religious motif in the opening of *Land in Trance*. *Antônio das Mortes* is littered with such endlessly repetitive, often irritating religious singing, which is mostly incomprehensible even for those who understand Portuguese. That all this maddening noise is not at all a studio trick, but direct recording of local singing traditions among the inhabitants of Milagres where the film is set, produces the disturbing sense of a land in actual trance. The reality of this trance is reinforced, both in Herzog and Rocha, by the circular movement performed by characters, vehicles and animals, and, in Rocha's case, also by the camera, giving the impression that not only those in the film, but also those making it are gyrating and out of control.

Chapter 3 looks at the trance phenomenon in Rocha's *Land in Trance* in detail, but here it is worth suggesting that, for Herzog as much as for Rocha, trance is that in-between, transitory state in which ideal touches material world, physics unites with metaphysics and art with the real. The extraordinary beauty of *Heart of Glass* clearly demonstrates how characters, colours, lighting and landscapes of classical and romantic paintings, by Georges de la Tour, Vermeer, Adolf von Menzel and, as always in Herzog, Caspar David Friedrich, spring to life in quasi-documentary images of Bavaria, its typical demographics, its dialect and a real, ancient glass factory. In *Antônio das Mortes,* it is the popular iconography which becomes animate in the northeastern *sertão,* including its kitschy colours and materials, such as the plastic flowers carried by the landowner's wife, her purple fluffy long gown and the scene of Saint George killing the dragon with his spear, a picture which decorates many a Brazilian home. Trance thus situates both *Heart of Glass* and *Antônio das Mortes* on the borderline of cinema and other arts, and, more importantly, favouring allegory, it allows for a historical connection between past and present events, facts and beliefs, religion and politics.

The uses of trance, on the other hand, are also where Rocha's and Herzog's aims diverge radically. The former's interest is to show how religious and other irrational impulses inflect politics and add complexity to political cinema; conversely, in Herzog, the emphasis is placed precisely on these inexplicable, irrational phenomena, to the detriment of politics, a realm in which the director is not specially versed and has made only rare and rather clumsy incursions (for instance, his untimely indictment of the Sandinista movement in *Ballad of the Little Soldier/Ballade vom kleinen Soldaten,* 1984). Rocha is always concerned with Realism, be it related to the phenomenological real or the reality of the medium, both of which result from an ethical-political stance. Conversely, Herzog's project is to change fiction into reality, one which brings him to grips with representation and ultimately to the opposite of medium realism, that is, narrative realism. One could say that it is the trance-inducing surplus of reality, as found in Cinema Novo, minus its political content, which introduced a watershed into Herzog's work, offering him fodder for his first serious venture into commercial narrative cinema, *Aguirre, the Wrath of God.*

Aguirre constitutes Herzog's most accomplished film within his Kinski-starred Latin American trilogy, and the one that actually lends some indexical resonance to its entirely representational follow-ups, *Fitzcarraldo* and *Cobra Verde*. Herzog is straightforward about his commercial intentions, when conceiving of *Aguirre*:

> In a way, by making *Aguirre* I set out to create something of a commercial film . . . The film was always intended for the general public and not the strictly art-house crowd. After looking at my previous films, it was quite clear that I had been serving only the niche market, and with *Aguirre* I made a conscious effort to reach a wider audience. If I could have been absolutely guaranteed an audience for the film I would have made it differently, probably rougher and less genre-orientated. (Cronin, 2002, p. 76)

Indeed, *Aguirre* achieved an international box-office response as no Cinema Novo films had ever done, partly thanks to the elements of period and adventure genres embedded in its linear narrative, but also, of course, to the trendiness of the subject and approach. The area of Machu Picchu, in Peru, where the film is partly set, was a favourite destination in those days among youths in search of some magical esotericism – a fact which became the butt of a joke in Fassbinder's *Rio das Mortes*. *Aguirre*'s esoteric overtones are reinforced by the new-age music of Popol Vuh (which, as noted above, is the title of a Quiché legend of Guatemala, adopted by the musician Florian Fricke for his ensemble) as applied to the hazy images of the Andes at the film's opening and other scenes. As usual, Herzog attributes the conception of *Aguirre* almost entirely to his own imagination, except for the basic historical facts:

> By chance, at a friend's house I found a children's book about adventurers that had a very short passage on Lope de Aguirre, a Spanish Conquistador who went looking for El Dorado and who called himself 'the wrath of God'. (Cronin, 2002, p. 77)

It is certainly yet another coincidence that the first script to Rocha's *God and the Devil in the Land of the Sun* was called *The Wrath of God* (see Chapter 1 for comments on this title). However, the fact that Eldorado is the allegorical land of *Land in Trance* is not. Herzog was clearly impressed with the monumentality with which Eldorado is portrayed in Rocha's film and the weight of reality the myth had acquired thanks to the real locations. This can be seen in the majestic opening of both films: in *Land in Trance*, an aerial shot over the sea leads to pristine mountains covered with thick forest as far as the eye can see, accompanied by trance-inducing *candomblé* chanting[12] (see more about this opening in Chapter 3). In *Aguirre,* the aerial shots of the Andes with the Popol Vuh hypnotic background music produces a similarly monumental effect. Characters in both settings are reduced to minuscule dimensions, which justifies their later delusionary, Quixotic behaviour towards such crushing environments. The protagonist's tragic pathos, in *Land in Trance,* is enhanced with the help of the operas *O Guarani,* by Carlos Gomes (one which Herzog directed in the Manaus Opera House years later), and *Othello,* by Verdi, as well as by Villa-Lobos's grandiose *Bachianas.* The use of Verdi is particularly significant as far as Herzog is concerned, as it makes the background sound to a series of scenes shot in the imposing interior of Rio's Opera House a feature which affects *Aguirre* and even more so *Fitzcarraldo,* whose very subject is the erection of an opera house in the jungle, with several scenes shot inside the Manaus Opera House.

The main purpose, in *Aguirre,* was to abolish the divide between representational and real worlds, and for this reason the entire crew and cast were submitted to the torments of location shooting in the Andes and the Amazon jungle and rivers. A sense of reality of events which supposedly happened centuries ago is achieved by characters clad from head to foot in inadequate garments and equipment, dragging with them large animals and trunks entirely unfit for locomotion in those cliffs covered with thick forest. As always, Herzog does not fail to express his intentions through explanatory lines placed on characters' lips, in the manner of authorial interferences, and thus Aguirre duly announces that 'We will stage history like others stage plays'. This phrase actually finds a better match in *Land in Trance,* in which the history of Brazil's discovery is allegorically staged on a beach with the presence of the Portuguese court representative and an Indian, both dressed in carnivalesque outfits, a priest in his cassock and the country's present-day tyrant Porfírio Díaz in a business suit. This follows the Brazilian carnival tradition of historical allegories combining different temporal layers, an arrangement which comes to a head with Diaz's coronation on the steps of his palace at the end of the film. One would not fail, moreover, to note the resemblance of the priest in *Land in Trance* (played by Jofre Soares, whose performance as the landowner in *Antônio das Mortes* had already echoed in *Heart of Glass*) with monk Carvajal, both of whom, incidentally, remarkably resemble the priest performed by Antonin Artaud in *The Passion of Joan of Arc* (*La Passion de Jeanne d'Arc,* Carl Theodor Dreyer, 1928).

The actual trump of *Aguirre*, however, lies in its prevailing aesthetic of silence, one which reflects the lack of encoded language and rational thought to account for nature's indifference. *Aguirre*'s aesthetic of silence is in fact the utmost expression of what Carroll has referred to as 'presence', apropos of Herzog, that is:

> A quality of experience wherein the percipient encounters a phenomenon that – because it is not readily assimilable via language or the routines of instrumental reason – evokes a feeling of strangeness or alien-ness such that, rather than prompting the percipient to discount the phenomenon as an hallucination, instils a sense of utter and inexplicable thereness of the object of attention. (Carroll, 1998, p. 285)

Kinski in particular benefits from the very few lines he is given, which preserves him from the facile hysterics he too often slips into in both *Fitzcarraldo* and *Cobra Verde*. Once again the enlightening parallel here is Rocha, whose films offer blank faces in silence as a counterpoint to trance and a mirror of nature's inertia vis-à-vis the hero's plights. In Rocha, silence is heavily gendered: it is often women in silence who watch expressionless their power-obsessed male partners sink into an abyss of religious and/or political verbosity. Examples are Rosa and Dadá in the face of delirious Corisco and Manuel, in *God and the Devil;* Sílvia mutely observing Paulo Martins's despair as he wavers between the populist and the dictatorial leaders, in *Land in Trance;* Dona Santa impassively watching Antônio das Mortes's class dilemma, in *Antônio das Mortes*; and, in the same film, the blind landowner's wife untouched by her husband's convulsive disintegration (Figs. 2.21–2.23).

FIGURE 2.21 Blank faces in *Land in Trance*

Figure 2.22

Figures 2.22–2.23 Blank faces in *Antônio das Mortes*

Women, whenever present, are also often mute spectators in *Aguirre*, pointed examples being Aguirre's daughter and Ursúa's wife, but silence also marks the behaviour of the Indian, the monk Carvajal and other characters turned indifferent to the promises of Eldorado (Figs. 2.24–2.26). Characters increasingly lapse into a stasis of blank faces looking straight at the camera, as Aguirre's expedition is caught in endless vicious circles which finally bring his raft to a standstill.

Silence relates to, but does not necessarily confirm, Deleuze's statement that 'Herzog is the most metaphysical of film directors', mentioned at the opening of this chapter. In his brief discussion of Herzog's auteurist motifs in *Cinema 1: Movement-Image*, which does not

Figure 2.24

Figures 2.25

go down to any kind of formal analysis, Deleuze identifies, on the basis of the recurrent figures of dwarfs and giants, a metaphysics which supplies all action with a double dimension. For example, Aguirre's heroic act of confronting the rapids corresponds, on one level, to the conquest of Eldorado, but also, on another level, to his ambition to become

FIGURES 2.24–2.26 Blank faces in *Aguirre, The Wrath of God*

the world's greatest traitor, by betraying his peers, the king and ultimately god (Deleuze, 2005, p. 189). As form, however, this metaphysics is itself 'betrayed' by the lack of depth not only of the natural surroundings, but also of characters reduced to the wordless catalepsy that precedes certain death. They are the negation of any possibility of transcendence, caught as they are in a permanent state of Spinozian immanence as defined elsewhere by the same Deleuze as 'a Life', which is no longer dependent on a Being or submitted to an Act:

> This indefinite life does not itself have moments, close as they may be one to another, but only between-times, between-moments; it doesn't just come about or come after, but offers the immensity of an empty time where one sees the event yet to come and already happened, in the absolute of an immediate consciousness. (Deleuze, 2001, p. 179)

An example of immanence privileged by Deleuze is that of the character of a scoundrel in a Dickens novel, who is in a coma, that is, not quite alive, but also not yet dead; his occasional signs of life awaken general sympathy, but once he appears to be actually reviving such sympathy reverts back to repulsion. This suspension of life between moments, according to Deleuze, produces a blissful state of neutrality beyond good and evil, which is in every respect comparable to the pure presentational physicality of the empty silence found in *Aguirre*.

This is also where Herzog's cinema comes closest to Cinema Novo's aesthetic of trance, as seen in the post-coup production of Guerra, Diegues and most of all Rocha, one deriving from a political crisis which affects subjective reasoning.

Presentational immanence is precisely what is lacking in Herzog's two subsequent Latin American instalments, *Fitzcarraldo* and *Cobra Verde.* These could indeed be seen as the representation for commercial purposes of the presentational realism Herzog had developed in *Aguirre* by cleverly resorting to Cinema Novo's aesthetic innovations and monumental locations. The disasters that plagued the making of *Fitzcarraldo* are not at all the result of nature's conspiracy against the director's artistic genius, but of a flawed project attempting to bring together a number of disjointed threads: the story of an Irish man who carried the parts of a ship over land between two Amazon tributaries; Herzog's fascination with the dolmens and menhirs of Carnac; his interest in opera; his eagerness to enter the celebrity world by casting the likes of Jason Robards, Mick Jagger and Claudia Cardinale (the former two abandoning the project half way through the shoot); plus a potpourri of decontextualized Cinema Novo citations, Nascimento, Lewgoy and Otelo, mentioned above, being just a few of them. Herzog's undisguised intention to outdo Hollywood by staging a sort of *African Queen* (John Huston, 1951) in the real jungle, however, only showed how resistant his cinematic conception remains to sutured narrative representation.

Cobra Verde is even more inclusive in its overarching ambition, with no better results. Here, in fact, Herzog attempts to cover Cinema Novo's contribution from the very beginning to its latest developments. *God and the Devil* lends it the blind *cordel* singer, the character of the hinterland bandit (Cobra Verde is in fact the personification of the 'Blond Devil', as the *cangaceiro* Corisco, a protagonist in *God and the Devil,* was called in real life), the desert littered with animal carcasses, the Iberian-style towns centred around a Catholic church. One can even detect some touches of Sebastião Salgado's photographs in the scenes shot in the goldmines of Serra Pelada. But it is actually from Diegues and his much later erotic comedy, set in the slavery period, *Xica da Silva* (1976), a far cry from his Cinema Novo days, that Herzog borrows the popular ingredients of slave period drama which prevail in the film. This includes the unconvincing and rather sexist image of a black queen wilfully delivering herself through an erotic dance to the utterly blond Kinski-Cobra Verde, very much in the manner of Zezé Motta in the title role of Diegues's soft-porn blockbuster. Always trying to outdo his models, Herzog multiplies the number of black slaves offering their bodies to the blond male by creating an entire army of naked female youths in Africa who dance and sing to the bandit. Needless to say, despite the location shooting which again subjected an international and voluminous cast to all sorts of unnecessary suffering, all this failed to lend any sense of realism to the film, least of all an obviously exhausted Kinski, at that point unable to do much more than scream and grimace even when rehearsing his own performances in spaghetti westerns. In the land of god and the devil, it is *Aguirre*'s aesthetic of silence which conveys the pure, inarticulate bliss of cinematic reality, one which is typical of a new wave self-questioning ethics of power drawing on sheer physicality.

Part II

The Reality of the Medium

Chapter 3

CONCEPTUAL REALISM IN LAND IN TRANCE *AND* I AM CUBA

In this chapter, I will look at two political films, *Land in Trance* (*Terra em transe,* Glauber Rocha, 1967) and *I Am Cuba* (*Soy Cuba/Ya Kuba,* Mikhail Kalatozov, 1964), which address the subject of revolution – a failed revolution in a hypothetical Latin American country, in the former; the 1959 Cuban revolution, in the latter – by revolutionizing the film form. This involves the application of devices, such as allegory, poetic language, synecdoche and personification, all of which are normally associated with anti-realism. In my analysis, however, I will dissociate realism from narrative mimesis, so as to describe, in these films, the migration of the realist drive from the referent to the sign, that is, from the objective world to the medium itself, generating what I call a 'realism of the medium'. I will argue that these films testify to the survival of an ethics of the real, typical of new cinemas, even when a world in transformation eludes realistic representation.

Granted, *Land in Trance* distances itself from the primacy claims typical of Cinema Novo, whose first phase was entirely devoted to exploration journeys into the Brazilian territories of poverty (the urban *favelas* in a first instance, then the dry hinterlands or *sertão*), whose reality it unveiled for the first time on screen. Nor could *I Am Cuba* be identified with any new cinema movements, as it was shot by a team of veteran Soviet artists and technicians, starting with director Mikhail Kalatozov and cinematographer Sergei Urusevsky, the celebrated duo who had won the Golden Palm at Cannes in 1958 with *The Cranes Are Flying* (*Letyat zhuravli,* 1957). Moreover, the Soviet crew worked in collaboration with no less experienced Cuban partners, under the imperatives (and constraints) of their respective socialist regimes, which included the advice from Che Guevara and Fidel

Castro themselves. My hypothesis here, however, is that anti-realist modes of address were employed, in both cases, precisely to enable a complete renewal of the film form through which new cinemas' typical realist drive could continue to thrive.

One could certainly argue that narrative anti-realism, in the form of self-reflexive devices, had been a common feature in Glauber Rocha's work from the very beginning, not least in *God and the Devil in the Land of the Sun* (*Deus e o diabo na terra do sol,* 1964), in which they abound in the form of theatrical acting, discontinuous editing and a multilayered, polyphonic soundtrack. However, as discussed in Chapter 1, self-reflexivity, in this film, was not meant to challenge the objective real as much as to forge a presentational regime allowing for the expression of the contingent real as experienced by crew and cast, in interaction with the deprived population of the Brazilian backlands. Rather than distanciation, self-reflexivity in *God and the Devil* signified complete identification between subject and object on the basis of faith in the radical transformation of both, that is, in revolution. *Land in Trance* comes just after the traumatic halt imposed by Brazil's 1964 military coup to what the intellectual middle classes, including all Cinema Novo filmmakers, then thought to be an unstoppable march toward social change. As a result, the physical link between the artists and their land, discussed in Chapter 1, was ruptured, creating a gap through which direct presentation gave way to a self-conscious representational regime, pushed to extremes of theatrical mise-en-scène and performance, in poetic, often operatic, registers.

As for *I Am Cuba,* its anti-realism is not due, of course, to organic intellectuals who become aware, in retrospect, of their misperception of reality, but to the complete foreignness of the Cuban culture and history to the Soviet crew. The realist drive encapsulated in the film is, however, obvious from the simple fact that it was conceived on the premise of location shooting with local population, despite the huge costs and complications the transportation overseas of a large crew and state-of-the-art equipment necessarily entailed. In this, it followed in the footsteps of other groundbreaking projects, characterized by the search for the exotic real, such as Flaherty's *Nanook of the North* (1922), set in the Arctic; Murnau's 1931 *Tabu,* set in Tahiti; Camus's 1959 *Black Orpheus* (*Orfeu* Negro), set in Brazil; the ill-fated Orson Welles's *It's All True,* equally shot in Brazil in 1942 and never completed; and Eisenstein's *Que Viva Mexico!,* shot in Mexico in 1931, and also remained unfinished. No doubt, the use of real locations and populations in all of them did not alter the fact that their images could not but be informed by foreign models. Likewise, *I Am Cuba* is mainly the vision of foreigners, according to testimonies of members of the crew themselves: 'As far as Cuba is concerned, we didn't know about their culture or their tongue, we only knew its location on the map', says the film's camera operator Sacha (Aleksander) Calzatti, in an interview in the Brazilian documentary *Soy Cuba: The Siberian Mammoth* (*Soy Cuba: o mamute siberiano,* Vicente Ferraz, 2005). Nevertheless, the filmmakers' contact with a previously unknown reality, in *I Am Cuba* as much as in its predecessors, meant a breakaway from their previous works and a breakthrough in film history which, even when surviving in the form of fragments, all these films ultimately accomplished.

I will return to how cinephile cross-referencing binds these films together. For the moment, let us raise another important point for discussion in this chapter, referring to the abundant use made in both films of devices hailed – not least by Bazin – as the quintessence of realist cinema. Obvious examples are the use of non-professional actors, location shooting, handheld camera, depth of field and the sequence shot. Except perhaps for handheld camera, a technique only made possible in the 1950s with the advent of lightweight cameras, all the other devices were at the core of Italian Neorealism and were celebrated by Bazin for the way they enabled direct presentation of contingent phenomena and the preservation of spatio-temporal integrity. However, in both *Land in Trance* and *I Am Cuba* these devices are employed, in combination with a highly stylized mise-en-scène and performance, with the opposite aim of erasing from the phenomenological world all spatio-temporal markers. Thus, in *Land in Trance* non-professional actors were utilized, for example, to play the crowds who follow and applaud the speeches made by José Lewgoy, a Brazilian screen and TV star, in the role of the populist candidate Vieira. These scenes could potentially have a startling documentary impact, but the result is instead one of estrangement, given that the cheering masses seem convinced that Lewgoy is a real politician and act in a completely different register from his. This unsettling effect is increased by the fact that all signs are removed that could possibly indicate that the locations are in Rio or anywhere in Brazil, as the story is set in an undetermined Latin American country (see, in this sense, Barreto, 2006). The realism resulting from such a strategy is thus a conceptual one: the reality of popular faith, regardless of contextual determinants which make the usual material of documentary realism.

Likewise, if *I Am Cuba* relates directly to a historical fact, the Cuban revolution, it purposely refrains from referring to any real political or historical facts. A brief newsreel footage in a drive-in cinema showing the dictator Fulgencio Batista colluding with the Americans is only there to cause the rebel students to set fire to the giant screen, in a dazzling display of the prevalence of the symbolic real over the phenomenological event. True enough, the film was almost entirely shot on location, however this is less aimed at capturing reality as it happens than to produce a conceptual real in the phenomenological world. Thus, for example, the shot of a peasant family hiding behind a waterfall was accomplished, not by finding the exact natural match for the scene, but by resorting to the extreme artifice of diverting the course of the river to the desired location. The film also contains some of the most spectacular sequence shots ever seen on screen, but these again serve the same purpose of attaching indexicality and real-life status to man-made phenomena.

Bazin lauded depth of field and the long take, as utilized in neorealist films such as *The Earth Trembles* (*La terra trema,* Luchino Visconti, 1948), because through them 'we see the whole operation; it will not be reduced to its dramatic or symbolic meaning, as is usual with montage' (Bazin, 2005, p. 43). Conversely, he criticised Eisenstein's and the Soviet montage cinema in general for their imposing a meaning through association 'which is not in the image, it is in the shadow of the image projected by montage onto the field of consciousness of the spectator' (Bazin, 1967, p. 26). Two eloquent examples should suffice to demonstrate that *I Am Cuba*'s long takes are not at all opposed to Eisenstein's montage cinema, on the contrary, events are enacted in a compressed, 'edited' form in the material world itself, before being captured in a single take.

In the first example, the long take starts with a scene on a high-rise rooftop, consisting of a rock band playing background music to a beauty contest. In a single shot, the camera focuses on each contestant at a time, then descends the building, wanders about for a moment capturing bikini-clad girls around a swimming pool and their courting men, who bring them drinks; it then plunges into the pool with one of them to film the bathers underwater. The acrobatics accomplished here refer not only to the camerawork, but also to the extraordinary compression of events which could not possibly have happened continuously, in the same place, starting with the fact that a high-rise rooftop is no obvious location for a beauty contest. If they are placed next to each other, this is thanks to several ellipses of time and space within the shot. Thus, if there is any reality conveyed through such a shot, it is not related to time and space, but to the vertigo the camera itself seems to experience as it follows the exorbitant pleasures of the elites in pre-revolutionary Cuba. Reality here is a conceptual one, produced by medium realism.

My second example is even more eloquent of how Bazinian spacio-temporal realism and Eisenstein's conceptual montage are conflated in *I Am Cuba.* In an extraordinary sequence shot of c. three minutes, portraying the funeral of the student Enrique killed in an anti-government demonstration, the camera starts rolling on the street where Enrique's body is being carried on a stretcher by his university companions, followed by the crowds. It glides backwards, then climbs up the outside of a house from whose roof onlookers throw flowers onto the crowds. It then enters the house opposite through a back balcony and into a cigar factory, where the workers stop rolling cigars to pass a Cuban flag from hand to hand. The camera follows this action across the rows of workers towards the front balcony from which they unroll the flag to the outside. The camera then finally exits the factory through this balcony to accompany the funeral procession from high up, as if in an aerial shot. Time and space compression and ellipses are again at work in a scene capable of bringing tears to the eyes of spectators such as this writer, not at all because of its capturing an unexpected, spontaneous event, and even less for its obvious emotional appeal, but because of the delirious accomplishment of a camera which seems to defy gravity and fly on its own. That is, because of the extraordinary assertion of the realism of the medium.

Bazin, it must be noted, was the first to recognize that 'one merit of the Italian film will be that it has demonstrated that every realism in art was first profoundly aesthetic' (2005, p. 25), and this is why he could place, alongside Neorealism, the highly sophisticated deep-focus cinematography employed in *Citizen Kane* (Orson Welles, 1941) which, for Bazin, 'restored to reality its visible continuity' (2005, p. 28). And this is also why for once he could defend Eisenstein's early achievements against the later Soviet cinema, dominated by socialist realism:

> *Potemkin* [*Battleship Potemkin/Bronenosets Potyomkin,* Sergei Eisenstein, 1925] turned the cinema world upside down not just because of its political message, not even because it replaced the studio plaster sets with real settings and the star with an anonymous crowd, but because Eisenstein was the greatest montage theoretician of his day, because he worked with Tissé, the finest cameraman of his day, and because Russia was the focal point of cinematographic thought – in short, because the 'realist' films Russia turned out secreted more aesthetic knowhow than all the sets and performances and lighting and artistic interpretation of the artiest works of German expressionism. (Bazin, 2005, p. 26)

I will come back in a moment to Eisenstein's 'realism' and mimetic project in the analysis of several techniques employed in both *Land in Trance* and *I Am Cuba*.

Let us first consider the intertextual relations between the two films, which are indeed so striking, that one would naturally assume that Rocha had seen Kalatozov's film before conceiving of his own. However, my investigation of this hypothesis has produced no conclusive results so far. Due to diplomatic barriers, Rocha had never visited Cuba before 1971, when he finally travelled there as an exile for a prolonged sojourn. Some sources consulted have suggested that he might have seen *I Am Cuba* during his first trip to Europe via Mexico City and New York, in early 1965.[1] This is however a remote possibility, as, according to the film's distribution notes, 'although brief mentions of the film appeared, the film was never shown outside of the Soviet Union and Cuba and was effectively lost until today' (n/d, p. 10). Thus, the film remained unseen until 1992, when it was screened for the first time at the Telluride Film Festival, during a Kalatozov retrospective, and subsequently restored and redistributed with funding provided by Francis Ford Coppola and Martin Scorsese. Furthermore, Rocha was a prolific writer and used to comment in writing on all his cinematic and cultural experiences, but no mention of *I Am Cuba* is to be found in any of his collected letters, articles, interviews and manifestoes published to this date, though a review of *The Cranes Are Flying* he wrote in 1960, four years before *I Am Cuba* was launched, suggests that he was familiar with Kalatozov's work (Rocha, 1960 and 1986, p. 219).[2]

The fact remains that Rocha had nurtured a bottomless admiration for Cuba, Fidel Castro and Che Guevara from the time of the Cuban revolution, in 1959. Since the early 1960s he had been working on a film script with the Spanish title of *América nuestra,* drawing on the Cuban revolution. From 1960 onward, Rocha was in regular contact with Alfredo Guevara, the president of the Instituto Cubano del Arte e Industria Cinematográfica (ICAIC), who accompanied all the work on *I Am Cuba* and who for several years made all possible efforts to overcome diplomatic obstacles and bring him to Cuba to shoot *América nuestra,* all to no avail. Che Guevara's death in 1967 put an end to the *América nuestra* project, though parts of the 1966 script of the film were used in *Land in Trance.* Thus, until further evidence is produced, I can only see the haunting coincidences between *I Am Cuba* and *Land in Trance* as an aesthetic affinity between filmmakers interested in interpreting social revolution through revolutionary filmmaking. The channel through which they unwittingly communicated over national borders was their passion for the film medium and devotion to an often overlapping pantheon of filmmakers. Above all, *I Am Cuba,* as much as *Land in Trance,* could not have been conceived without the experience of Eisenstein, his conceptual montage and 'mimesis of the principle' theory, as we will see below.

ALLEGORICAL REAL

Allegory is a structural device in both *Land in Trance* and *I Am Cuba,* intended in both cases to provide narrative figuration to a complex set of political concepts. As such, it constitutes a channel to the realist intention, when estrangement is interpolated between the observing subject and the objective real. As Greenblatt puts it, allegory is the thing itself, 'not particular instances of sin or goodness, but Sin and Goodness themselves directly acting in the moral world they also constitute'. But it is no less of the essence of allegory to acknowledge 'the darkness, the arbitrariness, and the void that underlie, and paradoxically make possible, all representation of realms of light, order, and presence' (1981, p. vii). Allegory thus embodies the very impossibility of the mimetic project subsumed under the concept of 'representation'. Greenblatt goes on to say that:

> [A]llegory arises in periods of loss, periods in which a once powerful theological, political, or familial authority is threatened with effacement. Allegory arises then from the painful absence of that which it claims to recover . . . (p. viii)

A similarly painful awareness of the absence of a trustworthy referent pervades *Land in Trance.* The apocalyptical tone adopted from the start suggests the traumatic loss at the film's origin, which deserves a brief retrospect here.

A liberal atmosphere had prevailed in Brazil since the mid-1950s, under the aegis of Juscelino Kubitschek's developmentalist government and its nationalist policy for the arts and sciences. From this period date the first *favela* films prefiguring Cinema Novo's national agenda (notably, Nelson Pereira dos Santos's *Rio 40 Degrees/Rio 40 graus,* 1955, and *Rio Northern Zone/Rio Zona Norte,* 1957). These were followed by Cinema Novo's groundbreaking films set in the *sertão* in the early 1960s. Power at that point had moved to the hands of the left-leaning president João Goulart (nicknamed 'Jango'), in office between 1961 and 1964. A sympathizer of Cuba and the socialist bloc, Jango was visiting China when the coup occurred which deposed him *in absentia*. What we see in *Land in Trance* is a representation of this sudden political setback by means of allegorical language, not so much because censorship might have prevented its direct portrayal, but because it allowed for the reevaluation of past perceptions of reality in the light of a convulsive present.

This changing perception can be traced back through the very titles of Rocha's films. *Terra em transe* has been variously translated into English as *Land in Anguish, Land in Trance* and, more recently, *Earth Entranced.* As stated in Chapters 1 and 2, I have chosen to utilize the English title of *Land in Trance,* because it preserves at least part of the allegorical value of both terms '*terra*' and '*transe*', crucial to this analysis, although the alliteration of the Portuguese words, in tune with the film's poetic language, is inevitably lost. The term *terra* (land) connects three Rocha films which became known as the *trilogia da terra,* or 'land trilogy', of which *Land in Trance* is the second part. They include *Deus e o diabo na terra do sol* (1964), which I am translating here as *God and the Devil in the Land of the Sun,* and *A idade da terra* (1980), or *The Age of the Earth.* Like the English word 'land', *terra* means both any given territory and the home country (that is, the motherland or the nation). But unlike its English equivalent, *terra* also means the planet Earth. In Rocha's trilogy, the term *terra* circulates through all these meanings. In *God and the Devil in the Land of the Sun,* the 'land of the sun' refers to the Brazilian dry backlands, or the *sertão,* which functions as a synecdoche for the entire Brazilian nation. In *Land in Trance,* the land is expanded to encompass all Latin American countries in a mythical 'Eldorado', where the Portuguese language is strewn with Spanish names, and whose main province is named after the Portuguese province of Alecrim, Portugal being Brazil's colonizer. In *The Age of the Earth,* the term *terra* is further expanded to encompass political processes of global resonance.

The evolution of these titles reflects the progressive dissolution of the national project whose defence, at the apex of Cinema Novo, was inseparable from the representation of Brazil through the *sertão,* whose images were held responsible for the national quality of its photography. As remarked by Galvão and Bernardet, in the 1960s,

> the photography of the northeast [had become] Brazilian cinema's 'trade mark'. It was valued not only for its adequacy to the reality conveyed, but also because it opposed a photographic style considered foreign. (1983, p. 204)

Land in Trance marks Rocha's departure from the 'land of the sun', which disappears together with the filmmaker's faith in the nation. The demise of the national project in Brazil's real history is thus what caused Rocha to break away from documentary realism and fully develop his allegorical, Latin American vision of the nation. As he declared at that time,

> the awareness that Brazil, Mexico, Argentina, Peru, Bolivia, etc. are part of the same bloc of North-American exploitation and that exploitation is one of the most profound causes of underdevelopment is becoming increasingly consistent and, more importantly, popular. The notion of Latin America overrides the notion of nationalisms. (Rocha, 2004c, p. 83)

Internationalization was thus seen as an alternative for keeping the country on the track of revolution, despite the recent installation of a retrograde dictatorship.

The same international, contagious character of the socialist revolution inspired the structure of *I Am Cuba*. In order to make the film's message universally applicable, Kalatozov told the scriptwriters – the Russian poet Yevgeny Yevtushenko and the Cuban novelist Enrique Pineda Barnet – to produce dialogue containing only the strictly necessary words, making them so expressive that there would be no need for translation (Barnet, n/d, p. 8). This resulted in highly artificial declamatory lines, in tune with the general poetic tone of the film, as we will see below. It is also revealing that Kalatozov encouraged the scriptwriters to watch the surviving rushes of Eisenstein's *Que Viva Mexico!*, on the occasion of Barnet's visit to Moscow to meet the Soviet crew (n/d, p. 8). As a result, an episodic structure was adopted for the latter that closely resembles that of the former. *Que Viva Mexico!* was originally divided in four episodes, framed by a Prologue and an Epilogue, which culminated in the apotheosis of Emiliano Zapata's revolution in the never-shot fourth episode, 'Soldadera', drawing on the female warriors who helped topple Porfírio Díaz's dictatorship, in 1910. *I Am Cuba* is also structured in four episodes, leading to the final triumph of the guerrillas of Sierra Maestra over the troops of dictator Fulgencio Batista. In *Que Viva Mexico!*, compression of history and geography was aimed at making the Mexican case exemplary of revolutionary processes worldwide. To that end, Eisenstein drew on what he called the 'horizontal montage' of Mexico itself, where history was 'presented not vertically (in years and centuries), but horizontally (as the geographical coexistence of the most diverse stages of culture)' (Eisenstein, 1985, p. 260). Thus, as Karetnikova explains, 'not far from the still matriarchal Tehuantepec lay plantations and lands with feudal customs, like the hacienda Tetlapayac, and next to that was twentieth-century Mexico City' (Karetnikova, 1991, p. 19).

Now, let us look at how history and geography are compressed in an organic, universalizing whole with the help of horizontal montage, in the overtures of both *I Am Cuba* and *Land in Trance*.[4] Proving to be siblings from their opening images, both go back to the early history of the Americas to explain the current political situation, and both resort to the discovery mythology to globalize the history of a single country. By calling attention to the prerogatives of the medium, they replace documentary with conceptual realism elicited through Eisensteinian horizontal montage.

I Am Cuba opens with long aerial shots gliding horizontally over the sea, leading to the Caribbean island's untouched hills and palm tree forests. In the black and white photography the sea presents a metallic glow, while the palm trees acquire a white shine under the sun. Carlos Fariñas's extradiegetic music during this opening combines light Afro-Caribbean drumming and flute sound, subsequently added to by the gentle plucking of guitar strings and a male choir. The camera, now handheld and supplied with a 9.8mm (extreme wide-angle) lens, continues in a pan across the sea and over land, eventually stopping before a white wooden cross on the beach above cliffs, bearing an inscription marking Christopher Columbus's visit to the island. On the horizon, behind the cross, a minute peasant family consisting of the parents, a child holding the father's hand and a baby in the mother's arms, wind their way. 'Cuba's' female voiceover then starts reciting the poem 'Soy Cuba' (I Am Cuba), which makes up the voiceover narration throughout the film:

> I am Cuba. Columbus landed here once. He wrote in his diary: 'This is the most beautiful land human eyes have ever seen'. Thank you, Mr Columbus. When you saw me for the first time, I was singing and laughing. I greeted the tufted sails, I thought they brought me happiness. I am Cuba. My sugar was carried away in ships. My tears were left behind. Sugar is a strange thing, Mr Columbus. So many tears go in it and still it's sweet.

Meanwhile, the camera in wide angle proceeds, now seemingly placed on the back of a canoe, capturing a black boatman from behind as he poles ahead in a flooded area past shacks and women doing their laundry. The camera follows the boatman in the water under the shacks, finally stopping at a footbridge, while the canoe continues under it. This combination of images and extradiegetic narration performs a vertiginous spatio-temporal compression. It juxtaposes the Biblical paradise, located in a mythical time, through the eyes of Columbus in his discovery of the new continent at the end of the fifteenth century. It goes on to signify the colonial times, represented by the peasants passing behind Columbus's cross, when the island was entirely taken by sugarcane plantations. And it finally arrives at the present day by showing the disastrous results of this foreign exploitation, with the population living in subhuman conditions in flooded slums. In this process (and in a matter of minutes), Columbus's portentous sailing ship mentioned in the voiceover narration is reduced to a miserable canoe in the images, while the shiny ocean gives way to murky swamps. Again realism here is of a conceptual order, despite location shooting and the liberal use of sequence shots.

Land in Trance's opening is kin to this in appearance and conception. As in *I Am Cuba,* the film is introduced by a long and slow aerial shot of the sea illuminated by the sun's metallic glow, occupying the totality of the frame. The camera that slides from left to right captures the sea's rounded surface as if it were the globe itself. The music in the background is Afro-Brazilian *candomblé*[5] drumming and singing, whose function during rituals is to induce mystic trance (I will return to the function of trance in both films shortly). Credits are superimposed on the images, while the camera glides over mountains covered with dense forest, followed by a valley in which a river winds its way. There are no signs of human presence in this pristine scenery, over which appears the title in parentheses: (Eldorado, inner country, Atlantic). This solemn arrival in Eldorado is then abruptly interrupted by various action sequences located in the present day, retelling the coup led by Porfírio Díaz, a present-day politician of Eldorado, named after the famous late nineteenth–early twentieth century Mexican dictator. After a triumphal parade in an open car, Díaz is shown arriving at a deserted beach, alongside a priest, a monarch (representative of the colonial power) and a native Indian, who together reenact in front of a wooden cross a ceremony redolent of Brazil's legendary First Mass in 1500 (Figs. 3.1–3.4). The latter two characters are dressed in extravagant outfits – the monarch with richly decorated crown and cape, the Indian with a tall feather headdress – like those employed in the composition of historical allegories during carnival in Brazil (the monarch is actually performed by Clóvis Bornay, a famous champion of carnival costume contests). Here again horizontal montage allows for

Figure 3.1

Figure 3.2

compression of history and geography, starting with the mythical Eldorado, followed by Brazil's discovery and First Mass celebrated by the Portuguese in the sixteenth century, interspersed with scenes of a contemporary world, the whole staged on a place, or 'land', bearing the shape of the entire globe.

FIGURE 3.3

FIGURES 3.1–3.4 Compression of history and geography: arrival in Eldorado in *I Am Cuba* and *Land in Trance*

It is unclear whether Glauber Rocha would have seen any of the several edited versions of *Que Viva Cuba!* made by third parties with the stock shot by Eisenstein and Tissé, prior to the making of *Land in Trance,* though several of his writings dating as far back as 1956 reveal that he was aware of, and enthusiastic about, this film.[6] In any case, the allegorical use of the dictator Porfírio Díaz as the embodiment of evil is suggestive of an intertextual relation. The reference to Mexico in *Land in Trance* is furthermore due to another Rocha idol, Luis Buñuel, whom he had first met in this country on his way to Europe, in 1965, an encounter documented in Rocha's brief appearance as an extra in Buñuel's *Simon of the Desert* (*Simón del desierto,* 1965). Whatever the case, *Land in Trance*'s allegorical, totalizing intentions, in tune with Eisenstein's horizontal montage, are evident here, affecting not only the settings, but also plot and character construction, the whole aimed at conveying reality as process.

Reality as Process: Trance in *Land in Trance*

As Ismail Xavier has noted, the allegorical world of *Land in Trance* 'condenses an endless number of questions and experiences into a few individual characters whose life courses, nevertheless, represent a national fate, the destiny of an ethnic group or of a class' (1997, p. 15). This can indeed be observed about all the characters. Paulo Martins, the film's (anti)hero, is at once a poet and a journalist redolent of a real journalist, Carlos Lacerda, whose articles are deemed to have effectively contributed to the military coup. On the other hand, as a poet, he can be seen as the filmmaker's self-reflexive alter ego whose first-person voiceover commentary, interrogating his political role and ethical stance as an artist, carries the narrative forward. Ambiguous by definition, he is committed to the elites, including the media tycoon Julio Fuentes and the multinational company Explint (*Compañia de Explotaciones Internacionales*). At the same time, he joins the communist party in their support of the populist leader Felipe Vieira, seen as a facilitator of social change. Vieira, in his turn, is a conflation of Jango and a number of other populist figures in Brazilian history, such as the dictator Getúlio Vargas (president of Brazil between 1930 and 1945, then again from 1951 until his suicide in 1954), with his demagogic speeches and empty promises to the masses. Like Jango, Vieira opposes no resistance when his power is usurped by Porfírio Díaz. Paulo, a former friend and later traitor of Díaz, is the only one to take up arms and resist, but ends up killed in a shootout with the police. His protracted death over sand dunes gives way to the convulsive flashback of his story, which accounts for the film's fragmentary, discontinuous narrative.

That such multifaceted, allegorical characters are equivalent to and interchangeable with the land they inhabit is made clear, among other things, through processes of naming and personification which are mental operations inherent to allegory (Barney, 1979, p. 21). In *Land in Trance,* the 'land' is named after a human state, that of 'trance'. As a result, it ceases to be a geographically situated and stable reality and becomes a process. This is in fact what the film's opening sequence described above, in which images of the Earth are combined with trance-inducing Afro-Brazilian drumming, suggests: a land falling into a trance.

Transe, in Portuguese, is an overarching word, which includes ideas of 'distress', 'risk', 'danger', 'hazard', 'crisis' and 'anxiety'. It suggests 'struggle', 'fight', the state of a medium possessed by a spirit as well as 'passage' and 'death'. In English, the word 'trance' has the more restricted meaning of a sleep-like state, caused, for example, by hypnosis, in which one concentrates on one's thoughts remaining oblivious of the world around. In the film *Land in Trance,* the term corresponds to the overarching sense it has in Portuguese. Ismail Xavier sees Rocha's use of what he calls 'the *transe* metaphor' as a way of characterizing the national crisis (1997, p. 82). 'Crisis' is no doubt an immediately identifiable feature binding together Paulo Martins and his country Eldorado, and it is significant that his protracted death, pointing a machine gun to the sky, takes place on a high, rounded sand dune, mirroring the shape of the Earth previously suggested by the ocean's rounded surface in the opening sequence. However, trance as a narrative device had been employed by Rocha since his first feature film, *The Turning Wind* (*Barravento,* 1961), set in a fishing village in Bahia, inhabited by Afro-Brazilians, in which *candomblé* trance brings the story to a head and defines its outcome. In *God and the Devil,* the state of trance affects tormented characters, such as the cowherd Manuel, torn between the opposing forces of god and the devil, not to mention the permanently entranced famished masses, prey to religious fanaticism. Ivana Bentes goes as far as identifying the process of trance as 'the first figuration of Rocha's thought and cinema':

> 'Trance' means transition, passage, possession, the process of becoming. In order to fall into a crisis or trance, one needs to be penetrated or possessed by the other. Glauber turned 'trance' into a form of experimentation and experience. [For him] to fall into a trance is to be in phase with an object or situation, to experience it from inside. (1997, p. 26)

Indeed, trance seems to filter Rocha's perception of reality throughout his oeuvre, until it becomes both form and content in *Land in Trance.* The film as a whole is situated within the transience of Paulo's crisis, that is, his passage to death, as, mortally wounded, he recollects his life. This comes in the form of flashes of memory in fairly random order, starting from the end, that is, the coup that deposes Vieira, going back to idyllic times of Paulo with Díaz and Sylvia (Paulo's first lover) dancing in a marbled palace; then of Paulo with Vieira and Sara (Paulo's second, communist lover) in a winter garden, concocting their political alliance; later with the press tycoon Júlio Fuentes and his depressive newspaper colleague Álvaro, both of whom he also meets at orgiastic parties in which they luxuriate in alcohol, jazz and group sex. These 'lumps' of memories, charged with synecdochic value, are in direct relation to Paulo's poetic language, which combines Mário Faustino's tragic poems with others authored by Rocha himself. Though Paulo's voiceover commentary only accounts for part of the images shown, his trance-like state contaminates all technical aspects of the film: the shaky, gyrating handheld camera, the theatrical mise-en-scène in sumptuous palaces in the middle of the jungle, the temporal zigzags, the whole enveloped in the sound of operas by Verdi (*Otello*) and Carlos Gomes (*O guarani*), as well as the dramatic *Bachianas brasileiras* n. 3 and 6 by Villa-Lobos, which alternate and overlap with extradiegetic gunshots and sirens. All colludes against logic and favours the exposure of the irrational element inherent to the state of trance, which, being conveyed through manipulation, draws the attention to the medium's material reality.

The film thus aligns itself with a cinema of poetry, as opposed to a cinema of prose, as argued for by Pasolini and Eisenstein, both of whom ranked high in Rocha's pantheon. Pasolini in particular defined cinema as a 'language of poetry' because of its 'fundamentally irrational nature' (Pasolini, 2005, p. 172). This statement is fitting not only to *Land in Trance* but to all other Rocha films, which resort to religious fanaticism and trance as a means to expose the irrational roots of politics itself. In his famous article 'Aesthetics of Dream', Rocha goes as far as defining revolution as fundamentally irrational:

> Revolution is the *anti-reason* which communicates the tensions and rebellions of the most *irrational* of all phenomena, which is *poverty*. . . . Poverty is everyone's maximum power of self-destruction and has such psychic resonance that the poor become a two-headed animal: one which is fatalistic and submissive to the reason that exploits them as a slave. The other, insofar as the poor are unable to explain the absurdity of their own poverty, is naturally mystical. (Rocha, 2004b, p. 250)

As for the irrational nature of poetry, it is a question which occupied Russian formalists, with obvious reflections on Eisenstein's cinematic theories. Khlebnikov and Kruchenykh, in particular, defended the concept of *zaum,* or a 'transrational language', to signify poetry and incorporate an irrational element through which the word becomes 'broader than its meaning' (Steiner, 1984, pp. 144ff.).

It is in the light of such 'transrational poetry' that one should understand Paulo Martins's 'anarchic' behaviour (as said in the film) as well as his contradictory views of the social classes, as expressed in a famous passage which sparked outrage among the Brazilian left-wing scene at the time. During Vieira's campaign, Paulo interrupts the speech of a trade-union leader by muffling him with his hand, then looks straight at the camera and exclaims:

> Have you seen who the people are? An imbecile, an illiterate, a depoliticised man. Can you imagine Jerônimo in power?

Paulo's poetic discourse, rather than justifying his contradictory political actions, unveils his Oedipal relationship with Díaz, as well as with Sara and Sílvia. He worships Díaz as the 'god of my youth', confirming his vision of politics as a matter of 'faith' ('The naivety of faith!', he exclaims), rather than conviction. Paulo literally expresses his disdain for reason, proclaiming that he 'prefers the madness of Porfírio Díaz'.

As Ismail Xavier points out, allegory and condensation of history in *Land in Trance* are used to create ambiguity and enigma rather than enlightenment (1997, p. 20). The same is true of its subjective narrative, which Xavier compares to Pasolini's theory of 'the free indirect subjective':

> in *Land in Trance,* whether a scene is explicitly subject to the poet's interior monologue or not, the entire narration is contaminated by the poet's state of mind. . . . The 'disturbed mind' is not only the character's but also that of the invisible narrator. (Xavier, 1997, pp. 66ff.)

Xavier finds similarities between this technique and what Eisenstein termed 'interior monologue', a discourse which combines 'the feverish race of thoughts' with 'outer reality' (1997, pp. 62ff.). Interior monologue is indeed a prevailing feature in *Land in Trance,* in which conversations easily turn into declamation, citation and recitation. Robert Stam refers to the film as 'a veritable essay on the intersection of art and politics' in which people 'find it normal to address each other in poetry' (1982, pp. 149 and 156). In Rocha's own view, 'the Latin American political avant-gardes [are] led by intellectuals, and therefore poetry precedes the gun' (2004d, p. 107).

Most importantly, poetry differs from prose in that it does not *represent* an object, but *is* the thing itself, and this is why the Russian formalists understood a poem as a synecdoche, a part of the organism or machine it stands for (Steiner, 1984, p. 138), that is, as material reality itself, rather than representation. Instances of poetic synecdoche abound in *Land in Trance,* in which armed resistance, for example, is signified by Paulo carrying a machinegun he never fires, or by the sound of gunshots which remain unmotivated within the diegesis (Figs. 3.5 and 3.6). Xavier talks about the gun as fetish in *Land in Trance* (1997, p. 69), whose direct ancestor is no doubt to be found in Eisenstein – for example, the synecdochic/fetishistic shots of boots as poetic symbols of the repressive machinery that proliferate in his early revolutionary works.

FIGURE 3.5

FIGURES 3.5–3.6 The gun as fetish in *Land in Trance* and *I Am Cuba*

Trance, Sexuality and the Christian Myth in *I Am Cuba*

The same equation combining allegory, personification, trance and poetry can be found in *I Am Cuba.* All episodes are centred on groups of allegorical characters, representing, respectively, the population of the urban slums, the middle-classes, the sugarcane planters on the plains and the guerrillas in the mountains, all of whom are exploited by the foreign (basically American) capital epitomized by the trading company United Fruit – an exact match to *Land in Trance*'s Explint. In episode one, René, a fruit seller and secret messenger for the revolutionary students, proposes marriage to the chaste Maria, unaware that at night she prostitutes herself to the Americans under the name of Betty. In episode two, a peasant (Pedro) and his two children are expelled from their sugarcane plantation by United Fruit. In episode three, university students conspire to overthrow Fulgencio Batista's dictatorship, ending with the sacrifice of several of them, including the episode's protagonist, Enrique. And in the final episode, Mariano, the father of a starving family in the mountains finally joins the revolutionary rebels in their march toward victory.

As much as in *Land in Trance,* processes of naming and personification lead to the state of trance, in a time of revolution. Like Paulo's embodied poetic voice, Cuba's disembodied female voiceover recites a poem about the country which regularly punctuates the film with its chorus 'Soy Cuba', while exemplary characters at the centre of each episode provide a conceptual definition of the country. Though this is aimed at internationalizing the Cuban case, the process of personifying the country as a woman is not dissimilar from devices normally used in nationalist narratives. As Susan Hayward notes,

> The nation pretends to be gender-neutral (in that it purports to dissolve difference) and yet the woman's body is closely aligned/identified with nationalist discourses. We fight and die for our mother-nation.

Hayward goes on to say that 'the colonized referred to the colonizing country as mother-country. When "she" is invaded by the enemy, she is "raped"' (2002, pp. 97ff.). Also in *I Am Cuba* colonial domination is presented from the outset as the invasion of a virgin land, an idea reinforced by sexual metaphors throughout the film. The camera seems to be constantly diving into and penetrating this woman-country from above or outside, and investigating its interior with a foreign, admiring gaze, as seen above with reference to the opening sequence, in which a small canoe standing for a degraded present-day version of Columbus's ship, penetrates the flooded slums. Cuba's female voice, though not directly attributed to her, echoes that of the character Maria/Betty, who is torn between two opposing forces. Incarnating the sanctified prostitute, a mixture of the Christian myths of the Virgin Mary and Mary Magdalene, she is divided between her need of money, brought in by the rich Americans, and the true love of her countryman, which is blessed by the church. This causes her to fall into a trance in scenes which astonishingly resemble the orgiastic parties in *Land in Trance,* steering the attention away from the narrative myth towards the sensuous reality of the medium itself.

These take place in a nightclub frequented by rich Americans who have at their disposal glamorous Cuban girls. A black crooner sings the romantic song 'Loco Amor', then gives way, at the request of a raucous American, to faster Afro-Cuban drumming, accompanying masked and costumed female dancers. Betty is a late comer, who is chosen by a 'prudish' American (as he is described by his comrades) apparently interested in knowing more about the natives. Later, loud jazz music starts that ignites a general frenzy of screams and dance, during which Betty is thrown into the arms of different men until she falls into an entranced, frenetic dancing. The camera meanwhile works its way through a highly symbolic setting of bamboo curtains, suggesting at the same time wilderness and a prison, capturing, as if in a trance in its own right, the clubbers' distorted, screaming faces (Figs. 3.7 and 3.8). After this orgiastic celebration, Betty ends up making love in her home with her American client. If no actual rape takes place here, this will be clearly suggested when the student Enrique rescues a girl from the hands of harassing American navy soldiers, just about to gang-rape her, a scene which provides a personified match to the desecration of the motherland by foreign intrusion.

This Christian, moralistic symbolism has been accused of 'engagement with patriarchal presuppositions' and endorsement of the idea that 'prerevolutionary Cubans were devout Catholics who were subsequently denied the right to religious practice' (Ching et al., 2007, p. 160). Correct in principle, such an indictment could only be acceptable if the film were trying to convey a faithful 'representation' of a country called Cuba. As we have seen above, however, no trace of such an intention is to be found in the entire film, whose overt artifice has the sole aim of conveying a sensory, medium-specific concept of revolution, and not at all a historical document of the real Cuban revolution. In fact, Maria/Betty is a collection of cinephile citations, hence

FIGURE 3.7

FIGURES 3.7–3.8 Trance-inducing orgies in *I Am Cuba* and *Land in Trance*

reminiscent of several other cinematic, mythical Marias, rather than any real one. The most obvious reference here is the peasant Maria in the second episode, 'Maguey', in Eisenstein's *Que Viva Mexico!*. In this film, though promised to the peon indio Sebastian, Maria is effectively raped by one of the hacendado's drunken guests, while her fiancé is buried in the ground up to his neck, and his head trampled by galloping horses.

Maria/Betty is close to yet another mythical Maria, that of *Metropolis,* by Fritz Lang (1926), in which the character is not only a double but a multiple woman, a true universal in what Gunning has called 'the Lang film that is most blatantly allegorical' (2000, p. 55). In *Metropolis,* Maria is Christian salvation for the poor, but also the evil robot working for the Lord of Metropolis. Moreover, she is the copy of the latter's deceased wife, hence the mother of his son who is in love with her, which completes the Oedipal triangulation – not dissimilar, incidentally, from the one seen in *Land in Trance,* between Paulo, Díaz and Sílvia, and between Paulo, Vieira and Sara. Maria, the robot, is portrayed as the reverse of the virgin, that is, the whore, who dances topless in the Yoshiwara club for a horde of lustful men, leading them into a collective trance. Later she is carried on the men's shoulders, shouting: 'let's watch the world going to hell', completing the combination of trance, sexuality and religion within an allegory of evil (Fig. 3.9).

Even the characterization of the non-professional actress, Luz Maria Collazo, who plays the virgin/prostitute Maria/Betty, followed a foreign model. In fact, she is almost a clone of Marpesa Dawn, the Eurydice of *Black Orpheus* (*Orfeu Negro,* Marcel Camus, 1959) (Figs. 3.10 and 3.11). This film, coincidentally shot in Brazil, proved very useful to the Russian crew in its drive to convey the idea of a 'tropical country' and a 'tropical people' to foreign audiences. The world of *I Am Cuba* lies, of course,

Figure 3.9 Orgy and trance in *Metropolis*

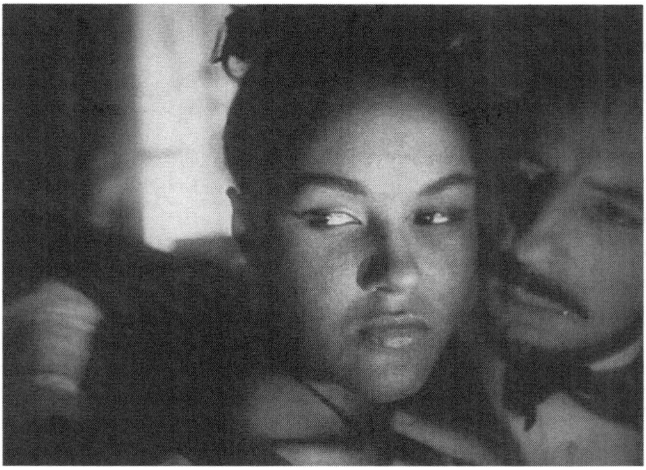

FIGURE 3.10

FIGURES 3.10–3.11 Cinephile characters: Maria/Betty in *I Am Cuba* is almost a clone of Marpesa Dawn (Eurydice) in *Black Orpheus*

at the opposite end from Camus' idyllic *favela*, inhabited by a happy people permanently dancing and singing samba, even when carrying water jugs on their heads. In any case, trance is again a decisive feature in this film, though this time it is the mythical Orpheus, rather than his beloved black virgin, who falls into a trance. Significantly, this happens when he is taken to an *umbanda* ritual, an Afro-Brazilian religion analogous to *candomblé,* here replacing Hades, or the hell of the Greek legend. All dancing women become entranced, and Orpheus with them, as the drumming picks up momentum, through which he is finally capable of communicating with Eurydice and inadvertently killing her by looking back at her. The power of this Afro-Brazilian ritual, filmed by Camus in documentary detail, was certainly not overlooked by Kalatozov, who made sure to introduce African wooden idols in the nightclub scene in which Betty falls into a trance, in *I Am Cuba*. However, in this film, poverty is denied all touristy interest when Betty shows her miserable quarters to her disgusted American client.

As always, the entranced state of the characters is used to call the attention to the reality of the film medium itself. For example, the shooting of Enrique's death is done through a subjective camera through which the image blurs like an abstract painting. A subjective point of hearing is also used to produce a sense of trance, for example, during Enrique's failed attempt to kill a vicious police chief through a telescopic weapon placed on the roof of a high-rise. His nervous, almost delirious state is conveyed here by his mental replaying of an old man's singing to the sound of his guitar, a sound which becomes diegetic thanks to Enrique's mental hearing, rather than any actual sound source.

Another more sophisticated procedure overlaps objective reality with the subjective view of the filmmakers. Let us look again at the whitening effect on the palm trees under the sun, in the opening aerial shots over the island. This effect was achieved with the use of negative stock sensitive to infrared rays, obtained from an East German film lab, according to the distribution pressbook (n/d, p. 10), or via the Russian army (according to the documentary *Soy Cuba: the Siberian Mammoth*). I am tempted to read this effect, with some poetic license, as Russian snow over Cuba, that is, the view of a tropical country through foreign, northern eyes. At any rate, such sophisticated technique, as everything else in the film, is meant to call the attention to its own reality rather than the real it captures as a given.

Mimesis of the Principle

Eisenstein agreed with the Aristotelian principle that imitation lies at the basis of artistic creation. 'Imitation is the way to mastery', he wrote. 'But imitation of what? Of the form that we see? No! . . . Mastery of principle is real mastery of objects!' (Eisenstein, 1993, p. 67). The question then was for him to define the principle hiding behind the visible form. Yampolsky defines it as 'the line', the structuring schema behind the objects:

> The linear nature of the 'image' allowed Eisenstein to elaborate the concept of the general equivalence of different phenomena on the basis of the similarity between their internal schemas. It was this concept, based on the psychology of synaesthesia and essential for the construction of the theory of montage, that linked together not the surface appearances but the inner 'graphemes' of objects. (Yampolsky, 1993, p. 179)

Yampolsky goes on to compare this linear schema to a 'bone structure', the skeleton that is in itself a recurrent trope in Eisenstein's films and drawings, not least in his *Que Viva Mexico!,* in which his fascination with the proliferation of skull masks in Mexican popular festivals prefigures the growing mysticism that will pervade his later works and thought. A structure that emerges to the surface of things is also associated with magic and mysticism in *I Am Cuba,* not least in the scenes of trance, with the masked dancers at the nightclub. And these are again reminiscent of *Black Orpheus,* in which a carnival participant disguised as a skeleton and representing death takes Eurydice away from Orpheus.

Yampolsky's association of Eisenstein's linear structure with his theory of vertical montage (1993, p. 179) is particularly relevant here. Originally, Eisenstein's vertical montage related to a link between sound and image, the music score being seen as a structural 'line'. As he reiterated: 'In all multiplicity of visual means of expression there must be those which by their movement are able to echo not only the rhythm but also the moving *line* of a melody. . . . Basically, this will be . . . the "linear" element in the visual medium' (Eisenstein, 1991, p. 335). But verticality in Eisenstein reaches beyond an editing device to inflect the conception of the images themselves, most obviously in his lavish use of stairs as well as high and low camera angles to elicit senses of power and oppression, ascent and fall, often encapsulated in the symbol of the Christian cross. The combination of horizontal and vertical lines, producing a symbolic cross, drawing heavily on Eisenstein's conceptual montage theories and imagery, can also be observed as both form and content in *Land in Trance* and *I Am Cuba.* In both films, this is aimed at bringing to the fore the inner reality of things, made palpable through medium manipulation (Figs. 3.12–3.15).

FIGURE 3.12

FIGURE 3.13

As discussed above, horizontality allows for compression of history and geography in the majestic opening of both films. In *Land in Trance,* this leads to the physical separation between the ruling classes and the masses. As a means to blur the boundaries between Latin American countries, the leaders of Eldorado are installed in palaces in the middle

FIGURE 3.14

FIGURES 3.12–3.15 Conceptual realism and verticality: stairs in *Battleship Potemkin, Metropolis, I Am Cuba* and *Land in Trance*

of an unidentifiable jungle, where they debate their strategies in isolation from the masses they supposedly represent. This is comparable, for example, with Charles Foster Kane imprisoned in his hilltop palace named after another mythical land, Xanadu, duly separated from the masses by barbed wire and a 'No Trespassing' plate, shot in close-up, in

Citizen Kane, especially if one considers that Kane is a media man involved in politics, just like Rocha's Paulo Martins. Palacial imagery is one of the most obvious tropes uniting Eisenstein to Welles and Rocha, the latter making ample use of the (unidentified) Rio opera house marbled terraces and stairs in connection with Díaz, to signify absolutist power. Moving away from the desperate masses on the arid backlands of *God and the Devil in the Land of the Sun* to focus on the powerful installed on the top of lush mountains and raised palaces, the camera in *Land in Trance* ends up conveying a foreign, uncanny view of the country, which is not so much unrealistic as suggestive of the leaders' complete alienation from reality.

Stairs are another recurrent trope in both *Land in Trance* and *I Am Cuba,* and here again the filmmakers were not short of models, from the Odessa steps in *Battleship Potemkin,* to the stairs to the underworld in Fritz Lang's *Metropolis,* to the endless steps of Xanadu in *Citizen Kane.* In accordance with Eisenstein's vertical montage theory, the magically unfolding, interminable steps in *I Am Cuba* have a musical, operatic element to them which enables the overstretched rendering of the ornamental masses of demonstrators fiercely climbing down from the university's classical building to confront the police. This is followed by the equally protracted enactment of Enrique's agony and death, as he steps ahead of the demonstrators and walks against the police bullets and water jets – reminiscent of those in the flooded underworld of Metropolis – until his final fall. Operatic tempo combined with the verticality of stairs also appear in *Land in Trance,* in which Paulo Martins is seen, toward the end of the film, struggling to drag his wounded body up the stairs of Díaz's palace, holding his never used machine gun, a scene which appears to be the sheer fruit of his delirious imagination. As Robert Stam observes, 'Paulo's death, co-extensive with the film, recalls the protracted agonies of opera, where people die eloquently, interminably, and in full voice' (1982, p. 156). Narrative realism could not be further from this, and yet this is sheer sensual experience of the delirious, irrational nature of power.

The cross-shaped 'line structure' behind *I Am Cuba* and *Land in Trance* is made explicit through the widespread use of the Christian cross with the synecdochic function of representing the church and religion as a whole. Maria/Betty is constantly holding her pendant crucifix, a token from her Cuban boyfriend who proposed to her in front of the cathedral. Her American client, on the other hand, is an apparently pagan crucifix collector who, after his night of love with Betty, takes away her pendant together with her hopes of an honest life. In *Land in*

Trance, Porfírio Díaz is constantly clasping an enormous cross to signal his allegiance to god and attachment to power. Here, Christian imagery is viewed under a critical light, in particular in the scene in which Díaz sticks his huge black flag of victory next to the bare wooden cross on the beach, during the reenactment of the First Mass. This is again reminiscent of Eisenstein's use of the same symbolism, for example, in *The Battleship Potemkin,* in which a church decorated with a cross awaits, at the foot of the Odessa steps, the masses entrapped by the police.

Especially in *I Am Cuba,* but also in *Land in Trance,* the line structure is where conceptual realism approaches expressionism, insofar as it overlaps a subjective projection with what is supposed to be the interior image of the object. In *I Am Cuba,* the camera's constant plunging into the interior of things tries to unearth from real settings a 'truth' enhanced through stylistic devices, for example, when Betty accepts that the foreigner penetrates the interior of her shack, in a flooded slum, which is tight, stuffy and wet. Its ceiling is too low, forcing her American client to lower his head, the floor is sloping, all is precarious and provisional, suggesting the disequilibrium, discomfort and instability of an expressionist setting. Expressionist deformation is most obvious in the orgiastic parties in both this film and *Land in Trance,* which again compare to the exaggerated frowns in the apocalyptic scenes of *Potemkin* and *Metropolis.*

Another geometrical formation, encompassing both horizontal and vertical movements, is the triangle, noticeable in the ornamental masses on the stairs of Lang and Eisenstein, but also in the triangular formation of the protagonists in *Land in Trance* and *I Am Cuba.* Lack of resolution is typical of intermediary characters, who are constantly agonizing between opposing forces (Figs. 3.16 and 3.17). Paulo, the poet, is always between two individuals whom he simultaneously loves and hates. He is also a journalist, a media man, who uses the power of the press to favour or destroy politicians, depending on his oscillating moods. In a male-oriented world, where intellectual and revolutionary roles are carried out by men, the intellectualized, revolutionary woman is also turned into a go-between, and it is interesting to observe how both *Land in Trance* and *I Am Cuba* arrived at similar aesthetic results to convey her social position, similar to that of a secretary. Sara, the mother figure, whom Paulo reveres and depends on, is introduced to us as 'the powerful woman behind the man', as she takes notes of Vieira's resignation speech. The triangular composition is achieved here with Sara between Vieira and Paulo, who strongly opposes Vieira's resignation. In *I Am Cuba,* Enrique rushes to his university when he

FIGURE 3.16

FIGURES 3.16–3.17 Triangulation in *I Am Cuba* and *Land in Trance*

hears the false rumour of Fidel Castro's death. There, he meets Alberto, the head of the student's union (played by Sergio Corrieri, later celebrated as the star of Tomás Gutiérrez Alea's *Memories of Underdevelopment/Memorias del Subdesarrollo,* 1968), who dictates a letter to a female student, quite in the same way, ignoring Enrique's clamour for immediate action against the repressive forces. Characters in doubt, who prevent the configuration of a fixed point of view, are another obstacle to representational realism, as they divert the attention from the story to the realism of the medium.

Concluding Remarks

As documented in Ferraz's film, the country in *I Am Cuba* was not, at the time, recognized as their own by Cuban audiences or even by those Cubans who were involved in its making. *Land in Trance* also had problems with censorship, but was finally released to a highly controversial reception, including accusations from left-wing militants, such as Fernando Gabeira, who stated at a public debate on the occasion of the film launch:

> *Land in Trance* does not offer any interrogation. I think that Paulo Martins is just a wannabe superman, who would inevitably lead to the reactionary theories he defends at the end. Therefore I think that the film, rather than an interrogation, simply makes a wrong statement about the possibility of revolution. (*Terra em transe* DVD, 2006)

Needless to say, with time these films have become unanimously recognized not only as cinematic masterpieces, but as accurate evaluations of the respective revolutions they were focusing on. My argument here is that this is due to their resolute rejection of representational mimesis, in the name of an ethics of the realism of the medium, that is, a determination to preserve their revolutionary principles within the film form. Cinephilia was a basic element in the construction of both films, confirming the drive among these filmmakers to intercommunicate through common tropes.

Land in Trance denies effectiveness to existing political proposals centred on the national question, championing instead the breaking of national and cultural boundaries. Rather than explaining the specific Brazilian case, it questions the role of the intellectual, including the one behind the camera, and suggests that revolution in art can only derive from the artist's despair and doubts that lead to the state of trance.

The composer and singer Caetano Veloso has said that the Tropicália movement, which revolutionized the arts in Brazil in the late 1960s, would not have existed were it not for the impact caused by *Land in Trance*. For him, the film revealed 'unconscious aspects of [the Brazilian] reality' and offered the means for his own breaking of boundaries between the national and the foreign, and between high and popular culture (Veloso, 1997, pp. 99ff.).

In a similar manner, *I Am Cuba* conveys little information on the Cuban revolution itself, and its propagandistic aims are as ineffective today as they were at the time the film was made. But it is a revolution in its own right. 'Each scene we filmed was like a battle, a combat, as if we were preparing a small revolution', says Sacha Calzatti in *Soy Cuba: The Siberian Mammoth.* And indeed this gigantic super-production, animated by an obsessive perfectionism, is a monument to the human capacity of invention and transformation. Because it failed to convey a clear image of the Cuban revolution, suggesting instead a high level of theatricality to politics and some attractive aspects of the orgiastic pre-revolutionary days, it was despised and forgotten both in Cuba and the USSR after just a few screenings, and consequently excluded from film history for several decades. A filmmaker such as Martin Scorsese, who, together with Francis Ford Coppola, was responsible for its relaunch in the 1990s, believes that he would have done a different kind of cinema had he been able to watch *I Am Cuba* in the early 1960s. In Scorsese's opinion, the entire history of cinema would have been different if the film had been duly shown at its time (*I Am Cuba* DVD, 2006).

Passion for cinema is, in effect, the very essence of *Land in Trance* and *I Am Cuba,* allowing identification through cinephilia, rather than through manipulation and illusionistic catharsis. Many Ann Doane connects cinephilia to indexicality, saying: 'what cinephilia names is the moment when the contingent takes on meaning. . . . The cinephile maintains a certain belief, an investment in the graspability of the asystematic, the contingent, for which the cinema is the privileged vehicle' (2003, pp. 83–4). Indeed, both films, while attesting to the international circulation of cinematic images, provide the living proof of the reality of the medium.

Chapter 4

THE WORK OF ART IN PROGRESS: AN ANALYSIS OF DELICATE CRIME

Beto Brant (b. 1964) is undisputedly one of the most creative contemporary filmmakers in Brazil. International audiences will probably be more familiar with names such as Fernando Meirelles (b. 1955) and Walter Salles (b. 1956), of a slightly older generation, but equally associated with the Brazilian Film Revival launched in the mid-1990s. The three of them, as was the rule among Revival filmmakers, made their names by addressing national issues through varied forms of revelatory realism. Salles and Meirelles, the former with *Central Station* (*Central do Brasil,* 1998) and the latter with *City of God* (*Cidade de Deus,* co-directed by Kátia Lund, 2002), attained international acclaim and went on to direct high-budget films abroad. Brant's own masterpiece, *The Trespasser* (*O invasor*), came out just a few months after *City of God* had taken the world by storm, however this and all his other films remain some kind of national treasure still awaiting due acknowledgement on foreign shores.

As I have commented at length elsewhere (Nagib, 2007), *The Trespasser*'s skilful combination of crime thriller and indexical realism resulted both in aesthetic accomplishment and a brilliant diagnosis of the problems affecting Brazilian society. After this cinematic breakthrough, Brant's interest naturally expanded beyond national borders, as had been the case with his older colleagues. But rather than engaging with foreign producers and casts, as Salles and Meirelles had done, he chose to address universal issues by further experimenting with presentational realism. The result was *Delicate Crime* (*Crime delicado,* 2006), a film that testifies to the return of the real in the aftermath of its critical and cinematic deconstruction. As I hope to demonstrate in this chapter, the film offers a fertile ground for the reframing of film theory in the post-theory era, as it undertakes a meticulous application and concomitant challenging of all the main principles defended by cinema's grand theory in the 1970s–1980s. While subscribing through form and content to grand theory's pièce de résistance, the demise of narrative realism, it celebrates reality as captured through the cracks of representation, thus offering the living proof of art's physical link with the historical contingent.

Though my approach will not be auteurist, I would like to start by pointing to some continuity indicators within Brant's oeuvre. All eight feature-length films he has directed so far have been literary adaptations, six of them made in collaboration with crime novelist Marçal Aquino. Adaptation may not even be the word when it comes to *The Trespasser*, a genuinely interactive work drawing on a novel in progress by Aquino, who then completed it on the basis of the finished film. *Delicate Crime,* Brant's fourth feature-length film, is yet another literary adaptation, this time of a novella by the celebrated Brazilian fiction writer Sérgio Sant'Anna. However, it steers away from the social-realist thriller genre which marks the Brant-Aquino collaboration, even though Aquino is once again credited as co-screenwriter and was even granted some fleeting appearances in the film. Instead, *Delicate Crime* stands out for its outspokenly hybrid, self-questioning language, in dialogue with currents in contemporary world cinema engaged with the challenging of representational truth, as exemplified by the work of Michael Haneke. One will not fail to recognize in *Delicate Crime* a reference to Haneke's *The Piano Teacher* (*La Pianiste,* 2001), which, like Brant's film, opens to the sound of Schubert's Piano Trio Opus 100, 2nd movement, Andante, functioning in both films as a diegetic device.

Cinema is a collaborative activity by nature, but *Delicate Crime* is markedly so. In the first place, the idea of adapting the Sant'Anna novella to the screen came from TV and theatre actor Marco Ricca, to whom it presented a particular interest for its focus on theatre making and criticism. Ricca's committed performance and creative input in *The Trespasser* had strengthened his bonds with Brant, who thus became the natural choice to direct the film. Ricca was involved with the project of *Delicate Crime* at all levels, as lead actor, co-script writer and co-producer. Multiple authorship in this film is further enhanced by the fact that it relies heavily on improvisation and the cast's own biographies; this gives it an overall appearance of a work in progress, open to chance and requiring engaged spectatorship to work through the narrative gaps.

On the other hand, the film is entirely programmatic in a very unusual way. Calling it an example of countercinema would not adequately account for its innovative aspect, in the first place because it seems to be the *result* of achievements of previous revolutions and countercinematic movements. From its opening images it demonstrates an awareness of, and an intention to respond to, the main questions film theory has been grappling with for the past 40 years: Brechtian alienation effects applied to the deconstruction of narrative illusionism; psychoanalysis as a means to unravel questions of point of view and gaze construction; the interplay of spectatorial and representational voyeurism, fetishism and exhibitionism; the female position as the passive object of the gaze; and, most importantly, issues pertaining to the representation of minorities, such as the disabled. I am not trying to suggest that the film crew and/or cast had read or were in the least concerned about any of such theory – although there are indicators that at least some of the scriptwriters (five in total) might have been. What seems relevant to note here is that this film could only have emerged from an environment where such ideas were well established and interwoven within the fabric of culture. Let us have a look at how it is constructed.

The film opens with an iconography of sadomasochist fetishism: the image of a female character, dressed as a nun and tied with ropes across her breasts and around her neck. In a medium shot which frames her from waist up, this character addresses the spectator directly, in a commanding tone, looking straight at the camera (Fig. 4.1). Her speech sounds like the fragment of some political discourse whose purpose is not immediately graspable:

FIGURE 4.1 Sadomasochist fetishism and feminist discourse: the opening image of *Delicate Crime*

> Nineteenth century, in the streets, the emancipation of the proletariat. In the patriarchal homes, the emancipation of the woman. A fierce, unequal combat, a struggle replete with female heroines and pioneers, idealists who believed in the possibility of a new world, a world in which the woman would be redeemed and the man would finally pay for his crimes and iniquities.

Let us first examine the content of this speech. It refers to events taking place in the nineteenth century, which led to the emancipation of both the working class and the woman. It therefore suggests that the world we are living in builds upon the conquests of those two revolutions. In this abrupt opening, however, all this sounds unmotivated. The spectator receives this vehement speech through a frontal shot, without any previous explanation and, more intriguingly, without the mediation of a fourth wall.

As is well known, the breaking of the fourth wall through direct address was a technique recommended by Brecht as a means to abolish the illusory separation between stage and audience, and cause the disruption of narrative illusionism. The difference here is that no fictional world has yet been introduced, and thus this opening sounds like an introduction to Brecht's theory itself, rather than to a self-reflexive film. The character's speech is artificial, poorly delivered, that is, delivered in an anti-naturalistic manner as if to conform to Brecht's recommendation that an actor, rather than embodying a character, should expose its artificiality by acting badly, awkwardly, unsympathetically, so that his/her person becomes apparent through the character (Brecht, 2001, pp. 136–40). Critical spectatorship, another of Brecht's proposals, is thus activated from the start, as the audience is led into questioning rather than obediently accepting what is being shown.

We are subsequently offered a wider view of the scene, though the point of it still remains obscure. We see a theatre stage on which actors play the members of a comical, stylized sadomasochist club (Fig. 4.2). A psychoanalyst with a suggestive German name, Johann Kraft, enters the club and catches his own wife in the act, only to be himself unveiled as a sexual pervert, who hypnotizes his patients in order to rape them. His wife then has her chastity belt removed by a female sadist, who announces the liberation of women and thus consecrates the dominatrix as the revolutionary feminist.

An abrupt cut and the scene changes completely. As soon as the spectator's critical consciousness has been activated by this intriguing overture, the figure of the critic emerges in the film fable, sitting at his desk and writing a theatre review. We then realize that the actress who

FIGURE 4.2 Theatre and spectatorship representation within the film (*Delicate Crime*)

had been speaking to us at the beginning was actually addressing the off-frame audience of a theatre within the film plot. This audience is represented by the point of view of the character now revealed as the film's protagonist, Antônio Martins, the theatre critic. And so it happens that the audience's point of view is confirmed as that of the critic, precisely at the moment where it is usurped by the figure of a critic within the fictional plot that he unleashes. Antônio reads out loud the few lines he has written about the play we have just seen:

> The spectacle disavows itself as such. It goes in and out of representation. . . . Instead of theatre, sex shop merchandising. The actors suffer, but the audience suffers even more.

A curious note about these lines from the critic's review is that they were written by Maurício Paroni de Castro, one of the scriptwriters, and the author of *Libertine Confraternity* (*Confraria libertina*), a fragment of which we had just seen at the opening of the film. As observed by Luiz Zanin Oricchio, Paroni indulged in the 'sadomasochist pleasure of bashing his own play and stage direction' (Oricchio, 2006, p. D6). In the film, these lines work as part of a metadiscourse which places the film in the intersection between voyeurism and exhibitionism, representational and presentational regimes. We were first challenged by the theatre actors through an exhibitionist direct address, but now a new voice has interfered, that of the critic, who takes over as first-person narrator and returns the film audience to their conventional voyeuristic position.

Spectatorial voyeurism was one of the main issues at stake among 1970s film criticism, which proposed Brecht as an antidote to the spectator's passive position prone to fetishism. This issue was first addressed by Christian Metz, who famously defined the film spectator as the voyeur who sees without being seen: 'The voyeur represents in space the fracture which forever separates him from the object', he said. This fracture, derived from a spacio-temporal gap, means that the exhibitionist component of the cinematic spectacle cannot be accomplished in the same way as in theatre, because the spectator was absent during the shoot (Metz, 1982, pp. 60 ff). What we are witnessing in the passage from the first to the second film scene is precisely this oscillation between theatrical and cinematic spectatorship: a Brechtian mode of address aimed at disrupting voyeuristic expectations, which is then reversed to satisfied exhibitionism within the fiction plot.

Implicit in this process is an ideological shift: once the diegetic critic is revealed, we become voyeurs of a feminist story mediated through a male point of view. This, in turn, makes room for another programmatic issue in psychoanalytic film theory relating to the gaze. This is explored in the next scene in which Antônio encounters the female protagonist, Inês, in a bar. The obvious reference here is Laura Mulvey and her foundational feminist essay, 'Visual Pleasure and Narrative Cinema', which defines the active male gaze as opposed to the passive female role as object of the gaze:

> The split between spectacle and narrative supports the man's role as the active one of advancing the story, making things happen. The man controls the film fantasy and also emerges as the representative of power in a further sense: as the bearer of the look of the spectator, transferring it behind the screen to neutralize the extradiegetic tendencies represented by woman as spectacle. (Mulvey, 1989, p. 20)

This formula is almost literally expressed, and brought into question, in the bar scene, which opens the book, but comes third in the film. The importance of the gaze construction in this scene is stated in the book's opening pages:

> I have never been a man who ostensibly looks at or approaches someone, as I find this tasteless and an aggression to sensitive women, among which I wouldn't hesitate to include her. But the walls and columns in the Café were mirrored. And through these mirrors, which reflected both of us, my observation could evolve, discretely and obliquely. In one or two moments, raising my eyes more abruptly from my glass, I could swear I was the one being observed with the same obliqueness, by those black eyes. (Sant'Anna, 2005, pp. 9–10)

In this excerpt, a direct link is established between gaze and power, and power being analogous to oppression against women. These topics will recur in the film in a variety of ways, as I will explain in a moment. Let us first consider how this works in the bar scene. Inês is first shown sitting at a table with friends, while Antônio, by himself, eats a sandwich at the counter opposite her. Inês's friends leave and Antônio and Inês glance at each other directly, without the mediation of a mirror as in the novella. There is also evidence of third parties' gazes in a caricature sketch of Inês and her friends lying on her table. All these gazes are placed in competition with each other and stir Antônio's jealousy, a theme which will take central stage in the plot. Antônio moves to Inês's table and the dialogue that follows revolves around power, as these lines demonstrate:

> Inês: 'I get everything I want . . . You were looking at me'.
> Antônio: 'It was you who were looking at me'.
> Inês: 'I was indeed looking at you'.
> Antônio, looking at the sketch left on the table: 'Is this how your friend sees you?'
> Inês: 'Can you see me there?'
> Antônio: 'A little, I barely know you'.

Inês is thus introduced as the offspring of a feminist, egalitarian era. She is a middle-class, liberated woman, free to do, and achieve, whatever she wants. She is the one who flirts with a man, makes the first physical advances (she takes Antônio's hand into hers and says that she loves when a man 'holds her firmly with his hands') and invites him out with the undisguised intention of sex. In this scene, if there is any victim within the male-female relationship, it is certainly the man. The spectator is given a brief close-up of the sketch left on the table. Inês is the lead character in this drawing, while the other guests are reduced to insignificant extras around her. She is the centre of gravity established by her agency, which confirms her as the active party when it comes to interacting with a man (Fig. 4.3). The fact that she is the one in control of the situation is confirmed by her prior knowledge that Antônio is a theatre critic who might present an interest for her, as she is also involved with art, albeit of another kind, as we will soon learn. He, however, has no idea of what she is, cannot explain the reason why he feels attracted to her and seems to be entirely subject to her whims.

This notwithstanding, the way we, as audience, are reading this relation may still be inflected by Antônio's male point of view, as he continues to be the narrator and thus the 'bearer of the look of the

FIGURE 4.3 Inês as the centre of gravity in the sketch left on the bar table (*Delicate Crime*)

spectator', in Mulvey's words. But the axiom of the passive female is challenged when the object of the gaze is suddenly revealed as a lack. As Inês stands up and grabs her crutches, it becomes clear that her 'plus' is actually a 'minus', a lacking leg. The focus of interest is thus diverted toward an absence which cannot conjure up the stereotype of the passive object of desire, but only its inexistence. Once in Inês's apartment, Antônio continues to feel embarrassed and lost for words, while Inês has no qualms in expressing directly what men first notice about her: the fault.

Another narrative theme further complicates this conundrum: drug date rape. This is a favourite subject in current newspapers worldwide and one which constantly reasserts the position of women as victims of male lust. Date rape drugs are those which a man surreptitiously drops into a woman's drink to make her unconscious and rape her, as the psychoanalyst is accused of doing to his patients through hypnosis in the beginning of the film. Here, drug date rape is introduced as yet another feminist issue, but in a way which suggests that this problem has already been historically resolved. Rape is a motif which will soon reemerge in the plot as the 'delicate crime' perpetrated by Antônio against Inês. For the time being, however, Inês is the one who ostensibly takes a pill in front of him, which she explains as a device 'to make life easier'. She takes the pill out of a 'black stripe' case, signifying in Brazil prescription drugs which can lead to addiction, such as sleeping pills, and washes it down with alcohol, known to intensify its effect (Fig. 4.4). Could this be read as an 'invitation to rape'? In what seems

FIGURE 4.4 Self-induced drug date rape (*Delicate Crime*)

to be a consequence of the drug she has taken, when Inês and Antônio are in her apartment she passes out in his arms and further sexual activity takes place which could potentially indicate drug date rape (note that this is still not the event later qualified as the 'delicate crime'). But was she not the one who took the drug of her own accord? Or is this once again what Antônio is leading the audience into believing, as the 'bearer of the look of the spectator'? Are we being deceived by a tale produced by Antônio's imagination, rather than the film's diegetic reality? Or are all those oddities part of the alienation effects pervading the narrative and intended to produce critical spectatorship?

Whatever the case, a general sense of discomfort prevails in the film, both on the level of the fable and its mode of address. Both protagonists seem uncomfortable and ill at ease in Inês's apartment. Inês, played by the real-life disabled actress Lilian Taublib, seems constantly out of balance and about to fall over, in particular when she lets go of her crutches. Antônio is unkempt and tastelessly dressed, as if no hair stylist or costume designer had been assigned to him. Played by an experienced actor such as Marco Ricca, he is at least convincing in his naturalistic rendering of embarrassment, but Inês's nervous giggling and abrupt utterances seem to stem, not from the character, but from the actress who incarnates her, an obvious beginner who cannot but make her true self all too visible through her persona. Discomfort is further enhanced by awkward camera positions and dim lighting in predominantly nocturnal settings, which invariably deny the spectator a privileged view of the scene. All these details suggest a precarious narrator, who seems to have no previous knowledge of the unfolding story.

Inês's apartment has a theatrical curtain at its centre, which hides a canvas in front of which she stands. And from there the film moves on to other, now professional theatrical stages, offering fragments of plays which were being performed in reality in São Paulo when the film was made. This time, of course, the viewer is already aware of Antônio's profession and can figure out that he is the one watching these plays, although, as in the opening scene, the theatre audience is left off-screen and the characters in the plays, particularly in the second case, address the camera directly, rather than one another, as if they were speaking to the film spectator and not between themselves. We are first shown a fragment of *Woyzeck* (in an adaptation by Fernando Bonassi called *Woyzeck, o brasileiro,* or *Woyzeck, the Brazilian*), the famous unfinished play found among Georg Büchner's manuscripts after his death in 1837, in which the soldier Woyzeck accuses his wife Maria of adultery. The second extract stems from *Leonor de Mendonça,* an 1846 play by Brazilian romantic poet Gonçalves Dias, in which again a woman, Leonor, is accused of adultery by her husband, D. Jaime. In both plays the female character is finally murdered by her husband, an outcome which is hinted at in the chosen fragments. This is the kind of fictional world Antônio lives in by profession, a world now left behind in the far removed nineteenth century of the three theatrical extracts shown, in which husbands retained the power of life and death over their wives. He is constantly reminded of how times have changed, not least by the actress of *Leonor de Mendonça,* with whom he has a one-night stand turned into yet another play, in which the actress, lying naked in his bed, bursts into laughter together with a packed theatre audience, while a baffled Antônio seems to be watching her from a voyeuristic, geographically unrelated standpoint. What had started as the realistic enactment of a date turns out to be Antônio's sheer imagination – or should it be read as an illustration of theatre's unrequited exhibitionist drive, once it is turned into film?

As fiction becomes increasingly inconsistent, the film opens up to the document, as three bar scenes based on sheer improvisation are edited in. In the three of them a renowned figure interacts with an unprofessional or little known actor: journalist Xico Sá and two transvestites; actor Adriano Stuart and an old drunkard; the famously outrageous film director Cláudio Assis and a lesser known theatre actress. Obviously improvised, the scene with Cláudio Assis is particularly effective in overlapping theatre performance, diegetic reality and real life. It consists of a couple sitting at a table engaged in a loud argument. Shot with the same frontal static camera as the other theatrical fragments we had previously seen, the scene gives us the initial impression of an extradiegetic excrescence within the plot. However, the quarrelling couple soon look at the camera and address someone off-frame. At that point a reverse shot shows us Antônio sitting at the counter opposite them as a silent observer, now revealed to be the originator of the point of view. As in the opening theatrical scene, he occupies the position which a moment ago was that of the film spectator. The uncovering of the voyeur, who suddenly acquires the active role of reciprocating theatrical exhibitionism, not only ties in the bar scene to the plot, but disrupts its realistic representation. And indeed at the end male and female characters are revealed to be only joking, embrace each other and leave the premises (Figs. 4.5–4.7).

FIGURE 4.5

FIGURE 4.6

FIGURES 4.5–4.7 Revealing the voyeuristic spectator: the improvised bar scene (*Delicate Crime*)

Meanwhile, the thin storyline going on at the level of the fable is as follows. Inês models for a painter, José Torres Campana – played by real-life Mexican painter Felipe Ehrenberg (who was at the time the Mexican Cultural Attaché in Brazil). She invites Antônio for the opening of this painter's exhibition, which he attends, and thus the viewer is introduced to the exhibition's centrepiece, the painting 'Pas de deux'. But it is only in a belated and unexpected flashback that we see Inês posing for this picture. In this flashback, the painter and the model are naked and engaged in different embraces during which he draws the sketches which are subsequently transferred to the canvas. Both processes (the drawing of the sketches and the actual painting) are shot while in progress, that is, Ehrenberg produced this painting during the actual shooting of the film (Figs. 4.8–4.11).

Once again, what we see in this scene is the actors leaping out of representation and into a presentational regime in which the production of an artwork is concomitant with its reproduction. Bazin once observed about the extraordinary film *The Mystery of Picasso* (*Le Mystère Picasso,* 1956), by Henri-Georges Clouzot, that its quality resided not in explaining the great painter, but in showing him in action (Bazin, 1997, p. 211) (Fig. 4.12). This suited to perfection Bazin's conception of ontological realism, but in *Delicate Crime* the filming of the work of art in progress goes beyond its documentary and indexical value to change fiction into the production of reality.

Indeed, the most startling aspect of the scene of the painting of 'Pas de deux' is that a real painter and a real model have agreed to create an artwork in real life while simultaneously playing fictional characters in a film (Figs. 4.8–4.11). The fact that this involves full nudity and physical intimacy between both, and that, to that end, the model, who is disabled in real life, had to remove her prosthesis before the camera,

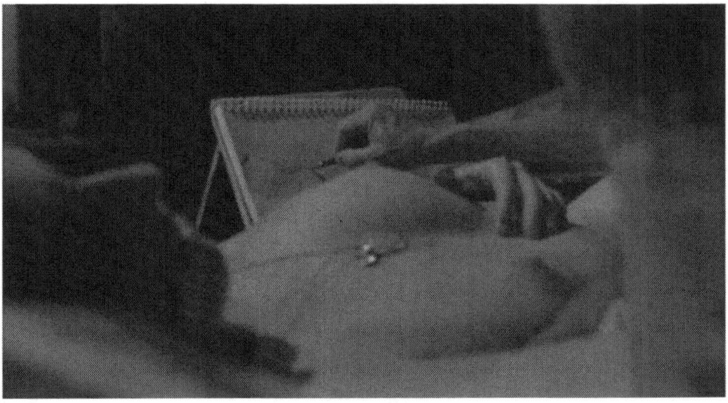

Figure 4.8

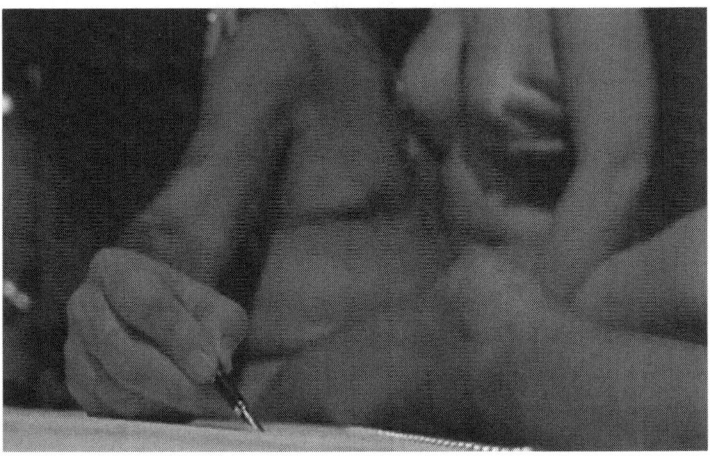

Figure 4.9

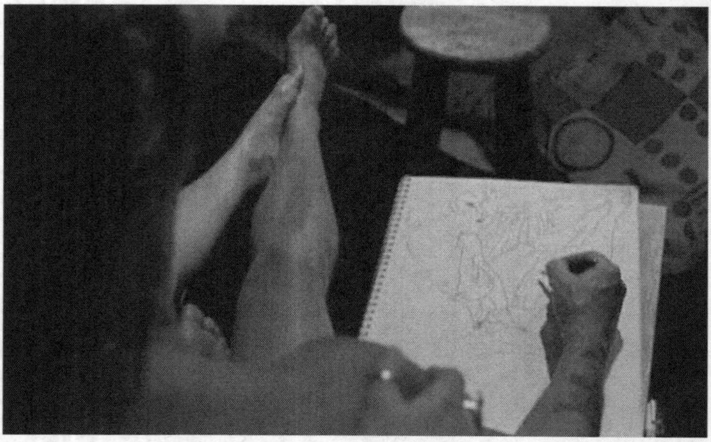

Figure 4.10

Figures 4.8–4.11 Leaping out of representation and into a presentational regime: the production of an artwork is concomitant with its reproduction (*Delicate Crime*)

indicates the transformative effect the film necessarily had in their actual lives, a fact confirmed by both Lilian Taublib and Felipe Ehrenberg in the extras of the DVD (2006).

Shown to us before we have seen how it was made, 'Pax de deux' has at its centre an erect penis next to a dilated vulva, both of which are

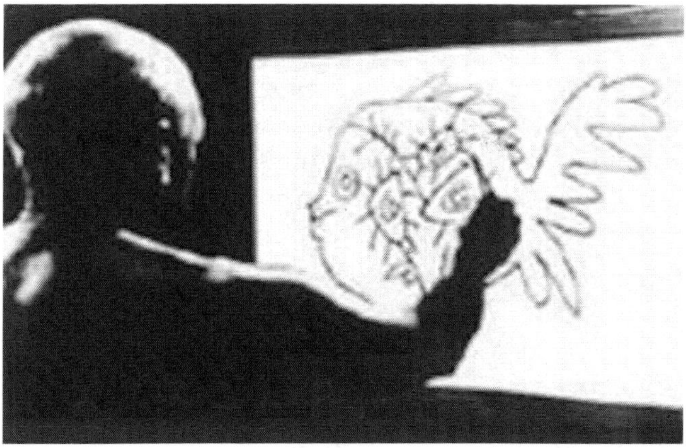

FIGURE 4.12 'The great painter in action': Picasso in *The Mystery of Picasso*

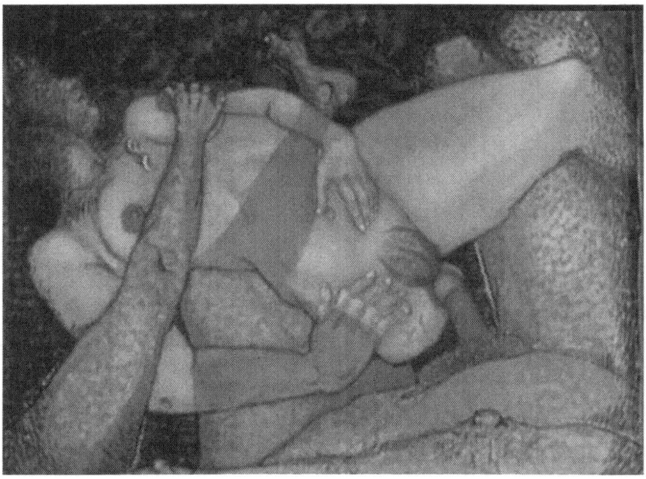

FIGURE 4.13 'Pas de deux': if the act of painting is taking place in reality, then sex must have happened as well (*Delicate Crime*)

the immediate focus of the viewer's attention. We are not given the image of the couple's genitalia during the creative work, however the ready picture leaves no doubt that, if the act of painting is taking place in reality, then something else must have happened in real life as well, namely sexual contact (Fig. 4.13). Due to its direct connection with the real, guaranteed by the necessarily contingent quality of sexual arousal, this painting, combined with the knowledge of how it was made, functions as a catalyst of all points of view and gazes within and outside the film. All of them are made vulnerable by the contagious power of sex, which binds crew to characters and these to the spectators, as it is hard to imagine how anyone, crew or cast or for that matter the viewer, would or should remain immune to the highly eroticized acts they were engaging in and filming.

This is also where all alienation effects and counternarrative devices spelt out like a mandatory grammar across the film, rather than creating critically distanced spectatorship, backfire into a sensorial, even material kind of identification, one which emerges from a post-countercinematic-feminist revolution and places all participants on an equal footing. The intention to reveal the apparatus within the scene, one of Brecht's main antiillusionistic devices, is blatant, as the painter Ehrenberg is subsequently interviewed within the film to explain in detail how that particular picture was produced. However, this revelation achieves the opposite effect to the one intended by Brecht, that is to say, its effect is general contagion rather than distanciation. This is due to the fact that the painting as well as the film medium which captures it, rather than following any a priori principles, are exposed to chance and risk as much as their own protagonists, and thus become themselves sensitized and eroticized by the contingent events.

One could even say that both contexts, the one within the film and the one from which the film has emerged, make up a world post-difference, where notions of normality have ceased to exist. It is a world in which, as Badiou puts it, 'Infinite alterity is quite simply *what there is*' (Badiou, 2002, p. 25). The disabled woman is different insofar as all individuals are different from each other and depend on how they are seen in order to make sense. Instead of a victimizing attribute, difference becomes the grain of originality essential to artistic creation. And indeed, if we look closely at 'Pas de deux', we will note that the erect penis is a substitute for the lacking leg. In it, art is the direct result of the gap in representation, which enables the emergence of the contingent real. Curiously, this image could be read as a literal translation of Laura Mulvey's assessment of the penis envy as applied to phallocentrism in American cinema:

> An idea of woman stands as linchpin to the system: it is her lack that produces the phallus as a symbolic presence, it is her desire to make good the lack that the phallus signifies. (Mulvey, 1989, p. 14)

But again the penis, despite its centrality in the picture, is still minute compared to the shadow of a leg depicted just next to it in the painting; it is the envy of a leg rather than the other way round. This sends us back to the question of victimization and the story of the rape, which makes up the core of the plot, as announced in the film's title. Antônio is jealous of Campana's portrait of Inês, which he deems to be mere pornography, and, after witnessing a quarrel between a jealous couple at the bar, he rushes in the middle of the night to Inês's apartment. She is not expecting him and does not welcome his outburst of passion, which ends in sex against her will. She then brings him to court for rape, to his total bewilderment, as he was convinced she had enjoyed their encounter, and had even written a love letter to her signed with his own blood the morning after. We are subsequently given an entirely realistic rendering of the trial, including both Inês's and Antônio's testimonials, shot in black and white for a stronger real-life effect, and in real judicial premises. Both defendant and victim seem to be equally worthy of sympathy, and we are not given the outcome of the dispute. It remains a question of point of view.

A final remark relates to how the antiillusionistic code, spelt out throughout the film as the main commandment for an ethical theatre and filmmaking, is finally turned on its head through an ethics of realism. Sant'Anna has a significant paragraph on the subject of prescriptive art criticism:

> the critic is a very special kind of artist, who does not produce any artwork, but who tightens up the net around those who do it, forcing them to demand more and more of themselves in the pursuit of that imaginary, mythic, impossible work whose co-author the critic would be. (Sant'Anna, 2005, p. 28)

This is also entirely applicable to Antônio in the film, who, with all his jealousy, is simply envious of the artist's brush, or, to be more precise, the artist's penis and the whole world of carnal sensuality from which art emerges. In a very touching scene, Antônio has his own vision of a 'pas de deux', with Inês bathed in blue light and dancing with her one leg and crutches to the sound of Schubert's Andante, whose use in the first theatrical fragment he had strongly criticized. Overcome with admiration, he sits there incapable of joining the dance, imprisoned as he is in his metadiscoursive exile. The intellectual world, which is that of the critic, is thus revealed as pure fiction, as opposed to the realm of material reality from which art is born.

Part III

The Ethics of Desire

Chapter 5

THE REALM OF THE SENSES, *THE ETHICAL IMPERATIVE AND THE POLITICS OF PLEASURE*

As he recounts in his article 'On Trial for Obscenity', Nagisa Oshima was once asked, by someone he defines as 'an extremely obnoxious German youth', why he made films. The answer he gave off the top of his head was: 'To find out what kind of person I am'. The young man then retorted: 'If that's all it is you might as well make them with 8mm film rather than in wide screen and color'. Oshima was left dumbfounded by this comment and, in his article, wishes he could have explained that one's desires are naturally related to beauty and therefore preferably expressed in widescreen and colour (Oshima, 1992, pp. 261–2). Earlier in the same article, however, he had unwittingly given a better answer to the question: 'Film directors want to shoot the dying. And they also want to shoot men and women (or men and men, women and women, or people and animals) having sexual intercourse' (p. 257).

At that time, Oshima was just coming out of the shooting of *The Realm of the Senses* (*Ai no koriida,* 1976),[1] which includes not only a whole plethora of sexual practices, but also the performance of real sex. And although no one actually dies in the film, of course, death is portrayed, on the level of the fable, as the ultimate consequence of sex. In his article, Oshima goes on to suggest that to capture in reality such extreme events is not only his own, but every filmmaker's innermost desire. As evidence he quotes the reaction to the film of Kaneto Shindo, an immediate predecessor of the Japanese New Wave (of which Oshima was the uncontested leader) not least in the seething sexuality of his films: '[Shindo] said, in a voice full of emotion, that he envied what I had done in *In the Realm of the Senses*. His eyes were wide and shining, the way children's are when they discover something they want, and a strange energy radiated from his small body' (1992, p. 257). As for shooting the dying, Oshima shows that he is not alone in considering this as a basic desire of filmmakers by quoting one of his lifetime companions, the actor Kei Sato, who had told him: 'When I learn that I'm dying of cancer, I'll let you film my death, Oshima' (p. 257).

There is nothing particularly new in all this insofar as death and sex have always been the touchstone of artistic creation. However cinema, thanks to its property of reproducing time and movement, adds an element of realism to this relation which has occupied film theorists from the very beginning, most notably the founder of realist film theory, André Bazin. In Bazin's ontological view, art of all times has sought to provide a defence against death and the passage of time, 'for death is but the victory of time' (Bazin, 1997, p. 9). Cinema, however, reaches beyond the preservation functions of painting, sculpture or even the death mask, because it satisfies, 'once and for all and in its very essence, our obsession with realism' (1997, p. 12). As for sex, he wrote:

> It is of the cinema alone that we can say that eroticism is there on purpose and is a basic ingredient. Not the sole ingredient, of course, for there are many films and good ones that owe it nothing, but a major, a specific, and even perhaps an essential one. (Bazin, 2005, p. 170)

Echoing the surrealists and ultimately Freud, Bazin attributes cinema's inherent eroticism to its affinity with dreams and the fact that all dreams are in essence erotic. However, he sets clear limits to its representation on screen in another often quoted passage:

> [T]he cinema can say everything, but not show everything. There are no sex situations – moral or immoral, shocking or banal, normal or pathological – whose expression is *a priori* prohibited on the screen but only on condition that one resorts to the capacity for abstraction in the language of cinema, so that the image never takes on a documentary quality. (Bazin, 2005, p. 174)

Central as it is to his phenomenology of film, death is also for Bazin intimately linked to sex in that it is 'the negative equivalent of sexual pleasure, which is sometimes called, not without reason, "the little death"' (2005, p. 173). He further expounds on this issue in his remarkable essay 'Death Every Afternoon', apropos of Pierre and Myriam Braunberger's documentary film *The Bullfight* (*La Course de taureaux*, 1951). The essay's title puns on Hemingway's essay book on bullfighting, *Death in the Afternoon*, a song of praise to violent death as a basic ingredient for creative writing (Hemingway, 2000). Hemingway's book was first published in 1932, a moment when bullfighting and its convulsive setting of a Spain on the brink of Civil War were enjoying particular attention among the French surrealists, including the surrealist dissident philosopher, Georges Bataille, and it is not a coincidence that two of Spain's most notable surrealist artists and filmmakers, Luis Buñuel and Salvador Dalí, were living in Paris at that time. Bataille's outrageous first novel, *Story of the Eye*, written in 1928, depicts the bullfight as the culmination of erotic experiments which include the devouring of a bull's testicles and the bull's horn piercing the fighter's eye (Bataille, 1970, p. 56), a motif also reported upon as a real event by Hemingway (2000, p. 22) and which reappears as the memorable eye sliced by a razor blade in Buñuel's *An Andalusian Dog* (*Un Chien Andalou*, 1929). Bataille's as well as Buñuel's works present multiple resonances with (and contrasts to) *The Realm of the Senses*, starting with the film's Japanese title *Ai no koriida*, or '*corrida* of love', an expression suggested to Oshima by his French producer, Anatole Dauman (Dauman, 1989, p. 228), probably himself inspired by Bataille's erotic milestone, and we will return to this in due course.

As for Bazin, he takes his cue from the shooting and editing of real bullfights, and the killing of *toreros* and bulls, to impose on the representations of death on screen the same limits he deems applicable to sex. This he defends on the basis of what he qualifies as cinema's 'exorbitant privilege' of moulding and repeating real time, understood in Bergsonian terms as *durée*, or duration, that is, a time which is immeasurable, irreversible and can only be lived as inner experience. In order to accept time flowing on screen, he says, spectators must make a 'concession of consciousness'. However death, as 'the unique moment par excellence' and consequently sex, 'the little death', 'radically rebel against this concession' because

> each is in its own way the absolute negation of objective time, the qualitative instant in its purest form. Like death, love must be experienced and cannot be represented . . . without violating its nature. This violation is called obscenity. The representation of a real death is also an obscenity, no longer a moral one, as in love, but metaphysical. We do not die twice. (Bazin, 2003, p. 30)

The consequence of showing real death in cinema thus constitutes, for him, an 'ontological obscenity', a transgression of the same order as 'the profanation of corpses and the desecration of tombs' (2002, p. 31). Needless to say, Bazin's view was largely conditioned by the moral standards of his time, as much as by his own religious convictions.

However, if Oshima's project violates Bazin's moral code by showing precisely the images he deems obscene, it provides eloquent evidence of the intrinsic relation between sex and the cinema he had intuited. It furthermore pays allegiance to Bazin's ontological thought by placing its bet on cinema's ability to adhere to objective reality and retrieve from it the authenticity of the original event. As for shooting the dying as referred to by Oshima, it is necessary to distinguish it from shooting death as described by Bazin with regards to filming or photographing bullfighting and death in war camps (2002), in which the photographer's position as a passive observer may be understood as concurring with the fatal event, an attitude which 'straddles the already relatively ambiguous border that separates ethical from unethical visual activity' (Sobchack, 2004, p. 254).

Instead, my point in this chapter will be to derive an unequivocal ethical stance from Oshima's choice to film live sex which culminates in (simulated) death, an ethics which secures continuity between a filmmaker's innermost desires and the resulting film. The election of *The Realm of the Senses* for the demonstration of this ethics is based on the fact that, as well as encapsulating a filmmaker's and his team's commitment to truth, it brings to full fruition an ideal of a whole generation of filmmakers as well as that of some of their predecessors, all of whom were interested in exploring cinema's indexicality and presentational properties. I am referring, in the first place, to the members of the so-called Shochiku Nouvelle Vague, who started at Shochiku in the late 1950s and were promoted to directors in the early 1960s, among them the notorious trio Masahiro Shinoda, Kiju Yoshida and Oshima himself. Of the same lineage are other Oshima contemporaries, such as Shohei Imamura, whose tendencies toward a maximum of indexicality combined with exhibitionist sex and violence were all too obvious in films such as *The Insect Woman* (*Nippon konchuki,* 1963), *Intentions of Murder* (*Akai satsui,* 1964), *The Pornographer* (*Erogotoshitachi yori: jinruigaku nyumon,* 1966) and *A Man Vanishes* (*Ningen johatsu,* 1967).

But *The Realm of the Senses* also sends us back to a generation immediately prior to them, the so-called second postwar generation, including the above mentioned Shindo, whose emotional reaction to the film well demonstrates his affinities, and most of all Masaki Kobayashi, of whom Oshima was a genuine follower. The daring approach to racial clashes in a Japanese war camp, as seen in Oshima's *Merry Christmas Mr Lawrence* (*Senjo no merii kurisumasu,* 1982), would not have existed were it not for Kobayashi's monumental war epic *The Human Condition* (*Ningen no joken,* 1959). In particular, the set designer Jusho Toda, responsible for the stunning sets of Kobayashi's *Harakiri* (*Seppuku,* 1962), among other films, transposed his classical, ritualistic modernism straight into 13 of Oshima's feature-length films, including the visually dazzling *Death by Hanging* (*Koshikei,* 1968), *The Ceremony* (*Gishiki,* 1971) and not least *The Realm of the Senses,* whose aesthetic balance and ritualistic atmosphere are largely owed to Toda's vision as developed under Kobayashi.

The Realm of the Senses is thus a catalyst of collective aspirations for the direct expression of physical experiences which only cinema can achieve, thanks to its property of adhering to phenomenological time and movement. It would be easy to describe it as a film which breaks all sorts of boundaries, but this would obscure the fact that it could only have been made *after* all sorts of boundaries had been broken, not least by the director himself. If *The Realm* is primarily the fruit of the process of sexual liberation that took place during the 1960s, both in Japan and the rest of the world, it is also a film of maturity, made by a director whose talent and creativity had been widely acknowledged at home and abroad, and was thus given freedom by a sensible producer, the French Anatole Dauman, to express his wishes without restraints. Above all, the film is the living proof that many so-called boundaries simply do not exist. Thus the following sections will analyse it with a view to revising established theoretical concepts drawing on such artificial boundaries, in particular those based on the opposition between sexual pleasure and intellectual enjoyment, which reflect on questions of genre, national identity, realism and spectatorship within and outside the fable. While querying their applicability, I will propose new modes of assessment based on an ethical stance that I believe informs this cinematic milestone.

Originality, Beauty and the Porn Genre

In its thrust to retrieve the aura of originality – of which Benjamin had famously stripped mechanically reproducible media – , *The Realm of the Senses* became as unique as the events it portrays with deliberate indexical intensity. Benjamin once stated that 'all great works of literature found a genre or dissolve one' (1999, p. 197). Of *The Realm of the Senses* one could perhaps say that it simultaneously founds and dissolves its own genre. Though in productive dialogue with many other genres (most notably Japanese soft and hardcore porn), the film eschews categorizations and could not have sequels or clones, not even in

Oshima's own oeuvre, because it exhausts its own aesthetics and subject matter, which is itself a story of fulfilment and exhaustion: sex that ends in death.

The true story at its origin already stands out for its singularity. It relates to the O-Sada incident, or the case of Sada Abe, a former geisha and prostitute who, in 1936, strangled to death and emasculated her lover, Kichizo Ishida, after several days of uninterrupted sex in a Tokyo inn. The most striking aspect of Abe's story is her devotion to pleasure above everything else in life. The voluminous material about her crime, which is increasingly coming to light in English,[2] leaves no doubt as to an entirely self-centred character, oblivious of society around her and even of her complacent family, someone whose feats, all to her exclusive benefit, are of the kind which elicits awe rather than sympathy. Despite her being a sex worker for the best part of her life before becoming a waitress at Kichizo's restaurant, one will not find in her story any references to pregnancies, miscarriages or abortions, or to her desiring to procreate or build a family. Her sexual activity, that she enjoys to extremes she herself at times deems pathological, is entirely sterile, an end in itself. It is true that Sada amassed a host of admirers particularly among female audiences (Johnston, 2005, p. 136), and there was a spate of severed penises in the wake of her crime (Schreiber, 2001, p. 190), but she could never be taken as a role model except at the price of social chaos and extinction. Bataille once found a name for such non-genital sex, the exclusive end of which is pleasure: 'expenditure', an unproductive activity which, though inherent in human societies alongside luxury, warfare, gambling and sacrifice, relies on the principle of loss and ultimately death (Bataille, 1967). *The Realm of the Senses* is not only a celebration of this unproductive character, but also succeeds in emulating Sada Abe in many ways, as I shall demonstrate.

Benjamin also states that 'the uniqueness of a work of art is inseparable from its being imbedded in the fabric of tradition' (1999, p. 217), and it is not a coincidence that Oshima, and even more so his exceptional art director and costume designer Toda, went back to the Japanese traditional arts, such as the erotic tales of Ihara Saikaku (1642–93), the colours and settings of kabuki theatre and in particular the iconography of Edo-period *shunga* (erotic woodblock prints) as a means to draw from a fairly recent event its ancient roots. The freedom with which Sada exercised her sex drive, at the height of Japanese repressive militarism, turned her into a character not only completely out of the norm, but also out of her time. Authors are unanimous in describing her as a remnant of the Edo period (1603–1868), when

Japan's capital was transferred to Edo (Tokyo), notable for its burgeoning sexual culture in its *ukiyo* or 'floating world' quarters, in sharp contrast to the severely repressive, sanitized early Showa Era (1926–1989). Even Sada's interrogator at her trial for murder observes that she is 'a woman in the smart, old Edo style who was sexy in a way one doesn't usually think of a geisha or restaurant woman' (Johnston, 2005, p. 124). Oshima complements this by saying that '[t]he aspect of Edo culture concerned with sex has an elegance and purity that provide a striking contrast to the crudeness and coarseness of today – although we may perceive it that way only because it has survived beyond its time' (Oshima, 1992, p. 244).

Accordingly, though set in a Japan with about half a century of European and American influence, all signs of this influence (such as automobiles, telephone poles, electricity, as well as western clothing, make-up and hair style) are carefully erased (Nagib, 1996, p. 160). And although the documentation of Abe's real story allows for the detailed reconstitution of the timescale of the events leading to Ishida's murder, the film editing avoids all temporal markers, with rare exceptions, such as a wintry, snowy surrounding, a seasonal indicator traditionally used as an erotic element in Japanese arts, as extreme cold contrasts with and reinforces the extreme heat of sex. As a result, it becomes fairly difficult to determine whether the story happens in the space of days, months of even years. The dislocation into Showa, and from there into a contemporary aesthetics, of a whole atmosphere of Edo *ukiyo,* alongside a narrative which obeys no temporal order other than its own *durée,* resulted not so much in presentification as in 'negation of objective time' in Bazin's terms, a time congealed, of mythic undertones, pertaining to the lovers alone. And thus the film fails to meet the requisites of the two basic Japanese genres, the *jidaigeki* (period dramas) and the *gendaigeki* (contemporary dramas), and therefore all other deriving subgenres.

The Realm of the Senses went on to become the apex of Oshima's career and a landmark in film history as a whole. As far as Oshima is concerned, the shooting of real sex was the result of a long learning process. In his writings, he repeatedly regrets not having had his cast engage in real sex in his previous films. As far back as in *The Sun's Burial* (*Taiyo no hakaba*), shot in 1960, Oshima had sensed the physical commitment of the actress Kayoko Honoo and wondered 'why it isn't permissible for real intercourse to take place at such times' (Oshima, 1992, p. 253). About a later film, *Pleasure of the Flesh* (*Etsuraku,* 1965), he expresses deep regret for not having cast 'pink' (Nikkatsu porn) actresses for the main roles, as this would have forced a resolve on his part, 'a resolve to forge ahead in the direction of complete expression' (1992, p. 257). Again, about another film, *Diary of a Shinjuku Thief* (*Shinjuku dorobo nikki,* 1968), he goes even further to suggest that he should have had Kei Sato, Fumio Watanabe and Rie Yokoyama perform real sex in a scene of rape: 'If I had done so, something would definitely have come of it' (Oshima, 1992, p. 258). These reflections demonstrate the long and laborious maturation process it took for the portrayal of real sex on screen in *The Realm of the Senses.* But this was to prove a one-off event in Oshima's oeuvre, despite his subsequent films being without exception devoted to erotic themes: adultery (*Realm of the Passion/Ai no borei,* 1978), homosexuality (*Merry Christmas Mr Lawrence,* 1982; *Taboo/Gohatto,* 1999) and bestiality (*Max My Love/Max mon amour,* 1986). Having suffered repeated strokes, Oshima has not been able to film since his wonderful *Taboo,* though he still makes occasional public appearances. Toda, however, whose auteurist contribution to Oshima's work cannot be overestimated, died in 1987 and thus deprived world cinema of one of its most talented and creative art directors.

Awareness of the uniqueness and innovative power of *The Realm of the Senses* has never ceased to grow. A wealth of studies and close readings continue to appear by the day all over the world. Newly restored celluloid copies and state-of-the-art DVD editions are periodically coming out, enriched with informative extras and additional footage.[3] The filming of real sex alone would not account for this feat, though it is true that real penetration had never occurred within Japan's prolific, but strictly invigilated, erotic industry. However the porn genre worldwide had often gone that far from the early cinema days, without necessarily bequeathing landmarks. To an extent, the film's impact could be ascribed to the sensational nature of its subject, but again Sada's story had been, and continues to be, profusely explored in literature, theatre and cinema, both in Japan and elsewhere,[4] in works which have rarely resonated beyond their limited space and time. A good example is *A Woman Called Abe Sada* (*Jitsuroku Abe Sada*), made by Noburu Tanaka in 1975, a year earlier than Oshima's film, which is more faithful to Abe's interrogation records than the latter and anticipates some of its scenes, but which fails to stand out even among Nikkatsu's softcore genre films.

In order to fully grasp what makes the originality of *The Realm of the Senses* it may be useful to refer back to the element of 'beauty' which, in his musings on the fundaments of filmmaking, Oshima defines as the object of desire which requires 'wide screen and colour' for its optimal rendering. Beauty, in art, has been connected to ethics as tantamount to being 'fair' and 'just' (Scarry, 2006), and the aesthetic balance tenaciously pursued in the film may, in a way, respond to such an aspiration. Within a Japanese performing arts tradition, beauty is associated with 'truth' (Kawatake, 1990, pp. 234ff.). Rather than with accurate mimesis or logical order, it is connected with the senses and unmediated physical experience:

> The sense of beauty through eyes and ears, sight and sound – these are treated as the first consideration, not only for actors and other stage performers but for the entire stage and the theatre as a whole. (Kawatake, 1990, p. 86)

We will see in more detail how the film reflects an endeavour to appeal to the spectator's five senses, including the non-cinematic ones of touch and smell.

As far as cinema is concerned, however, beauty and real sex are more often than not incompatible terms. Corny settings, unattractive performers, clumsy acting, thin or nonsensical narrative lines and general bad taste are the usual encumbrances of hardcore porn films, whose exclusively commercial function is to provoke sexual arousal. In contrast, what immediately strikes you about *The Realm* are its impeccable compositions, its obsessive balance of settings, costumes, proportions, shapes, colours, sounds and, not least, its stunningly beautiful as well as skilful leading actors, Eiko Matsuda (Sada Abe) and Tatsuya Fuji (Kichizo Ishida). The film's assistant director, Yoichi Sai, makes the fitting remark that, while looking for male actors for the protagonist role, the main concern was the 'photogenic' aspect of their penises, rather than their size as usual in the porn genre (Sai, 2003). In her perceptive analysis of the film, hardcore theorist Linda Williams describes *The Realm* 'as the first example of feature-length narrative cinema anywhere in the world to succeed as both art and pornography – as both genital maximum visibility and the erotic subtleties of line, color, light, and performance' (2008, p. 182). This means that the necessarily contingent, unpredictable quality of real sex had to be achieved and captured through maximum planning, a near-impossible equation as Oshima himself points out: 'From the beginning, I was asking the impossible: that they [the cast] act and have sexual intercourse at the same time. However, this demand was satisfied' (Oshima, 1980, p. 323; 1992, p. 264).[5] It is in this fusion of apparently incompatible terms, staged representation and presentation of reality, that the film's uniqueness seems to reside.

As a rule, sex in art films, explicit though it might be, is part of a complex network of feelings, moods, psychological states and cultural standards which infuse it with guilt, frustration and disappointment as a means to cohere with what Freud called the 'reality principle' as opposed to the 'pleasure principle'. *The Realm,* however, combines realism with gratifying sex and undisturbed fruition of pleasure, meant to infect cast, crew and audiences alike, as no other films, not even Oshima's previous or later outputs, have ever been able to do. Such an extraordinary result was enabled by a number of favourable circumstances. In the first place, Oshima was lucky to find an actress such as Eiko Matsuda, with the ideal face and body to play the title role and psychologically prepared for it. Though she had never worked in a film, she was part of Shuji Terayama's troupe Tenjo Sakiji, or 'children of heaven' (inspired by Marcel Carné's *Les Enfants du paradis/Children of Paradise,* 1945), famous for their daringly surrealist stage and screen experiments. Tatsuya Fuji, an experienced Nikkatsu and television action film star, was another lucky strike, after an exhaustive search for actors who could combine excellent acting skills and self-confidence in their sexual performance before a rolling camera. Decisive in this context was Oshima's long-standing relationship with the prolific Japanese softcore porn film industry, the Nikkatsu 'pink' and 'roman porno', which hosted in its ranks many left-wing activists. Koji Wakamatsu, the most notable and politicized of them, agreed to take up the role of the film's Japanese producer and help the team through the difficulties and necessary secrecy of shooting real sex within the walls of a Japanese studio, in this case, the Daiei studios in Kyoto (Wakamatsu, 2003). Another contribution from the softcore porn industry was the cinematographer Hideo Itoh, who had shot all of Wakamatsu's films, and the brilliant actress Aoi Nakajima (sadly now deceased), who plays Toku, Kichizo's wife, and appears in the film's first explicit sex scene. Behind the cameras, she was also the one who helped Fuji reach the required stage of arousal, while the crew waited with all lights switched off in an atmosphere of general sexual tension and contamination (Sai, 2003).

Most important of all was the freedom of creation secured for Oshima by his exceptional producer, Anatole Dauman. More than a businessman, Dauman was a film patron for whom artistic value came before all commercial concerns, as one can easily tell by his portfolio of uncompromising auteurs, including the likes of Godard, Bresson, Wenders, Varda, Marker, Ivens and Schlöndorff. Their relationship, which would continue until *The Realm of Passion,* started with *Death by*

Hanging, which called international attention to Oshima's uncompromising political stance against the Japanese establishment, and I will refer back to this film in a moment. However, Dauman's sympathy derived from an aspect which had escaped most critics at the time – impressed as they were with Oshima's political verve and modernist aesthetics – namely, his exceptional skills at shooting sex scenes. It was on that basis that he decided to commission him to make an outright erotic film, which Oshima's 'wishful thinking', according to Dauman, took as an invitation to shoot a 'pornographic' film (Dauman, 1989, p. 228; Oshima, 1992, p. 258). Oshima then submitted two projects to Dauman, who chose the O-Sada incident, all the while emphasizing that the approach should go beyond the director's usual countercinematic devices:

> If I had followed Oshima's original idea, the action would have centred on the judicial suit brought against the heroine, a narrative form already used in *Death by Hanging*. 'Keep to the representation of a couple drunk with sexual passion', I told him. And to make myself better understood, I added: 'Shoot a *corrida* of love'. I believe that was what Oshima most wanted to do from the depths of his being. (Dauman, 1989, p. 228)

The accuracy of Dauman's intuition is confirmed by the lines I highlighted at the beginning of this chapter, in which Oshima lays down his ethics of desire. However, it was not until three years after this proposal, when he heard of the final demise of French censorship, that he decided to start working on the project (Oshima, 1992, pp. 258ff.). In order to escape the claws of Japanese censors, he devised a strategy of shooting in Japan and smuggling the negative stock to France for development and editing. Thus, enjoying total freedom of creation and economic ease, he was finally able to make a positive film about Japan.

The Eroticized Nation

This was surely a surprise to many who knew Oshima for his combative style of filmmaking. Even his assistant director, the 'pink' novice filmmaker Yoichi Sai, reveals how disconcerted he was to find no politics but only 'a love story' when he first read the script of *The Realm of the Senses* (Sai, 2003). However, many critics insist to this day on seeing *The Realm of the Senses* as a corollary to Oshima's transgressive countercinematic style, both on the formal and on the political front. Joan Mellen, for example, ends her finely observed study of the film, which makes a volume of the BFI Film Classics series, with the conclusion that it

> portrays, in what may be the most brilliant dystopic vision ever to appear on film, the tragic consequences of individual resistance to a culture that denies freedom and thwarts human fulfilment. (Mellen, 2004, p. 84)

Whether or not Japan corresponds to such a view in reality, the fact remains that this evil country is simply not present in the film and, for this reason, *The Realm of the Senses* is *not* a dystopic film but, much to the contrary, a celebratory, even utopian, in any case entirely positive, vision of Japan, though certainly of a very different Japan from that Mellen is talking about. In fact, sex and the nation are not separable terms in Oshima's oeuvre, which is a relentless pursuit of Japan's erotic core, as a brief retrospect will evidence.

Before all those favourable circumstances described above allowed him to make his erotic masterpiece, negation and 'self-negation' had been an essential part of Oshima's platform. In an article dating back to 1960, when still a novice as a film director, he had famously proposed, for Japanese upcoming directors, a process of constant 'self-negation' as a condition for the configuration of an auteurist project able to resist stagnation in patterns of genre (Oshima, 1992, pp. 47–8). This principle was still resonating when, in 1988, he gave me an interview in which he compared himself to a phoenix being constantly reborn out of its own ashes (Nagib, 1988, p. B-7). At stake here was a Sartrean call for responsibility and a rejection of all self-victimizing representations, which had become so common in postwar Japanese cinema. A primary requirement for a socially responsible filmmaker was the abolition of all boundaries between public and private spheres, to the extent that questioning oneself, and this 'self' being Japanese, translated in Oshima's films into negation of the nation Japan.

As a result, self-negation was exercised in the form of a ferocious attack on national allegories, with 'Japan' (Nihon/Nippon) becoming a recurrent term in the films' very titles: *Night and Fog in Japan* (*Nihon no yoru to kiri,* 1960), *A Treatise on Japanese Bawdy Songs* (*Nihon shunka-ko,* 1967) and *Japanese Summer: Double Suicide* (*Murishinju: nihon no natsu,* 1967). And so it happened that a defiled *hinomaru* (the 'disc of the sun' or the Japanese national flag) became Oshima's personal, auteurist signature throughout his filmography. In the early 1960s it functioned primarily as scorn for the *taiyozoku,* the 'sun tribe' of a very popular mid-1950s Nikkatsu genre focusing on a hedonistic, beach-loving youth fuelled by the new values of the American occupiers in postwar Japan. This is entirely the case, for example, in *The Sun's Burial* (1960), where the image of a blazing sun burning over a murderous rape in an Osaka slum offers an outrageous funeral to Japan's rising-sun symbol together with its sun-tanned, Americanized youth. Later, thanks to the addition of Toda's iconographic input, the sun is removed from its mythical, ethereal sphere, and brought down to earth, objectified and materialized as cloth and paint. It becomes a plaything in the hands of the characters, in particular in their sexual experiments. The motif of the sphere and the hole, combined with sexual killing by strangulation, becomes recurrent from Oshima and Toda's first collaborative work, *Violence at Noon* (*Hakuchu no torima,* 1965), based on a *fait divers* of a serial killer who rapes his victims after strangling them. The red disc is painted in a funereal black and set fire to, then used as bedding on which a university teacher is gang-raped, in *A Treatise of Japanese Bawdy Songs.* The erotic circle of the lace and the rope is subsequently connected with that of the rising sun in *Death by Hanging,* another account of rape and murder committed by a Korean who is sentenced to death by hanging, turning the circle of the rope into a circular motif within the film plot itself, which climaxes with a giant Japanese flag serving as a drape to wrap a pair of naked incestuous Korean lovers. And in *Diary of a Shinjuku Thief* the blood of a violated virgin expands into a red sphere on her white bed linen (Figs. 5.1–5.4).

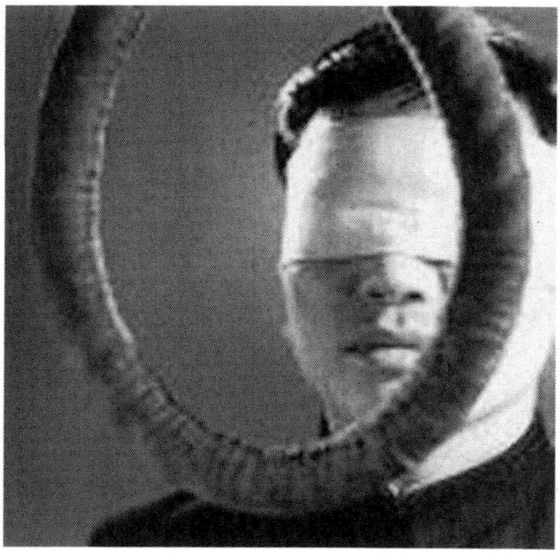

Figures 5.1

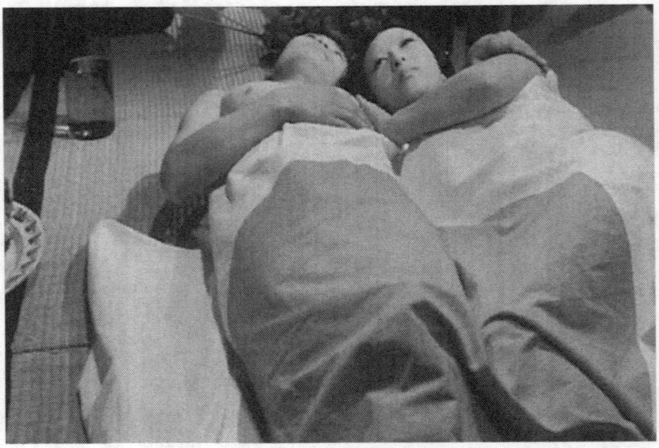

FIGURES 5.2

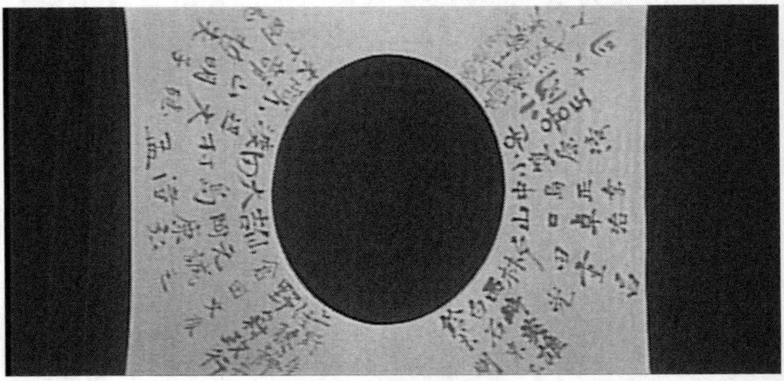

FIGURES 5.3

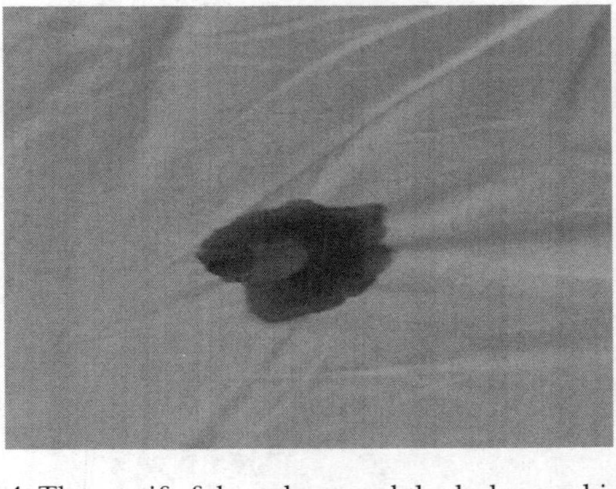

FIGURES 5.1–5.4 The motif of the sphere and the hole, combined with sexual killing by strangulation: *Death by Hanging* (5.1 and 5.2), *Boy* (*Shonen,* Nagisa Oshima, 1969, 5.3) and *Diary of a Shinjuku Thief* (5.4)

The association of the Japanese flag with sex is so obsessive that it betrays a fascination with the icon itself, with its round shape suggestive of the vaginal hole, or the 'solar anus', to resort to Bataille's imagery, who adds to this association the element of sexual killing, as expressed in *The Solar Anus* and other of his writings. Moreover, beyond all metadiscourse and self-reflexivity, there is an obsession with the motifs of the rope, strangulation and necrophilia per se, regardless of the social causes behind these crimes. By the time of *Violence at Noon*, Oshima had found a name for the crime of strangulation followed by rape: 'crime of conviction', whose causes were not to be found in society or any other external motivations, but within the agent himself (Oshima, 1992, pp. 107ff.). Hitchcock's *Rope* (1948), with its story of a gratuitous murder by strangulation associated with necrophilia, homosexuality and rope symbolism, is a confessed influence here, one which is notable as early as in *Night and Fog in Japan* (1960), whose extremely long takes owe as much to this film as to the famous Mizoguchi sequence shots so cherished by the French Nouvelle Vague directors.

In this context Sada Abe was the ideal character to focus upon, once total liberty to the filmmaker was granted, as she enabled the understanding of the country through a sex culture detectable even in its national symbolism. This is proved, in the first place, by the fact that, in real life, she saw no barriers to the expression of her desire and, interestingly, found very little resistance to her behaviour and practices in the society around her. The detailed and straightforward answers she gave in her police interrogation (Abe, 2005), an extraordinary document from which Oshima drew most of his script, indicate not only patience and sympathy on the part of her interrogator but a bottomless tolerance for her extravagant habits from her family, employers and lovers, even when she lies to them, betrays them and steals from co-workers for gambling or other inconsequential purposes. On all these occasions she receives minimal or no punishment, and goes on to squeeze out yet another sizeable sum from her betrayed protectors, among them the kind and respectable Professor Omiya, who also features in *The Realm*. The film is entirely faithful to the real story in this respect, featuring a whole society that bows to Sada's whims, as exemplified in the scene in which she threatens the head-waitress with a knife at Kichizo's restaurant, where she works. Rather than being rebuked, she is met with her boss falling head over heels for her. The same kind of docile behaviour is to be found even on the part of Kichizo's wife, who begs Sada not to quit work in their house when she is caught spying on their love-making.

In real life, the public reaction to Sada's crime was no less baffling. Beyond the obvious media sensation it naturally caused, the incident was greeted with genuine fascination, not least on the part of the jury, who gave her a mere six years in prison for the premeditated murder of a thoroughly innocent man. Johnston notes sympathy for her crime in particular on the part of female audiences:

> The *Yomiuri* called interest in the case 'Sada mania' and referred to the young women in attendance as 'Sada fans'. This implied that there existed considerable sympathy for Abe, quite possibly because many young women themselves wished they could 'monopolize' a man they loved. (Johnston, 2005, p. 136)

Oshima, in his turn, emphasizes the warm reception from Japanese society as a whole:

> The common people roared out shouts of liberty from the depths of their hearts. They offered Sada Abe a storm of 'bravos' . . . They knew that this was [a case] that crossed the entire history of Japan up to today, from the most distant times when sexuality stood for love and beauty. (Oshima, 1980, p. 11)

Johnston concurs with the idea that Sada was a late remnant of a more flexible erotic culture of a pre-modern Japan, in which sexual experience before marriage was expected from women and men alike (2005, p. 29).

In short, Sada and Kichizo represented precisely the Japan Oshima admired and identified with, a country in which sex was not at all repressed, even if it ultimately led to death. It was certainly not the militarized, repressive Japan of the early Showa Era, but another, historical, perhaps mythical, surely personal country, whose defence was the whole point in his previous films. It took more than a decade and a foreign investor for this to happen, but then in *The Realm of the Senses* the motifs of strangulation and the *hinomaru* could make a glorious and entirely positive comeback, in widescreen and full colour as befits 'beauty', in Oshima's understanding of the term. Sex becomes a means to embellish rather than defile the national flag and, accordingly, the red and white of the *hinomaru* are splashed over the entire film so as to respond to the contagious nature of the lovers' sexual passion. The literalization and objectification of the national flag, as cloth, burning red and freezing white, as befits the extremes of carnal love, are the means through which the country acquires material reality.

Sex in Red and White: Double Suicide

Oshima had been exploring the aggressive power of red since his first colour film, *Cruel Story of Youth* (*Seishun zankoku monogatari,* 1960), but it is in *The Realm* that, with the indispensable help of Jusho Toda, the complexity of red, from its function in the Japanese traditional arts to its symbolic use in the national flag, is fully deployed in all its shades of rose, brown, wine and purple. In his essay 'On Beauty in Kabuki', the painter Ryusei Kishida once wrote:

> This colour of red was originally something primitive, with no possible touch of refinement. It is immature, with a good measure of barbaric flavour about it. It is heretical, in some cases bringing to mind blood and fearsome devils. While it is a rich colour, it is never elegant but has instead a common rustic flavour. Yet kabuki has gone beyond this and used it as the means to create before discerning eyes a strangely beautiful world which is both rough and fragrant. (Kawatake, 1990, p. 101)

This aggressive elegance of kabuki red is here recovered through Sada's ebullient sexual imagination. Already in the opening scene, the viewer is presented with a nocturnal shot of a light brown, transparent *shoji* (sliding paper door) through which swaying shades of white washing on a line, in the manner of flags in the wind, are visible. A reverse shot shows us Sada in her dormitory flanked by other sleeping servants, her wide open eyes looking intently at the swaying shadows, her head resting on a wine-coloured, penis-shaped small pillow, covered with a white cloth (Fig. 5.5). As the combination of these props

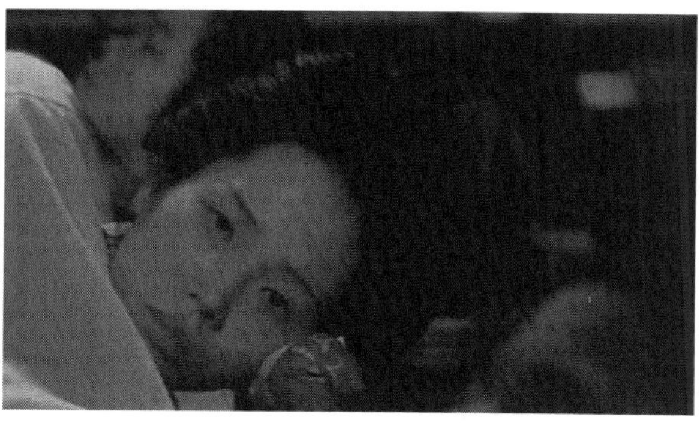

Figure 5.5 The *hinomaru* as sex symbol: Sada's penis-shaped red pillow, covered with a white cloth

suggests, it is the thought of sex that keeps her awake. Another servant approaches and takes her place next to her, and as she lifts the white cover Sada's red kimono is unveiled into which she inserts her hand to caress her immaculately white breast. Both women then leave to spy on Kichizo being dressed in the early hours by his wife, Toku, who carefully ties a *fundoshi*, or white loincloth, around his waist. This reveals that the white linen previously seen by Sada through the *shoji* is actually Kichi's *fundoshi*. The dressing operation turns into the first explicit sex scene in the film, with Toku duly raising her red kimono topped with a white apron before Sada's greedy eyes and moist, fleshy red lips.

As in Oshima's previous films, literalization and objectification of the *hinomaru* motif are again at work here, but this time with the aim of enhancing the sensual atmosphere. The gently falling snow over the servants' red, pink and brown kimonos, in their spying expedition, contrasts with and emphasizes the heat of their sexual lust. The white of Sada's smooth skin – repeatedly noted in the dialogue – is an invitation to touch. Throughout the film the white-red motif is reiterated as an attribute of the characters themselves. Traditionally, the beauty of the Japanese woman is connected to the whiteness of her skin. In particular geishas, as seen in the film, have their faces and necks, and from the nape of the neck to the kimono's neckline, covered in white make-up. Eiko Matsuda, who plays Sada, does not wear this heavy white make-up, but the natural whiteness of her skin contrasts with the darker complexion of Tatsuya Fuji, thus reinforcing the sensual attractiveness of the red-white contrast. As far as skin is concerned, the care with colour goes down to Kichi's own penis, of a tone that matches the purple of Sada's kimono in their first sexual encounter. The combination is intentional and had been indicated in the film script:

> [Kichizo] stretches out his hand and touches the lips of her vagina and then shows her his hardened penis, erect and red-brown, almost the same colour as Sada's kimono. (Oshima, 1980, p. 15)

Granted, that loathed Japan of Oshima's previous films is still a ghost lurking in the corners, but now reduced to minimal proportions of small *hinomaru* banners in the hands of children, also dressed in red, who tease with it the flaccid penis of a drunkard sleeping in the snow. The miniature flags reappear in the celebrated scene in which Kichizo, entirely absorbed in his world of sexual passion, walks against the flow of soldiers marching to war, while the crowds wave their little banners at them. The purpose here is clearly to dismiss all political discourse as irrelevant within this universe of sexual freedom and beauty, governed by no politics other than pleasure (Figs. 5.6 and 5.7).

That Sada, in real life, should have killed her lover by strangulation fitted Oshima's imagery and imaginary to perfection, as far as the overlapping of the round *hinomaru* with sex and killing is concerned. The flipside of the 'demon' in *Violence at Noon,* the woman is the one who

Figures 5.6

Figures 5.6–5.7 The loathed Japan of Oshima's previous films makes brief appearances in the form of *hinomaru* banners in *The Realm of the Senses*

strangles the man for sexual satisfaction, a fact which has fuelled debates on the film's possible feminist point of view (see Sharp, 2008, Standish, 2008). The complication is that, as much as society is absent to explain the demon's criminal behaviour in the earlier film, Sada lacks an enemy. Feminist attitudes are reactive and necessitate the configuration of a repressive situation in order to be activated. Kichi is clearly not the representative of any repressive male-chauvinist institution, although this was an overwhelming presence in Japan in the mid-1930s, with the ultra-conservative samurai revival in the Japanese army which Oshima would portray so well in a later film, *Merry Christmas, Mr Lawrence.* This conservative rise is only very briefly indicated in the film with the aforementioned soldiers' parade and plays hardly any role in the plot. Strangulation here is exclusively presented as an advanced stage of Sada and Kichi's *corrida* of love, after they have promised each other never to let their pleasure wane. Kichi agrees to let himself be choked because he had tried this on Sada before without feeling sexually moved. Sada then takes the lead, chokes him and succeeds in obtaining yet another erection from his exhausted body. On a second attempt, now carried out with the help of a typically red kimono sash, she finally kills him, but not before she gently slaps his face to wake him up and make him aware that she will be pulling till the end.

This role reversal and mutual acceptance of the rules of the game certainly do not cancel out the fact that Sada is the powerful one in the film, which is clear in her autocratic and abusive personality with whoever is around, young and old alike, including a scene of paedophilia in which she aggressively caresses a male and a female child. Her display of power finally comes to a head when she severs Kichi's penis and testicles in a pool of bright-red blood. Even here, however, it is not entirely clear whether she is usurping male power – which Kichi never had over her anyway – or rather becoming one with him, as she writes with blood on his body: 'Sada and Kichi together'. In any case it is her insatiable, unstoppable thirst for pleasure, more than any political power, that the film is perpetuating in its dazzling final shot from above the immobilized bodies of Sada and the dead Kichi. He lies on his back, and she on her side, facing him, dressed in a light, open-front pink and silver kimono, her bloody fingers delicately resting on his stomach as a signature to the message she wrote on his chest, while clutching his excised organs in her left hand above his head. Rather than murder, this is a perfect picture of double suicide, despite Oshima's voiceover announcing that Sada, in real life, survived and was found carrying her token, with a rapturous smile on her face. Mellen has fitting remarks, here, on the way this image, suggestive of double suicide, reverses what she calls 'the classical and humiliating upside-down positioning of lovers who have been discovered to have committed double suicide, traditionally the woman's head was placed alongside the feet of the man' (Mellen, 2004, p. 70), an image which makes a magnificent ending of another film, Masahiro Shinoda's *Double Suicide* (*Shinju ten no Amijima,* 1969), based on the bunraku play by Chikamatsu Monzaemon (1653–1725).

The idea of double suicide is also part of Sada's real story, with less feminist and more scabrous details. According to her account, she had become prey to jealousy and could not bear the thought that Kichi would be having sex with his wife or anyone else. After it became clear that she would not be able to have him for herself alone, she started to plan his killing. She bought a knife to that end, but then started the choking game which was nothing but a way to interweave sex and murder. In her first attempt, Kichi survived with a badly swollen, purple face, which prevented him from leaving the inn room where they were lodging. This gave her the opportunity for a second attempt, but she first administered him some twenty pills of a soporific called Calmotin, and only then succeeded in strangling him to death (Abe, 2005, pp. 198–9).

Despite all these avowed circumstances, Sada's murderous act was still partly interpreted as double suicide by the jury, given that she was preparing to kill herself at the moment she was arrested by the police, who found the various suicide notes she had written. She willingly delivered herself, according to her account, with the hope of receiving capital punishment, but this was not to happen and she survived until her disappearance to an unknown destiny in 1970. *Shinju,* a ritual double suicide between lovers who for any reason are being forced to terminate their liaison, has a long tradition in Japan and features amply in Japanese literature and theatre, most famously Chikamatsu's bunraku plays, such as the one adapted by Shinoda quoted above. Sada and Kichizo were also facing imminent separation, as sooner or later he would need to return to his wife. An interesting variation of *shinju* is *murishinju,* or 'forced' double suicide, which occurs when one of the parties cannot summon up the courage to kill themselves and agrees to be killed (or is simply murdered) by their partner instead, a theme Oshima had exploited in *Double Suicide: Japanese Summer* (the word in the original Japanese title is *murishinju*). Sada's case would fall into this category, if one accepts (as the jury members seem to have partly done) that Kichizo had agreed to be killed by strangulation, so as to achieve yet another erection. As in the film, rather than a threat to social hierarchy, this seems to indicate the resilience of a cultural tradition within which the murderous act would make some kind of sense.

Oshima is framing his storytelling within this tradition, alongside the fitting choice of traditional decoration, iconography and music. If there is any feminist point of view, it in no way detracts from customs deeply ingrained in the Japanese culture, customs which Oshima deems liberating and perfectly adequate to express this interior, red-hot world to the public eye, as acted out with utter realism and the inherent contingency of real sex in *The Realm of the Senses*.

Anti-realism and Artistic Real

Oshima's radical defence of visual and carnal pleasures, as conveyed in *The Realm of the Senses* in the form of an ethical platform for the expression of desire, came out in 1976, the same year that Laura Mulvey published her groundbreaking feminist attack on visual pleasure derived from American cinema (Mulvey, [1976] 1989). These diametrically opposing aims which were at that time at the forefront of respectively the avant-garde Japanese Cinema and European left-wing film criticism suggest that Oshima's enthusiastic reception in Europe in the early 1970s may have been based on some important misunderstandings. As I will endeavour to show, these misunderstandings become thoroughly apparent when it comes to the critical appraisal of *The Realm of the Senses*.

'Anti-realism' was the order of the day at that time, and a corresponding theory had been evolving from the late 1960s, particularly in France and the UK, with reflections all over the world, in the form of a prescriptive programme aimed at deconstructing subjective identification as produced by the 'realist' narrative style of the so-called classical Hollywood cinema. 'Anti-realist' filmmaking was epitomized by Jean-Luc Godard, a countercinematic, non-narrative paradigm against which all other filmmakers were measured. On the basis of these assumptions, several pioneering concepts in film studies were developed whose usefulness and applicability endure to this day. Among them, the notion of the cinematic 'index', as formulated by Peter Wollen in his famous 1969 essay 'The Semiology of Cinema', which identifies Bazin's ontology with the indexical sign, in Peirce's terms, because it stresses 'the existential bond between sign and object' (Wollen, [1969] 1998, p. 86). Few concepts in film studies have been more widely utilized than Wollen's indexicality, which is also entirely applicable when it comes to Oshima's adherence to the contingent with the performance of real sex in *The Realm.* However, Wollen's intent was certainly not to defend realism as style, as Bazin had done, but to celebrate Godard's Brechtian, self-reflexive cinema as an expression of 'Peirce's perfect sign', insofar as it presented 'an equal amalgam of the symbolic, the iconic and the indexical', that is to say 'conceptual meaning, pictorial beauty and documentary truth' (Wollen, 1998, p. 106).

Oshima's first success in Europe, *Death by Hanging,* on a first approach seemed to fit this programme like a glove, and this explains much of the applause he received at the time in Europe. The film is a masterly Brechtian take on racial discrimination in Japan, in which a Korean rapist and murderer is sentenced to death by hanging. The execution proceeds, but the convict fails to die, becoming amnesiac instead. The film then evolves with the authorities representing his crime to him so as to revive his memory and carry out a new execution in accordance with the Japanese law, which requires a convict's full awareness of his crime before being killed. Roles are thus reversed, with the authorities playing the part of criminals and the Korean, that of their impassive spectator.

Death by Hanging was prevented from premiering at Cannes in 1968 because the festival was interrupted by the May rebellion, but caused a considerable stir at parallel showings in France. The *Cahiers du Cinéma,* which had surrendered to cinematic *japonisme* since their discovery of Mizoguchi in the early 1950s, immediately adopted Oshima into their pantheon of celebrated auteurs, while *Death by Hanging* was hailed by one of its most distinguished writers, Pascal Bonitzer, as the quintessence of antiillusionism and denunciation of 'spectatorial "foreclosure" from the film story', and a 'metaphor of the impossibility of the spectator's action' (Bonitzer, 1970, p. 34). Stephen Heath, the main representative of Oshima's devotees on the pages of *Screen,* subsequently joined the chorus by calling attention to 'the radical importance' of *Death by Hanging,* whose self-questioning narrative structure located it in a 'negative hollow' between form and content (Heath, [1976, 1981], 1986, p. 412). This welcoming reception reflects the veritable war then being waged by both French and British critics against narrative cinema and what was then referred to as 'realism'. Because Japanese cinema was normally at odds with the 'realist' conventions of the so-called Hollywood classical cinema, Japanese directors in general were regarded as 'rebellious' by European critics, regardless of whether they were, like Mizoguchi and (a late Western discovery) Ozu, hegemonic at home (see Nagib, 2006). And so it happened that Oshima, the rebel par excellence, came to crystallise the very kind of countercinema they were craving for. Turim explores at length the Brechtian dimension of this film, starting by noting that:

> Not only is *Death by Hanging* a strategic readjustment of Brechtian devices of distanciation to cinematic form, it invites specific comparison in its treatment of the hanging to that at the end of Brecht's *The Threepenny Opera* (1928). It also invites comparison to his *Caucasian Chalk Circle* (1948). Justice is on trial. For this reason and for its dark humor, its theoretical connections to Brecht are significant. (1998, pp. 63)

Brecht's epic theatre was based on the notion of *Verfremdungseffekt* (variously translated as an effect of 'alienation', 'distanciation' or 'estrangement'), whose point was to appeal to reason (*Verstand*) rather than feeling or empathy (*Einfühlung*) (Brecht, 2001, pp. 16, 23). Its purpose was to call the spectator's attention to the ideological content of conventional, 'bourgeois' theatre which operated through processes of spectatorial 'identification' and 'illusionism'. Revolutionary though this proposal was, it did not break away from well-established Western traditions. On the philosophical front, it embraces a Christian-inflected body-mind dualism harking back to Kantian metaphysics. 'Distanciation effect' chimes in particular with Kant's notion of 'disinterest' as formulated in his Critique of Judgement, which defines a subject's relation to artistic beauty as an attitude of detached contemplation through which the subject remains unaffected by the physical existence of an art object (Gaut, 2007, p. 29).

Brecht's 'neo-Kantianism' had been the subject of heated discussion already in the pages of Screen, the most outspokenly Brechtian of film journals in the 1970s. In his defence of Lukacsian realism, Mitchell (1974, contested by Brewster, 1974) had aligned Brecht's concept of *Verfremdung* to Shklovsky's formalist concept of *ostranenie*, based on processes of de-routinization and defamiliarization triggered by works of art. Mitchell argued that:

> Formalist aesthetics is Kantian, topped with modern phenomenology (Husserl was an influence: one sees in Shklovsky's formulation how the 'what' of a work of art can be 'bracketed' . . .) . . . Or to put it another way: the 'what' of representation turns into the 'how'. (Mitchell, 1974, p. 75)

Barthes, another highly influential figure on film theory in the 1970s alongside Brecht, further expanded on this 'bracketing of contents' with his idea of 'third' or 'obtuse' meaning, that which is 'discontinuous, indifferent to the story and to the obvious meaning (as signification of the story)' and for this reason has a 'distancing effect with regard to the referent' (Barthes, 1977, p. 61). It is, in essence, the same idea he puts forward in his insightful book about Japan, *L'Empire des signes* (1970), in which the country is defined as an empty centre with meanings dispersed around its fringes – and from which the French title of Oshima's film, *L'Empire des sens,* derives. Heath translated this idea into the notion of 'excess' (1975) to define film elements with no narrative function, but endowed with the power to reveal further meanings of a film, not least the 'arbitrariness' of its narrative structure (Thompson, 1986, p. 140).

The Kantian idea of 'disinterest' has recently returned to the debate in connection with ethics and processes of 'othering' as put forward by Lévinas and discussed by Derrida (Gaston, 2005). It has also been compared to notions of beauty as a function of 'disinterested contemplation' and 'artistic detachment' as found in both traditional Zen and modern Japanese philosophy (Odin, 2001). However, notions of 'otherness', as derived from Kant and related philosophical sources, or Japanese 'detached contemplation' which is discernible in filmmakers akin to Zen-Buddhism such as Ozu, could not be farther removed from Oshima's and his generation's aesthetic aspirations. Zen emphasizes in-between spaces and nothingness, as expressed respectively in concepts of *ma* and *mu,* and certainly Ozu – whose grave is simply marked with the *mu* Chinese character on his own request – shunned any physical contact in his films, except for extremely rare and highly emotional handshakes. However, the concept of *ukiyo,* the floating world which celebrates life's ephemerality and a corresponding attitude of *carpe diem,* is no less attached to Zen philosophy, and it is the recovery of this atmosphere of liberty which animated Oshima and the filmmakers of his generation. Rather than the elements of modernity capable of matching Western philosophical abstraction, what interested these filmmakers about Japanese arts and philosophy was a tradition of the cult of the body and the physical environment able to back their daring approach to material reality. As Dominique Buisson argues,

> In contrast to the Judaeo-Christian West, where sex is always associated with evil, Japan does not condemn pleasure as such; sex does not imply any personal guilt, having as its sole limit, according to the Confucian moral, not to disturb the public order and not to stain one's name with an indelible shame. Japanese sexuality is connected with immediate joy, rather than with the Western conception of love. (Buisson, 2001, p. 63)

This is what Dauman so perceptively intuited in Oshima's work when he commissioned from him an outright erotic film. Oshima showed how well he understood the message by focusing on Sada Abe, a modern character whose mindset dated back to the Edo period or even farther to Heian (794–1185), when exceptional female writers such as Murasaki Shikibu (*The Tales of Genji*) and Sei Shonagon (*The Pillow Book*) spent their lives refining their sexual knowledge and practical experience. The anti-metadiscourse par excellence, Sada's literalness is exemplarily illustrated by the way she put into practice what Freud had famously defined as the female 'penis envy', by simply taking possession of her lover's penis and testicles in their materiality. Not only did she continue to carry this token inside her garments wherever she went, before her arrest, but she cuddled, sucked and tried to insert it into her body (Abe, 2005, p. 205). Repulsive though this mere idea may sound, the sensual understanding she had of a woman's love for a man is at times intensely moving:

> People have made an incredible fuss since they found out what I did, but there are lots of women who fall hopelessly in love with a man. Even if a wife doesn't like sashimi, if her husband likes it she will naturally start to like it, too. And there are lots of wives who sleep with their husband's pillow in their arms while he is away. For some women the smell of the quilted kimono of the man they love might make them feel ill. But there are lots of women who think that the tea left behind by the man they love or the food that he has already had in his mouth are delicious. (Abe, 2005, p. 208)

Such statements resulted in moments of rare beauty in the film, for example, when Sada locks herself in a train lavatory to unpack and dive her face into Kichizo's kimono she is carrying with her. Or when he dips slices of mushroom and other vegetables in her juices before mouthing them and sharing them with her, a scene which comes straight from Sada's own account (Abe, 2005, p. 194). Vivian Sobchack derives an ethics from the aesthetics based on the 'experience we have of ourselves and others as material objects' (Sobchack, 2004, p. 296). This she calls 'interobjectivity', which 'lies in the *subjective* realization of our own *objectivity,* in the passion of our *own* material' (Sobchack, 2004, p. 310). In Oshima's film, a similar process can be observed in the emphasis placed on the, ultimately utopian, continuity through which a subject aspires to incorporate and become the beloved object.

Sada was furthermore the living proof of the continuity between art and reality. The knife she bought when she first thought of murdering Kichizo was suggested by a theatre play she had watched at the Meijiza in between encounters with him (Abe, 2005, pp. 192, 194). Upon her release from prison, she herself became part of a theatre troupe, directed by Mikihiko Nagata (who would later turn to screen writing), performing a one-act play called *A Woman of the Showa Period* (*Showa ichidai onna*), based on her own story. Abe even appeared in a documentary film by Ishii Teruo, *Love and Crime* or *History of Bizarre Crimes by Women in the Meiji, Taisho and Showa Eras* (*Meiji-Taisho-Showa, ryoki onna hanzaishi*, 1969) (Johnston, 2005, p. 161).

Donald Richie has a marvellous piece on his encounter with Sada Abe, in the bar she had been working in since 1952, which shows how she had come to fuse performance and real life:

> After the war, released from prison, she got herself a job in Inari-cho, in downtown Tokyo: at the Hoshi-Kiku-Sui – the Star-Chrysanthemum-Water – a pub. There, every night workers of the neighbourhood . . . would gather to drink saké and shochu and nibble grilled squid and pickled radish. And every night around ten, Sada Abe would make her entrance. It was grand . . . Always in bright kimono, one redolent of the time of her crime, early Showa, 1936, Sada Abe would appear at the head of the stairs, stop, survey the crowd below, and then slowly descend . . . The descent was dramatic, with many pauses as she stared at her guests below, turning a brief gaze on this one and that. And as she did so, progressing slowly, indignation was expressed . . . The men invariably placed their hands over their privates. Fingers squeezed tight, they would then turn and snicker. Above, the descending Sada Abe would mime fury, casting burning glances at those below who squeezed and giggled the more. She slapped the banister in her wrath, and merriment rippled. (Richie, 1991, p. 33)

As well as contiguity between art and life, this account testifies to a participative audience which is precisely the kind Oshima was aiming at with *The Realm of the Senses.*

The Participative Voyeur and the Eroticized Apparatus

Indeed, while Mulvey denounces the position of the spectators in the cinema as 'one of repression of their exhibitionism and projection of the repressed desire onto the performer' (1989, p. 17), *The Realm* replaces voyeurism with exhibitionism, so as to encourage scopophilia and identification to the point of pushing the passive voyeur, both within the film fable and on the level of spectatorship, into physically and actively joining the erotic play. A lot has been said and written about voyeurism in the film, and indeed, in its 20 scenes of sexual situations, there is practically none that is not being either secretly or openly spied upon by someone. This has been literally drawn from Sada's account, who reiterates that, in the inns she frequented with her lover, 'whether the maid or anybody else came to the room I wouldn't let go of Ishida' (Abe, 2005, p. 194).

Going beyond this description, in *The Realm,* the voyeur is there to be noted and invited or even forced by an all-powerful Sada to participate in the sexual act. Rather than punished for their intrusion, the voyeur is often rewarded with sex with Kichi, in stark contrast to the sliced eyes of Bataille and Buñuel, both of whom are directing their aggression against a repressive system grounded in Catholicism. An eloquent example is the case of the elderly geisha, Kikuryu, who collapses in ecstasy when penetrated by Kichi, which causes him, moreover, to remark that he felt as if desecrating 'his dead mother's corpse', a phrase with a curious Bazinian ring to it. Sada and Kichi find, reveal or even create voyeurs wherever they go, forcing them to confess to their current status with regard to sex, like the virgin servant who is keeping herself for a future husband or the impotent restaurant cook, who remains unmoved at the sight of Sada's exposed pubis. Bataille's eyes (including the eyes of a bull and a priest) and other round-shape avatars, such as the bull testicles which Simone, in *Story of the Eye,* inserts in her vagina, are here replaced by a boiled egg, which Kichi inserts into Sada's vagina and makes her return by squatting and pushing like a hen – and the egg comes out intact. Rather than any repressive religious or social force, it is the empire of desire which is here at work, leading all characters to attest to their physical, all too human, condition.

Recently, there have been perceptive readings of this scopophilic mechanism, for example, by Sharp who, in his minutely researched and beautifully illustrated book on the Japanese erotic film industry, remarks that the *The Realm*

> rejects the standard voyeuristic *nozoki* position, or rather it subverts it so that most of the scenes are witnessed by women, as opposed to men . . . Sada later not only asserts dominance in the bedroom; she more or less 'performs' with Kichi for the benefit of the various female third parties . . . (Sharp, 2008, p. 192)

More often, however, voyeurism in *The Realm* has been seen as the introduction of an intermediary instance, as a means to generate a distancing effect. 'The movie prohibits all immediate contagion, all sexual emotion. Rarely has voyeurism been so discouraged', writes Pascal Bonitzer, Oshima's most devoted critic at the *Cahiers.* This is because, as he puts it, 'the spectators see themselves in the film. . . .

The third person's eyes are constantly included in the scene to be challenged' (Bonitzer, 1976, p. 51). Such denial of sexual contagion continues to reverberate in Mellen, who states: '. . . the film permits little vicarious arousal by a spectator' (2004, p. 36) and, in another passage: 'Deliberately, Oshima refuses the easy palliative of audience identification' (2004, p. 72). How would these critics then explain the ubiquitous presence of voyeurs in porn films, in which they are obviously meant to *cause* spectatorial identification and arousal? That this is also the voyeur's function in *The Realm* is evident, among other things, in the didactic nature of the camera movements, in charge of Nikkatsu softcore cinematographer Itoh, who guides the viewer/voyeur's gaze towards arousing sights, and the careful positioning of actors' legs, torsos and arms in such a way as not to block a detailed view of sex organs, penetrations and fellatios, including what in the porn genre would be called 'the money shot'. All of these are performed with utter realism so as to expose the state of sexual excitement that cast (and, one would suppose, crew) themselves were in during the shoot. It is hard to imagine how any viewer can (or should) remain immune to 'vicarious arousal' in the sight of this.[6]

In this respect, *The Realm of the Senses* is no different from *shunga,* which inspired so many of its pictorial compositions, and whose function is no other than to provoke sexual arousal and satisfaction in the fashion of contemporary porn films. An image found in Timon Screech's excellent *shunga* book ingeniously illustrates the inextricable continuity between artistic contemplation and physical enjoyment in the Japanese art Oshima and Toda were clearly looking at when they made *The Realm.* The print shows a man who has rolled up a picture of a 'beautiful person' (a prostitute) until only her face remains visible; he then shapes a body out of clothing and ties to it a so-called 'Edo Shape' (*azumagata*), or artificial vagina, made from leather or velvet and stuffed with boiled *konnyaku* (a jelly made of a special kind of potato), which allows him to perform sex (Screech, 1999, p. 20). Abstract thinking thus finds continuity in real intercourse (Fig. 5.8).

Such an aversion, on the part of some critics, to sexual contagion relates to, and often derives from, Brecht and his body-mind dualism. In an early book which he would probably not subscribe to entirely nowadays, Robert Stam explains that 'as well as rejecting compassion and fear, Brecht's non-Aristotelian theatre also rejects any possibility of erotic involvement' (Stam, 1981, p. 154).[7] Typically, Stam singles out Godard as an example of how cinema can 'eschew the dangers of sexual images' and 'sabotage the eroticism of the image', as well as avoid

Figure 5.8 The *azumagata* allows the picture viewer to perform sex: abstract thinking finds continuity in real intercourse. (Anon., *Man using a portrait and an 'Edo shape'*, monochrome woodblock illustration from an unknown *shunga* book, c. 1760)

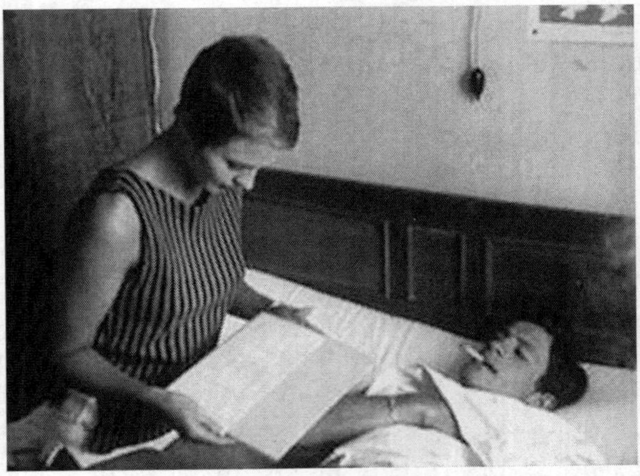

Figure 5.9 Reading disrupts sex in *Breathless*

'the traps of art as an ersatz for libidinal satisfaction', 'the spectator's voyeuristic involvement' and 'scopophilic concupiscence' (Stam, 1981, pp. 155–6). It is indeed a fact that, in Godard, intellectual activity inevitably collides with and interrupts the sexual act. In his first feature film, *Breathless* (*À Bout de souffle,* 1960), for example, reading disrupts the sexual involvement between the protagonists in a famously long bed scene, in which intercourse is only suggested under the bed covers (Fig. 5.9). In stark contrast to this, a *shunga* print by Harunobu Suzuki (1725–70), on which a scene of *The Realm* was based, shows that singing and reading (a poetry book lies open next to the male lover), that is, intellectual activity, not only does not disrupt sex, but enhances it with artistic beauty, poetry and music being conducive to sexual arousal. Sitting on her lover's penis in exactly the same position as seen in the *shunga* picture, Sada, in the film, sings to the shamisen for Kichi to disguise their sexual activity, in case his wife is overhearing them through the thin paper door. Her singing then gradually changes into moans as she climaxes, which supplies her artistic/intellectual performance with a physical ending (Figs. 5.10 and 5.11).

FIGURES 5.10

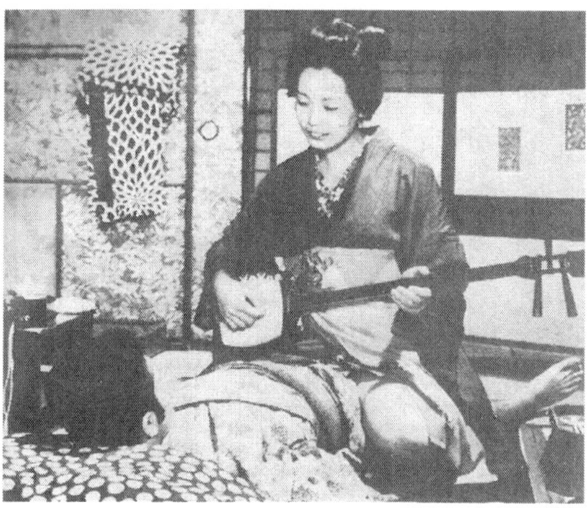

FIGURES 5.10–5.11 As in Harunobu's *shunga*, Sada's artistic performance has a physical ending. (Woodblock print by Harunobu Suzuki, 1725–70)

Another Harunobu *shunga* print makes this point even stronger. Here, calligraphy and love poems (intellectual pleasure) are the very motor of sexual activity (carnal pleasure) as a teacher leads the hand of his pupil on the writing of a love poem, while he penetrates her (Fig. 5.12).

Averse to this idea though many of Oshima's admirers might be, the fact remains that *The Realm of the Senses* is an authentic antithesis to Godard, as Williams rightly remarks:

> Though Oshima's politics and avant-gardism could sometimes make him seem like a Japanese Godard – a filmmaker whose metacinematic qualities he indeed did emulate in some of his earlier films – the narrative of this particular film, which is straightforward, is very un-Godardian. (2008, p. 186)

As much as any other filmmaker, Godard was obsessed with sex in the liberating 1970s, and a film such as *Number Two* (*Numéro Deux,* Jean-Luc Godard, 1975) abounds with fellatios, anal sex and female masturbation. However, these images are constantly and purposely dislocated from their aim of producing pleasure, which makes them 'obscene' in the Sartrean sense of disruption between consciousness and the body, or a body 'caught up in acts which reveal the inertia

FIGURE 5.12 A calligraphy lesson leads to sex in *The Spell of Amorous Love.* (Woodblock print by Harunobu Suzuki, c. 1766–70)

of the flesh' (Sartre, 1943, p. 452). Body-mind continuity is what, in *The Realm,* avoids this sense of obscenity of the unconscious flesh, by candidly exposing bodies entirely and consciously drenched in sexual lust. Lacan reportedly said of *The Realm* that it was 'the most chaste film I have ever seen' (Mandiargues, 1989, p. 237). This curiously echoes Sada, who said of Kichi that: 'Emotionally he was a very simple man. Even little things would make him happy. He tended to show his emotions and was as innocent as a little baby' (Abe, 2005, p. 193). Sada seems to have touched a point: the direct expression of emotion and desire averts all sense of obscenity, dirt, sin and guilt. And this is why, in the film, the lovers can relish their own smell, even if it disgusts a non-participant voyeur, and find each other juices, including Sada's menstrual blood, delicious. The latter example, incidentally, is also directly drawn from Sada's account, which is even more poignant than its screen version: while in the film Kichi licks his blood-smeared fingers after playing with Sada, in the real story he goes down on her, despite her uninviting condition. This is not just the film breaking one of Japan severest sexual taboos but the inexistence of taboos in the pleasure world Oshima was focusing upon.

But even when Oshima was openly embracing Brecht, as was the case in *Death by Hanging,* the result was far from pure alienation effects. This is precisely what *The Realm,* as the apex of the director's career, summing up his most daring experiments, shows: how questionable the very idea of alienation effect is. Congnitivists, such as Smith, have long dismissed 'the commonplace, with very ancient roots in Western culture, concerning the purportedly antagonistic relationship between reason and emotion' and 'the idea that undergoing empathy deadens our rational faculties' (Smith, 1996, p. 132). Instead, he says, 'emotion is integrated with perception, attention, and cognition, not implacably opposed to any of them' (Smith, 1996, pp. 132–3).

Interestingly, Brecht was under the influence of the Chinese theatre when he first formulated his idea of 'alienation effects'. According to his translator John Willett, Brecht used the famous expression *Verfremdungseffekt* for the first time with reference to the Chinese actor Mei Lan-fang and his theatre company, when they performed in Moscow in 1935 (Brecht, 2001, 99n). *Verfremdung* is a neologism intended to replace in an art context the concept of *Entfremdung* in the Marxist sense of a worker's alienation from the product of his/her labour. In his article 'Alienation Effects in Chinese Acting', Brecht lists a series of devices he deems 'antiillusionistic' in the Chinese theatre, all of which he would later employ in his own epic theatre, including the rejection of realistic mimesis, the use of symbols, the actors' emotional control, the absence of a fourth wall and the construction of the sets before the eyes of the audience (Brecht, 2001, pp. 91ff.). All these devices had the aim of making visible the theatrical 'apparatus'. This is pertinent here insofar as most Japanese art forms derive from the Chinese and include all these supposedly 'distancing' devices, as can also be observed in *The Realm of the Senses,* close as it is to Japanese traditional arts.

As far as cinema is concerned, since the 1970s the so-called *dispositif cinématographique,* or the cinematic apparatus, has become a central concept, for it describes the ways in which identification and illusionism are produced in order to create an 'impression of reality' (Baudry, [1970, 1975] 1986). Psychoanalytic and semiotic theories embraced the concept of cinematic apparatus as the phenomenon of the spectator's regression to the mirror phase, as defined by Lacan. The revelation of this apparatus in the scene, as carried out by Godard, would consequently prevent identification and enable the formation of critical spectatorship in Brechtian terms. Japanese theatre is famous for this kind of recourse, as seen, for example, in the bunraku puppet theatre, where the puppet manipulators are fully visible alongside their puppets. Most critics who believe *The Realm* prevents sexual contagion are in fact identifying the visible voyeurs in the film with this kind of purportedly 'disruptive' figure. Let me resort once again to Harunobu's *shunga* prints as a means to demonstrate that the visible apparatus in the Japanese traditional arts, rather than preventing erotic contagion, is itself eroticized, that is, a mechanism through which reason and emotion remain intertwined, as is also the case in Oshima's film.

Despite the beauty and obvious artistic value of so many *shunga* prints, their primary function, as I have pointed out above, was sexual arousal and satisfaction. For this reason, they were also called *makura-e,* or pillow pictures, and *warai-e,* or laughing pictures ('to laugh' signifying 'to masturbate') (Screech, 1999, p. 14). However, the self-reflexive elements abounding in them could easily suggest detachment and distanciation in the very same way Brecht had understood the workings of the Chinese theatre. In order to test this assumption, let us have a look at this Harunobu print (Fig. 5.13). In it, the lovers not only do not look at each other (do not look for excitement on each other), but look in opposite directions. At a first glance, this could suggest distraction, detachment, lack of attention or even indifference towards sex.

FIGURE 5.13 Two apparently independent activities are in fact inextricable. (*The Spell of Amorous Love*, woodblock print by Harunobu Suzuki, c. 1766–70)

A closer look, however, reveals that the two apparently independent activities are in fact inextricable, because the woman is actually drawing sexual inspiration from the sight of pedestrians (potential voyeurs) walking in the rain (water seen as an erotic element), while the man is expecting the same from an object off-frame (possibly other voyeurs). What they see flows through their eyes and minds, so as to inspire the activity of their lower bodies. As in onanistic activities, sexual desire is aroused by the sight of a third element.

In this print, several of the 'alienation effects' described by Brecht with reference to the Chinese theatre can be identified:

- Symbolism: the woman's toes are contracted, expressing sexual arousal (Klompmakers, 2001, p. 17), although nothing else in her body indicates that.
- Emotional control: as in Brecht's description (2001, p. 93), the characters are not in trance, there is no exaltation or eruption.
- The absence of mimetic realism: facial expressions are only slightly indicated with single strokes, male and female faces are very similar, resulting in mimesis of the idea rather than of the form; the unnatural position, even contortionism of the bodies simultaneously conveys the characters' sexual and intellectual activities to the viewer.

This other Harunobu print (Fig. 5.14) perfectly illustrate the idea of an 'eroticized' apparatus, in the form of the participative voyeur, who maintains a self-reflexive, ironic attitude, while expressing his own sexual arousal. I am referring to the miniature man, Maneemon, the protagonist of a series devoted to his adventures, as reproduced in Klompmakers (2001). Maneemon is the alter ego of Harunobu himself, reduced to miniature size thanks to a magic potion he has taken in order to be able to spy on his own characters. Here, a man makes love to an adolescent, who in turn masturbates. The boy's gaze is turned toward the sleeve of his kimono, which has a masculine pattern, the iris, whose leaves are associated with the blade of a sword. The man's gaze is turned toward the boy's organ while he masturbates. The patterns on the futon also indicate sexual love, with the motif of the stylized chrysanthemum which resembles the anus. Maneemon, the 'eroticized apparatus', descends to the tea house's second floor, flying in on a kite, which he still holds in his left hand. The written comments reveal that the scene excites him so much, that he needs to fan himself – his samurai outfit, including the sword, indicates the condition of the man and homoeroticism as a common practice among samurais (Klompmakers, 2001, pp. 62–3). What becomes obvious here is the general sexual contagion, including the painter himself, who is not only the excited voyeur within the image but also the artist indulging his erotic imagination. His activity mirrors and suggests that of the

Figure 5.14 The voyeur's activity mirrors and suggests that of the viewer (*Elegant Horny Maneemon*, woodblock print by Harunobu Suzuki, c. 1768–70)

viewer, who is also supposed to engage in onanistic or other sexual practices while looking at the print.

The same can be observed throughout *The Realm of the Senses*, most strikingly in the scene with the elderly geisha Kikuryu mentioned above. She arrives as Kichi and Sada are naked making love, politely congratulates them on their energy and is hardly able to hide her own excitement as she starts playing the shamisen and singing. A frontal shot captures her through the half-opened shoji in centre frame, with Sada on top of Kichi to the left. Sada then starts to interrogate Kikuryu in a dialogue which actually suggests Sada's envy of the voyeur position. She finally offers Kichi to the geisha. The camera then reverses to show Sada through the half-opened shoji while Kichi makes love to Kikuryu in the hallway. Alternate reverse shots show both that Sada is becoming excited with this sight and that Kichi is looking at her for his own arousal. In the role of this eroticized voyeur, Sada is given tighter and tighter close-ups, with her thick, red, trembling lips occupying the whole screen; at this point, Kikuryu gives her climatic sigh, which seems to come from Sada's own lips as she dubs her (Figs. 5.15–5.19).

The revelation of the voyeur's lust takes place here through literal unmasking: Kikuryu loses her wig and exposes her actual dark skin below her whitened face and neck, her wilted body revealed under the shiny, elegant red and white kimono, redolent yet again of the *hinomaru*. Revelation and general contamination of desire, that is to say

Figures 5.15

Figures 5.16

Figures 5.17

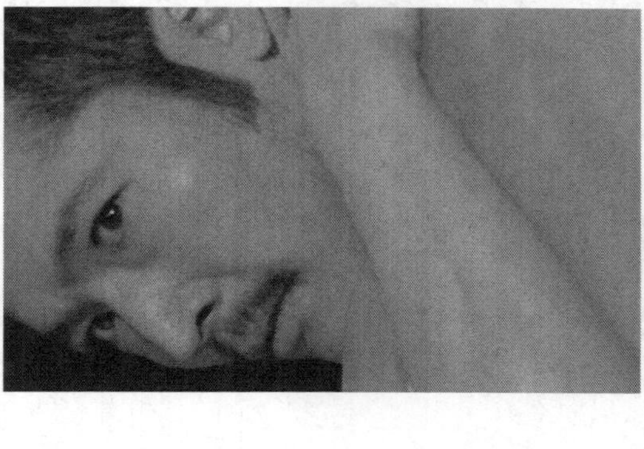

Figures 5.18

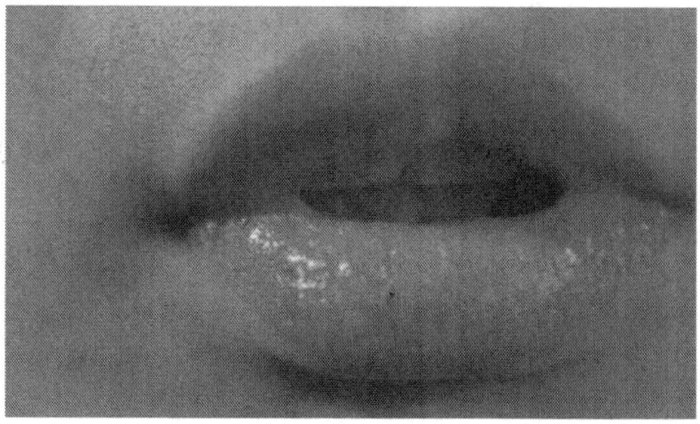

Figures 5.15–5.19 Reversing and merging active and passive voyeurism: Sada dubs the geisha's ecstasy

the unmasking and celebration of total identification, which cause the reversibility and equivalence of spectators and participants at all levels, is shown to be the rule in this world of passion, and are propounded as a unifying, ethical principle connecting art, intellect, the film medium and the body.

Part IV

The Production of Reality

Chapter 6

HARA AND KOBAYASHI'S 'PRIVATE DOCUMENTARIES'[1]

Life is acting.
Kazuo Hara

A victim of severe cerebral palsy slowly drags his tiny, lame body on all fours across the zebra crossing of a busy Tokyo avenue, while cars and motorbikes drive dangerously close by him. A woman gives birth to a child entirely by herself in front of a static camera in an uninterrupted sequence shot. A former WWII soldier pays an impromptu visit to one of his comrades nearly 40 years later, now a frail old man, and assaults him while the camera carries on rolling. A popular novelist has three quarters of his liver removed in front of the camera. These scenes, drawn respectively from *Goodbye CP* (*Sayonara CP,* 1972), *Extreme Private Eros: Love Song 1974* (*Gokushiteki erosu: renka 1974,* 1974), *The Emperor's Naked Army Marches On* (*Yuki yukite shingun,* 1987) and *A Dedicated Life* (*Zenshin shosetsuka,* 1994), exemplify the radical kind of realism embraced by director Kazuo Hara and his lifetime companion, collaborator and producer Sachiko Kobayashi.[2] Their films are so confrontational towards their characters, so intrusive into their private lives, so exposing of their intimacy, that one wonders how they could have possibly been made. The filmmakers' daring and uncompromising mode of address of the most explosive social issues is, on the other hand, undeniably effective. Rarely has cinema been so politically active, while refusing to send any straightforward political message. Hardly ever has it been so supportive of minorities of gender, race and disability, while remaining thoroughly averse to victimization.

In this chapter, I will look at the four films listed above, all of which have commonly been defined as 'documentaries' on the basis of their use of real characters and locations, but which have extended the frontiers of the genre to hitherto unknown realms. As I will endeavour to show, these films testify to an auteurist realist project based on physicality pushed to the 'extreme' – as expressed in the title of the duo's second feature – as a means to go beyond realism as style and turn the act of filmmaking into producing, as well as reproducing, reality. My analysis will first consider the extent to which these films express and transcend their historical time, marked by the late developments and ramifications of the Japanese New Wave. I will then move to an examination of the films' phenomenological time, that is, the protracted periods they have taken to be produced as a means to adhere to a character's life span and allow for the emergence of the revelatory event. And finally I will address the conflicting authorial subjectivities at work within each film, in order to evaluate the ethical imperative – as well as consequences – of this unique realist project.

Historical Time

Hara and Kobayashi's career harks back to the late 1960s, a moment when Japanese cinematic aesthetics and modes of production were undergoing a revolution triggered in the early years of the decade by the emergence of the Japanese New Wave. Hara started as a still photographer in the mid-1960s, working for the *Asahi* newspaper from Yamaguchi, in the south of Japan, where he was born in 1945. In 1966, he moved to Tokyo to attend the Tokyo College of Photography, while making a living by working at a school for disabled children whom he also photographed. These pictures led to his first photo exhibition, at the Nikon Salon, in Ginza, in 1969, where he met another photographer, Sachiko Kobayashi, herself a victim of disability caused by polio. Their relationship quickly progressed into their first collaborative motion picture, *Goodbye CP,* a film about a group of adult individuals affected by cerebral palsy, shot in the early 1970s and released in 1972, and to their marriage in 1973. From this very first film Hara and Kobayashi set in motion a radical method of physical approach to reality which would remain practically unaltered through their subsequent films and become their distinctive auteurist signature. Let us examine how it relates to the cinematic new wave and realist tendencies of that time.

As John Hill, quoting Raymond Williams, observes with relation to the British New Wave films, 'it is usually a "revolt" against previous conventions which characterizes a "break towards realism" in the arts', as a means 'to communicate a new, and more fundamental, "underlying reality"' (Hill, 1986, p. 59). Such a 'break towards realism' certainly applies to most cinematic new waves and new cinemas in the world, starting with Italian Neorealism and including the Japanese New Wave. This adds to a perception that representations of 'pain and deprivation are more real than pleasure' (Grodal, 2002, p. 87), meaning that many of these films have immersed themselves into the world of the dispossessed and underprivileged, especially in postwar periods.

The early revolutionary films of the Japanese New Wave were all about unveiling a deep and more real Japan, that is to say an underlying reality of poverty, illegal businesses, petty crimes and general amorality which thrived in the country in World War II's long-lasting aftermath. And this was in frank opposition to the conciliatory humanism until then prevailing in the films by studio directors, such as Kurosawa, Ozu and Naruse. However, this 'social realist' phase, together with its national agenda, was already receding and giving way to new developments by the time Hara and Kobayashi emerged on the cinematic scene. At least a decade older than the duo, most Japanese New Wave directors, such as Oshima, Shinoda, Yoshida, Imamura and Suzuki, had started within Japan's studio system in the mid-1950s and launched their groundbreaking works in the early 1960s. By the late 1960s, most of them had already abandoned their respective studios and gone out to the streets in search of a stronger indexical backing for their fiction films, many even turning to documentary filmmaking, an emerging genre in Japan which would climax at the turn of the decade.

Hara and Kobayashi's initial output is entirely in tune with the independent street film style of that time. If most of *Goodbye CP* is set in Tokyo's Shinjuku station area, where the CP victim Hiroshi Yokota recites his poems, this follows the lead of someone like Oshima, who in the late 1960s also had his camera out in Shinjuku focusing on avant-garde theatre troupes and interventionist artists. Oshima's 1968 *Diary of a Shinjuku Thief* (*Shinjuku dorobo nikki*) stars the outrageous graphic designer Tadanori Yokoo in the role of a shoplifter in Sinjuku's famous Kinokuniya bookshop, in which, years later, Hara would meet the novelist Mitsuharu Inoue, the star of his 1994 film *A Dedicated Life.*

The immediate aesthetic result of this opening up for the contingent was a shift from a representational to a presentational regime, and from illusionistic voyeurism to self-reflexive exhibitionism, including the revelation of the cinematic apparatus within the scene. An example is *A Man Vanishes* (*Ningen Johatsu,* 1967), the first independent film directed by Hara's mentor, Shohei Imamura, after he left Nikkatsu, in which the walls of a stage are torn down to unmask fictional devices within a documentary film and expose the theatrical quality of real life. Building on such groundbreaking experiments, Hara and Kobayashi used the street film format to abolish any notions of a double-layered reality opposing inner and outer worlds, society and the individual, real life and acting. Thus, going public, for them, became equivalent to going extremely private. As Hara himself remarks: 'In the 1970s it became clear that we should question ourselves. . . . My films are not intended to debunk the state power, but to expose this power structure within ourselves' (Nagib, 2007).

This project is first put to practice in *Goodbye CP*, a film which pushes presentational, exhibitionist realism through to its ultimate consequences. In order to simultaneously expose disability to the world and demonstrate what the experience of the street is for the disabled, the camera not only *focuses* on cerebral palsy victims, but *becomes* one of them. An example is the opening scene, in which the poet Hiroshi Yokota, the most severely affected CP victim in the group in focus, rejects his wheelchair and crosses a wide avenue on all fours, struggling to control his movements and constantly losing his thick spectacles with his involuntary head jerks. The shaky, aleatory handheld camera meanwhile seems itself affected by CP, as it follows Yokota at ground level, experiencing together with him the rough touch of the tarmac surface and the frightening closeness of the wheels of cars and motorbikes driving past him. Yokota's roaming of the pavements of Tokyo culminates in the recital of his poem 'Legs' at Shinjuku station, during which the low camera, sharing the character's impaired sight and limited visual field, captures the legs around him like bars in a prison (Fig. 6.1). *Goodbye CP* has been described as a 'documentary focused on how CP victims were generally ignored or disregarded in Japan' (Doll, 2007, p. 4). Whether this is the case or not in Japan, the fact remains that not a word or image in the whole film suggests it. The camera's unprivileged positioning and restricted view, combined with the discontinuous editing, prevent the formation of any objective verdicts on a country or its society. Instead, the horror of exclusion is conveyed from the inside of disability, without the need of identifying a baleful 'other'.

Hara and Kobayashi's rejection of oppositional schemes encompasses the search for a 'spiritual' or 'metaphysical' reality beyond the 'apparent reality', which Raymond Williams defines as a common realist impulse (1978, p. 533). *Goodbye CP* is eminently physical, not only

FIGURE 6.1 *Goodbye CP*: Yokota recites his poem 'Legs', while the camera captures the legs around him like bars in a prison. (Copyright © by Shisso Production)

for its stress on the characters' sensory experiences, but also for its open address of sexual taboos, in this case, the sex lives of the physically disabled. The interviews conducted by the crew with the CP group unveil the excruciating difficulties they experience to fulfil their needs, including one account of rape. Here again Hara and Kobayashi are building on the example of their immediate Japanese predecessors, whose realist repertoire, more than in any other world new waves, resorted to sex as a privileged vehicle for the physical and therefore 'real' experience of the world. Homosexuality, paedophilia, incest, rape and sadomasochism were among the practices insistently focused on by Imamura, Hani, Oshima, Matsumoto and others. Their method excluded any moral judgments on their subjects while often requiring from casts their bodily engagement in sexual representations, as epitomized by *The Realm of the Senses* (*Ai no koriida,* Nagisa Oshima, 1976), entirely based on real sex among the cast, as we have seen in Chapter 5.

I once defined as 'corporeal realism' this tendency of fusing performance and real life, typical of the 1960s-70s in Japan, which often relied on modern, self-reflexive cinematic devices to give expression to Japanese traditions of the cult of the body and the physical environment (Nagib, 2006). Hara and Kobayashi's second film, *Extreme Private Eros: Love Song 1974*, released two years ahead of Oshima's erotic masterpiece, is a perfect example of this trend. Carrying the date it was

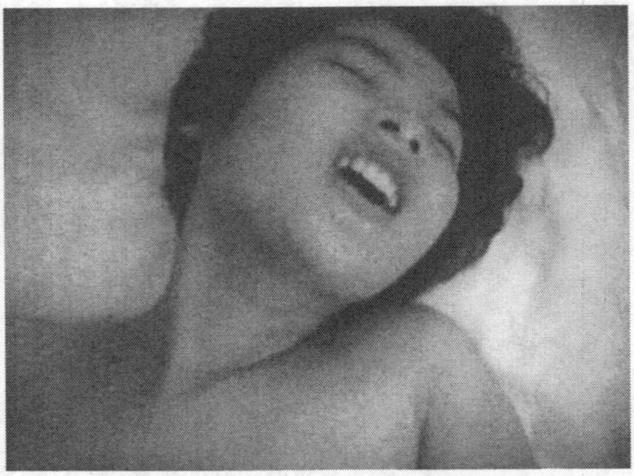

FIGURE 6.2 Lovemaking with the camera: Miyuki Takeda in *Extreme Private Eros: Love Song 1974*. (Copyright © by Shisso Production)

made in its own title, the film reflects even more explicitly than *Goodbye CP* the libertarian atmosphere of the period as it documents the sex life of Hara's previous wife, Miyuki Takeda, together with that of Hara and Kobayashi themselves, as both feature in the film. Once again the camera is a character in its own right, with its needs, desires, frustrations and pains. At one point, it even becomes apparent to the spectator, through a shaky, blurry sequence of images, that Hara is shooting his own lovemaking with his former wife (Fig. 6.2).

Takeda, in her turn, is the period's typical heroine, with her intuitive feminism, pan-sexual drive and rejection of family ties, all of which culminate in an extreme act of independence, when she gives birth, entirely by herself, in front of Hara's turning camera, to the child of a black American soldier. As well as exposing her own intimacy, wonderfully represented by the birth of her child, Takeda's sexual curiosity leads the camera on an exploration journey to the underworld of prostitution in Okinawa, including the revelation of a large contingent of black-Japanese children.

Both *Goodbye CP* and *Extreme Private Eros* resort to typical low-budget techniques, such as 16mm handheld camera, black-and-white stock, discontinuous editing, asynchronous sound and an interview-based narrative structure redolent of cinéma vérité. This Hara attributes to second-hand knowledge mediated by the Japanese TV documentaries being produced at that time, including those by Tsuchimoto, Imamura, Oshima and Ogawa, who were themselves influenced by vérité and the

French Nouvelle Vague (Nagib, 2007). New as a genre, within a television system which was just completing a decade of existence, these documentaries became a privileged ground for political and artistic experiments at the turn of the 1960s to the 1970s. Despite the generation gap, Hara played a role in this movement, among others, as an assistant director to Imamura in some of his TV documentaries.

It was Imamura who, in the late 1970s, first envisaged a TV documentary on the protagonist of *The Emperor's Naked Army Marches On,* Kenzo Okuzaki, a former WWII soldier who had served more than 13 years in prison, three of them in solitary confinement, for having murdered an estate agent and shot steel *pachinko* balls with a sling at the Emperor. Imamura's project was finally scrapped by the television company because of its direct address of the taboo subject of the Emperor's responsibility for the war. Hara and Kobayashi then took it in hand and shot the film independently, with money borrowed from friends and Okuzaki himself. Even though here the camera is more stable and the editing more sutured than in the duo's previous vérité films, revelatory realism is again stretched to its limits through the film's unrestricted involvement in Okuzaki's obsession. His (and therefore the film's) mission is to extract from some of his former comrades the truth about the killing of two lower-rank Japanese soldiers in New Guinea, when the war had already ended. After repeated interviews with the veterans, in which Okuzaki often resorts to violence in front of a rolling camera, one by one they finally confess to the crime of cannibalism.

Jeffrey and Kenneth Ruoff (2007, p. 9) describe *The Emperor's Naked Army Marches On* as 'one of the most scathing and engaging indictments of Japan's Fifteen-Year War and of Emperor Hirohito's role in it'. If this is undoubtedly Okuzaki's message repeatedly hammered throughout the film, the film's own point of view is anything but an indictment of Japan. Instead, it is in Okuzaki's volatile behaviour, fuelled by dubious principles of selfless honour, that one is more likely to identify the nefarious elements of the war ideology.

Finally, *A Dedicated Life,* launched 22 years after *Goodbye CP,* in 1994, is a far cry from the artisanal vérité style adopted in the early Hara-Kobayashi films, with its sophisticated mixture of colour and black-and-white stock, including a plethora of materials, such as interviews, lectures, archival documents and even fictional inserts. Nevertheless, the radical revelatory drive of the early films is still very much at work here too. The film is a relentless investigation into the very nature of artistic fiction through a scrutiny of novelist Mitsuharu Inoue's life, including a physical search into the writer's own body, as he goes through liver surgery and finally dies. It is then revealed that most of Inoue's autobiographical data was sheer fabrication and his entire life nothing but acting.

Phenomenological Time

Hara and Kobayashi's films seem to feed on the utopian search for the coincidence between life-span and creative time. With a film career dating back to 1972, they have brought out no more than five features in 36 years of collaborative work to date.[3] All but one – *The Many Faces of Chika* (*Mata no hi no Chika,* 2004), a fiction film entirely conceived and written by Kobayashi and only directed by Hara – are character-based documentaries. Each of them has taken several years to be completed for reasons unrelated to budgetary constraints, which have always been there of course, but derived from an uncompromising option for freedom of creation and unlimited shooting time. Time and freedom are the binomial which has regulated the duo's independent filmmaking so far and proved crucial to their intended aesthetic results. As Hara explains with relation to *The Emperor's Naked Army Marches On*:

> It was really a film that could only be made independently. I had no money, but I had time and freedom. Time and freedom were weapons to make a film about a taboo subject. The reason that lots of people came to see my film was that I used the power of time and freedom. (Ruoff, 1993, p. 107)

In keeping with this method, the shooting of *Goodbye CP* and *Extreme Private Eros* stretched, in each case, over a period of three years. *The Emperor's Naked Army Marches On* took longer, from 1982 to 1987, while the making of *A Dedicated Life,* planned to last for a decade, was shortened to five years by the death of its protagonist.

In all cases, maximum adherence to a real life span was a condition for the films' existence, that is to say shooting would continue for years if necessary, until a decisive event – wished for, but unpredictable – would take place which would become the film's raison d'être and draw the shooting to a close. This is the means through which one or more climaxes, as well as a coherent narrative structure, were secured in each of these films. Let us have a closer look at how these moments come to existence and how they function within the films.

In her remarkable book, *The Emergence of Cinematic Time,* Mary Ann Doane develops a concept of 'event', with relation to early cinema, which combines constructiveness with contingency. She explains:

> Insofar as the cinema presented itself as the indexical record of time, it allied itself with the event and the unfolding of events as aleatory, stochastic, contingent. It was capable of trapping events in all their unpredictability and pure factualness. However, the fact of its own finitude – the limits imposed by both the frame and the length of the reel – resulted in the necessity of conceiving the event simultaneously in terms of structure, as a unit of time, as not simply a happening, but a significant happening that nevertheless remained tinged by the contingent, by the unassimilable. (Doane, 2002, pp. 140–1)

Hara and Kobayashi's filmmaking seems to stand out precisely for the way it hinges on this 'significant happening', which is at the same time unpredictable and structural to the films. But how are they achieved? Raymond Williams, in his famous 'Lecture on Realism', refers to 'realist intentions' which are mediated through a specific ideology (Williams, 1977, p. 64). This is applicable to Hara and Kobayashi insofar as there is a clearly identifiable 'intention' – though not obviously mediated by ideology – which structures the unpredictable event in their films. This intention is actively exercised in the manner of a provocation, aimed at causing physical and psychological stress to its subjects, so that they are led or even constrained to open up and reveal their innermost motivations. The moment and content of this revelation, however, cannot be predicted, and so waiting is a condition for it to happen.

Take the case of *Goodbye CP.* The radically physical, exhibitionist shooting method utilized here results in mounting tension among the CP group, leading to some of them wanting to quit the film. This finally comes to a head when Yokota's wife, another CP victim, reacts furiously against what she considers the portrayal of her husband as a freak and orders an immediate halt to the shooting or she will divorce him. Rather than stopping, the camera keeps on rolling as the defining moment has not taken place as yet. At long last, however, the climactic and most exhibitionist scene of all is produced, in which Yokota naked, in the middle of a Tokyo flyover, struggles to stay upright on his knees. After several minutes of his mute staring at the camera, we hear on the asynchronous soundtrack his impromptu speech, which reveals the shattering effect the film has had on him:

> *We set out to make this film to show that we can't do anything. But I was hoping I could do something to make a different kind of film. That was what I thought. But while we went through the process of making the film, my hopes were completely shattered. How can I say,*

> *after all on many levels I require some form of protection. That's the only way I can survive. I could never be on my own. That realization made me feel totally empty. To be honest, I'm not sure how I can move on. That's how I feel.*[4]

Yokota's naked, wobbling, mute figure, about to be run over by passing cars as he stares at the camera, has the effect of a Barthesian *punctum,* with its inexplicable power of reality which pierces, hurts and mortifies the viewer, regardless of the latter's will (Barthes, 1982, pp. 26.7); or of a Lacanian *objet petit a,* whose opaque formula indicates an irreducible remnant of the Real (Lacan, 2004). But his final speech is a genuine event for its structuring intentionality combined with its unpredictable revelatory contingency (Fig. 6.3).

The same applies to the other three documentaries. *Extreme Private Eros*'s several parts are demarcated by intertitles of dates – 1972, 1973, 1974 – which indicate several periods of waiting for events to take place. One of them is Takeda's pregnancy, and in fact one of the reasons for the film's existence was that she had expressed to Hara her wish to give birth in front of a rolling camera. The film must therefore wait for her to become pregnant, which finally happens when she has a three-week affair with a black American soldier, Paul, stationed in Okinawa. Then another nine months must elapse until Takeda is ready to deliver. Although all this was intended and predictable, its outcome, her baby which pops out in a pool of blood right toward the camera,

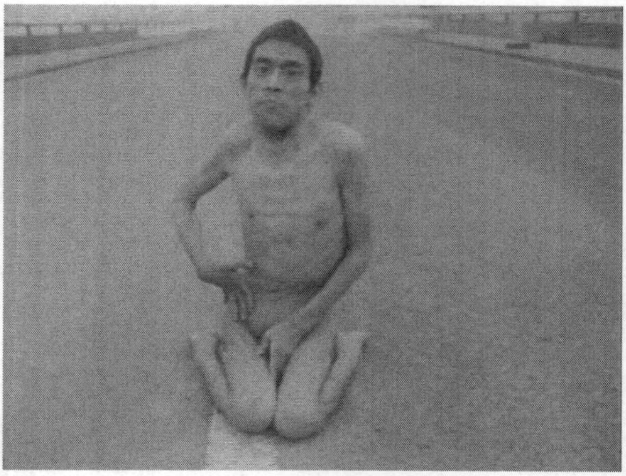

FIGURE 6.3 Yokota's naked, wobbling, mute figure, about to be run over by passing cars as he stares at the camera in *Goodbye CP.* (Copyright © by Shisso Production)

on the floor of Hara's tiny Tokyo apartment, without any help from third parties, has the *einmalig* quality of Benjamin's auratic events (Benjamin, 2007, pp. 211–44). It compares in all aspects to the uniqueness of death which, together with real sex, Bazin had deemed unrepresentable on screen (Bazin, 2003, pp. 27–31).

On the subject of representations of birth and death on screen, Sobchack states that

> although birth and death are each processes and representations of liminal moments of bodily transformation and both threaten the stability of cultural codes and conventions with their radical originality, in our present culture death is the more subversive transformation of the two. (2004, p. 233)

And indeed the representability of death is the sole limit Hara and Kobayashi have encountered and not surpassed in their two following films, not for lack of subversive will, of course, but because this would amount to concurring on the production of the liminal event.

In *The Emperor's Naked Army*, Okuzaki, who had already spent time in prison for murder, is clearly moved by an uncontrollable desire to kill again. This is certainly not the aim of the film, but it is one of its possible outcomes, as Okuzaki's increasingly violent behaviour suggests. He has an obsession with the figure of Koshimizu, the man who had ordered the execution of two lower-rank soldiers, from Okuzaki's own unit, both of whom were accused of desertion. Okuzaki did not participate in the firing, as he had been captured in the final months of the Pacific war in New Guinea, but he visits one by one his surviving comrades in different parts of Japan to interrogate them on the real reason for the killings, given that at that point the war had already ended. The process of finding out the current addresses of the veterans, visiting them, comparing answers, visiting them again, takes several years. However, all of them finally confess to the fact that, under the appalling conditions they were in, cannibalism had become the last available resort. As *kurobuta* ('black pork'), a euphemism for the natives, had become hard to catch, they had to turn to *shirobuta* ('white pork'), that is their own mates. This is the startling, structural revelation of the film, but not yet its end. Koshimizu is visited twice by Okuzaki in the film, but at a certain point it is revealed, through captions, that Okuzaki has attempted to kill him, only managing to seriously injure his son. Okuzaki is again imprisoned and here the film ends, after reporting the death of his wife shortly thereafter.

It is not a secret that Okuzaki had invited Hara to shoot his killing of Koshimizu (Ruoff, 1993, pp. 109–10; Nagib, 2007). According to

Hara, the murder attempt happened while he was taking advice from Imamura and a lawyer on how to deal with Okuzaki's frightening offer to kill in front of a rolling camera (Nagib, 2007), but it is also true that the camera never stopped rolling when Okuzaki physically assaulted the war veterans during his interrogations, sending one of them, who was recovering from an operation, back to hospital. The film thus leaves no doubt that all confessions (whose details were unknown to all, including Okuzaki) were obtained under duress, that is, prolonged, intentional action, with unforeseeable consequences.

I will approach the ethical aspect of this method in the last section of this chapter, but let us first note the second case verging on the limits of representability, *A Dedicated Life,* which follows the daily life of the novelist Mitsuharu Inoue in his last years until his death from cancer. Inoue never bowed to Hara's coercive methods (Ruoff, 1993, p. 104), but welcomed the film crew during several years of his life and even allowed them to film the removal of most of his liver, though not his actual death. Almost by way of revenge, the shooting continues after he has passed away so as to uncover the sheer fabrication of his autobiography.

Conducive to the revelation of the unpredictable contingent as it may be, intention also entails manipulation, and Hara and Kobayashi have profited fully from 'the limits imposed by both the frame and the length of the reel', in Doane's words, to produce intended readings of their films, as in the case of *A Dedicated Life.* In contrast to their almost religious allegiance to phenomenological time as far as the creative process is concerned, the resulting product is nothing but montage and action cinema. The opening of *Extreme Private Eros* is an interesting and deliberate example of this manipulation, as it shows still photographs of Hara's former wife, Miyuki Takeda, and their little son, edited in the manner of a slideshow. Here, the film sends us back to the very origins of cinema (still photographs put side by side and set into motion) by accelerating the speed of the stills of the child, to give the impression that he is actually walking. More significantly, the discontinuous editing is constantly reminding the viewer that the intertitles and captions indicative of time progression, in both *Extreme Private Eros* and *The Emperor's Naked Army,* are no guarantee of a linear chronology.

Rather than on common people and their uneventful lives, as usually seen in realist films, Hara and Kobayashi focus on extraordinary characters engaged in transformative action, which defines the exclusion of non-action scenes in a film's final cut. If the filmmakers occasionally make use of the sequence shot, such as for the childbirth in *Extreme Private Eros* or Yokota's crossing of a Tokyo avenue on all fours, in *Goodbye CP,* this is due to the exceptional character of the events in focus, which take on a life of their own after being intentionally provoked. Hara and Kobayashi are foreign to what Cesare Zavattini once defined as the neorealists' drive to 'remain' in a scene which 'can contain so many echoes and reverberations, can even contain all the situations we may need' (Zavattini, 1966, p. 219). Zavattini's view was famously hailed by Bazin as the ultimate realist achievement in *Umberto D* (scripted by Zavattini and directed by Vittorio De Sica in 1952), exemplified by the scene of the maid grinding coffee, in which 'nothing happens' (Bazin, 1972, pp. 79–82). The revelatory power of empty moments as this became the distinctive trait of such epitomes of modern cinema as Antonioni (MacCann, 1966, p. 216) and the principle behind the work of a documentarian such as Frederick Wiseman, who seems entirely averse to the cut. However, dead time, or the patient waiting for epiphanic revelations that do not depend on the filmmakers' will and intention, does not feature in Hara and Kobayashi's films. Unlike Wiseman, Antonioni or Rossellini, Hara and Kobayashi are not interested in spontaneous happenings, because their aim is to produce reality.

Active Subjects

Hara and Kobayashi's working system is basically collaborative, starting with the way both of them interact. This is how Kobayashi replied, when I asked her about her interest in directing films:

> From the very beginning I was interested in directing but at the same time I love collaborating as a team. And when it comes to shooting the film, Hara has the tendency of stepping forward and I have the tendency of stepping backward. Hara can be a strong presence and a strong signature in a film, which probably I am not. But when we decide to shoot a film, we discuss, I get involved in the scriptwriting and all other aspects of the film. I'm not interested in actually directing, but I am involved in the whole process of making the film. (Nagib, 2007)

This collaborative system was very much in vogue when they started as filmmakers. Nornes, in his book on the collective Ogawa Pro (2007), gives a full account of the revolutionary output resulting from such collaborative method as seen in the famous Sanrizuka Series, which between 1968 and the mid-1970s documented as well as stirred mass demonstrations against the construction of Tokyo's Narita Airport. Hara was close to Ogawa's collective and even considered entering it at a certain point (Nornes, 2007, p. 132; 2003, p. 153).

Hara and Kobayashi's documentaries have drawn on this collective mode of production also with relation to the cast involved. All four of them have been in a way 'co-authored' by their stars, who are not only interesting personalities, but also either accomplished or amateur artists: Yokota is a poet; Takeda is an aspiring visual artist, actress and dancer; Inoue is a famous novelist; and Okuzaki, though not by profession, is perhaps the best actor of all. What really matters here is that all of them suggested and agreed to perform the most daring acts of their lives before the camera.

This shared authorship between crew and cast, however, eschews any idea of a harmonious conviviality, resembling much rather a battle of egos on a filming arena. *Goodbye CP* was partly conceived and financed by The Green Lawn Association, formed by the CP group, who therefore felt entitled to decide about the directions the film should take. This is one of the reasons for the conflicts among the cast and between these and the crew described above, but another evidence of their authorial competitiveness is the fact that most members of the CP group, in the film, are carrying photo cameras which they point at passers-by as well as at the crew members themselves, thus constantly swapping places between subjects and objects in the film.

As for *The Emperor's Naked Army Marches On,* the main problem faced during the shoot, according to Hara (Nagib, 2007), was Okuzaki's insistence on directing the film himself, which he had co-financed, arriving at a point where he threatened to destroy all footage shot thus far. *A Dedicated Life,* in its turn, can be seen as two overlapping films, one relating to Inoue's biography as he sees it, and another, corresponding to Hara and Kobayashi's contrasting view of it.

But it is in *Extreme Private Eros: Love Song 1974* where the battle of authorial egos becomes most apparent. As his voiceover commentary reveals, Hara decides to make the film because he cannot come to terms with the fact that Takeda has left him and moved with their son to Okinawa. The film then develops in four stages, over three years: two trips by Hara to Okinawa; a third trip, in which he is accompanied by his current companion, Kobayashi; and a fourth phase when Takeda returns to Tokyo to give birth to her child. In his first visit, Hara finds Takeda living with a female lover, Sugako. They are fighting, and he films the fights. After a few days in these circumstances, Hara concludes, in voiceover commentary, that it is his presence in their apartment that is causing them to fight. The conflict, which is real, is however not only provoked by the director, but also performed by Takeda as a public display of her love for Sugako, which is certain to hurt Hara.

Takeda is no naïve character. She had artistic ambitions of her own. The stills edited at the beginning of the film show her next to some of her paintings, and she was also active as a photographer and film actress (Nornes, 2003, pp. 145–6). In *Extreme Private Eros* she is living for the film, making a film out of her own life and obviously delighting in it. This is however not readily accepted by the filmmakers. If she defies Hara by getting together with Sugako and then Paul, the American soldier, to the point of bringing Hara to tears in his sole appearance before the camera, he makes sure to bring his current companion, Kobayashi, to Okinawa to help him out with the film and drive Takeda mad with jealousy. And if Takeda delivers a baby by someone else in front of his camera, Kobayashi does the same, shortly after, and this time to a child by Hara himself (Fig. 6.4).

Hara refers to this film as 'self-documentary', and he is known in Japan as the pioneer of the 'private film' (Nornes, 2007, p. 131), a first-person documentary genre which has its followers in the country up to this day. Commenting on the mid-1990s development of first-person documentaries or 'I-Movies' in the US, Patricia Aufderheide observes that 'the first-person saga has become a feature of venues once identified as feisty bastions of left-wing perspectives' (Aufderheide, 1997).

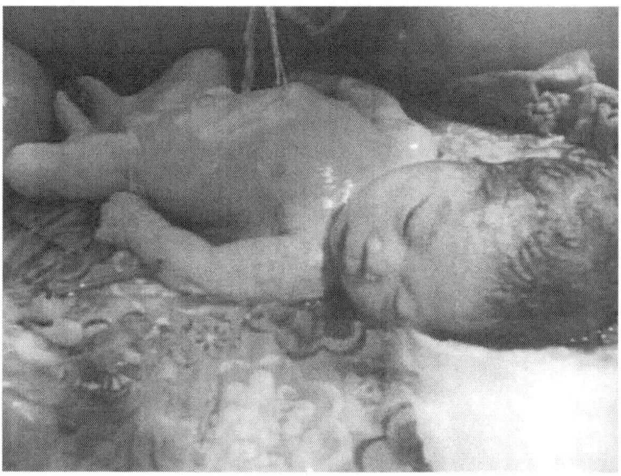

FIGURE 6.4 Birth equals death in its originality: *Extreme Private Eros: Love Song 1974.* (Copyright © by Shisso Production)

Indeed the end of the socialist era in the early 1990s caused documentary filmmaking, to a considerable extent, to retreat from the public to the private sphere, making room for the identification between the personal and the political (Aufderheide, 1997). *Extreme Private Eros* precedes this trend by nearly two decades, also as concerns typical I-Movie journeys of discovery of one's own identity, as noted by Renov (2005, p. 243), who describes the genre as the 'stage for claims from ethnic, gay, lesbian and disabled minorities'. The fact is that the fight for individual expression has a particular meaning in Japan, a homogenous society marked by long military traditions. In the cinema, it had started in the early years of the Japanese New Wave and was entirely politically motivated.

As early as 1960, Oshima had proclaimed that 'new films must, first and foremost, express the filmmaker's active involvement as an individual' (Oshima, 1992, p. 47). The word used by Oshima to signify this is *shutaiteki,* a term very much in vogue at the time which means an 'active subjectivity'. An individual endowed with an 'active subjectivity' is one in direct opposition to a uniformized society, who rejects victimization and takes full responsibility for the social consequences of his/her acts. An 'active subjectivity' is actually a merging of subject and object, an individual's intimacy turned into the stage for social happenings, on which the boundaries between public and private spheres cease to exist.

Thus what may sound like a purely narcissistic exercise in Hara and Kobayashi's films would perhaps be more accurately described as the crumbling of the usual filming hierarchy (the subject above the object, the director above the crew and the cast) through the productive clashing of active subjectivities behind and before the camera. It is a process of general empowerment and emancipation which frontally opposes the 'romance of victimization', which according to Aufderheide, quoting Baxter, derives from first-person narratives in American storytelling, not just on television, but in literature and politics (Aufderheide, 1997). Impossible to say who are victims and villains in the Hara and Kobayashi films, which also means that the filmmakers are exposed to the same stresses and risks as their characters.

In *Goodbye CP,* the crew is stopped by the police in the streets, their camera seized while still shooting, as one can tell by its aleatory focus on an empty sky for a few moments. In *Extreme Private Eros,* Hara is beaten up by thugs who are not happy with the feminist pamphlets Takeda is distributing in the streets of Goza, Okinawa, which also brings the shooting to an abrupt halt. Finally, in *The Emperor's Naked Army,* the crew is not only facing threats from the police and from extreme-right activists for filming a man who publicly announces his hatred for the Emperor, but is also at risk from working with Okuzaki himself, a murderer who intends to carry on killing.

The multiple authorships and exhibitionist methods applied to both casts and crews thus make it difficult if not impossible to identify an ethics of the documentary gaze, as classified by Vivian Sobchack (2004, pp. 226.57 [1984, pp. 283–300]), Bill Nichols (1991, pp. 84–5) and commented on by Linda Williams (1999, pp. 176.89), as this would presuppose a single subject positioning represented by the camera. The exposing scenes in the films are all shot in full accordance with, often on the suggestion of, their adult actors, even the most radical ones, such as the childbirth in *Extreme Private Eros* and Yokota's naked pose on the road in *Goodbye CP.* It could be argued, of course, that if Okuzaki has agreed to and is steering the ways he is being filmed in *The Emperor's Naked Army*, the camera is not, for this reason, entitled to observe passively as he goes about making justice with his own hands. Even here, however, it must be said that in all cases where violence took place in front of the camera, help was immediately asked for from the police, by the crew and often by Okuzaki himself, in his theatrical stunts of bravery.

I will conclude by suggesting that Hara and Kobayashi's films are thoroughly and consistently ethical for their commitment to the truth of the unpredictable event, in Badiou's sense. This they exercise through what Rancière termed 'the inherent honesty of the film medium' (2006, p. 2), that is to say, the film's indexical property, all the while retaining their drive to politically interfere in the production of the real, regardless of the risks for cast and crew this may entail. Their films thus make room for both the contingent and intention, the combination of which accounts for their ethical realism.

Chapter 7

THE SELF-PERFORMING AUTEUR: ETHICS IN JOÃO CÉSAR MONTEIRO

. . . he was incessantly looking for a diamond in the mud. He held it in his fingers, at each film. He dropped it and looked for it again, desperately, in his next film.
Manuela de Freitas, actress in João César Monteiro's films for 30 years

It seems appropriate to conclude this book by focusing on the Portuguese director João César Monteiro, in particular on his so-called autobiographical films, for a number of reasons. Monteiro is widely recognized as Portugal's greatest film director alongside Manoel de Oliveira. His oeuvre of more than 20 feature-length films has been the subject of detailed studies worldwide, not least in Portugal, but most notably France. Within his oeuvre, it is his autobiographical phase which has drawn international attention, including the João de Deus (or John of God) trilogy – *Recollections of the Yellow House* (*Recordações da casa amarela,* 1989), *God's Comedy* (*A comédia de Deus,* 1995) and *The Spousals of God* (*As bodas de Deus,* 1998) – as well as another two self-starred films, *The Hips of J.W.* (*Le Bassin de J.W.,* 1997) and Monteiro's last opus before his untimely death in 2003, *Come and Go* (*Vai e vem,* 2003). It is generally accepted that this phase peaks with *God's Comedy,* which scholars such as Paulo Filipe Monteiro do not hesitate to qualify as 'one of the best Portuguese films ever made' (P.F. Monteiro, 2007, p. 203). My interest in this phase of Monteiro's work (and probably the latent reason behind his international acclaim) relates to the exemplary way it summarizes the issues on ethics and realism at stake in this book.

As far as the title of Part IV, 'The Production of Reality', is concerned, he comes closest, among the works and auteurs analysed throughout the book, to Hara and Kobayashi's mode of expositional and exhibitionist first-person documentaries examined in the previous chapter, despite the outspokenly fictional character of all his films. Like the

Japanese duo, Monteiro not only enacts but provokes the film events as much as possible in the phenomenological world. The heightened degree of risk-taking physicality required for this, in its turn, is in many ways comparable to that contained in Herzog's cinema, as analysed in Chapter 2. Also like Herzog, Monteiro, as a self-performing auteur, incarnates a kind of almighty, god-like creator, who is even named as such: João de Deus (or John of God) is the protagonist's name, or rather the director's 'heteronym', as he likes to call it, in four of his films. Not to be overlooked, of course, is the self-parody deriving from this procedure, in stark contrast with Herzog's cinematic self-inscription, entirely impermeable to irony and humour, as we have seen.

Physicality and production of the real forcibly centres, in Monteiro, on eroticism, which brings him close to Oshima, whose exhibitionist and intentionally contagious eroticism was studied in detail in Chapter 5. As in the films of his Japanese counterpart, Monteiro's Eros is a voracious borrower of Bataille's sexual imagery, including a whole plethora of milk baths, eyes, eggs, testicles' and anus's avatars of all sorts, as well as the worshipping of non-genital sex and prodigality extolled in Bataille's expenditure theory. João de Deus, a male Sada Abe, delights in throwing away piles of money for the exclusive sake of pleasure, to the point of being reduced to indigence over and over again in each film. In common with Oshima, Monteiro cultivates erotic pleasures as resistance to political oppression, Portuguese Salazarism, alongside all forms of fascism, being a favourite target in his work. And if for Oshima oppressive Christian traditions have never been an issue, Monteiro fervently embraces Bataille's anticlerical furore, via Portugal's long undercurrent of anticlerical traditions and typical pornographic humour.

Attached like few filmmakers to Bazinian phenomenological realism by means of the sequence shot and the long take, combined with location shooting, natural lighting, diegetic sound and non-professional acting, Monteiro is no less a fierce (though hardly Brechtian) adept of the realism of the medium, as analysed in Chapters 3 and 4. Self-reflexivity, national allegories, cinematic intertextuality and intermedial citations are an all-pervading presence that comes to a head in his most theatrical film, *The Hips of J.W.* A common denominator across the assessments of Monteiro's films is indeed his encyclopaedic knowledge of all other arts, in particular music and literature, but also of world cinema, all of which are interwoven in an inventive citation network of flamboyant imagery, language and sound, flavoured with brilliant irony and humour. Equally knowledgeable critics delight in decoding the diverse sources of his aesthetic devices, resulting in profoundly erudite as much as insightful readings, such as Bovier's (2007), which will inform some of the analysis below. It seems relevant to note that intermedial relations and intertextuality are a common denominator among filmmakers (several of them addressed in this book) subscribing to the reality of the medium, such as Glauber Rocha, Alexander Kluge, Pier-Paolo Pasolini, Luis Buñuel, Jean-Luc Godard, Jean-Marie Straub and Danielle Huillet, many of whom are explicitly or implicitly interwoven within Monteiro's filmography.

The reason why I propose all these procedures be reexamined here in relation to one another is that they derive, I contend, from an ethics. Hence, in the following sections, I will examine the term 'ethics' as regards Monteiro's use of the autobiographical genre, auteur prerogatives and both phenomenological and medium realisms, so as to test its applicability within and beyond the realm of representation.

Ethics of the Impossible Real

I am certainly not the first to refer to 'ethics' with relation to Monteiro's method of filmmaking; on the contrary, this is a recurrent term in critical assessments of his work as well as in his cast and crew's testimonials. Why this should be the case, however, is less than obvious, in particular if ethics is understood in the sensu lato of an 'ethics of representation', that is, one conforming to the limits of human rights and equality. In Monteiro's films considered autobiographical, the protagonist, played by the director himself with exhibitionist realism, is invariably a thoroughly and purposely unethical character. On the level of the fable, not only does this character excel in betraying and cheating all around him, in particular the frail and defenceless, but he is also an incorrigible womanizer with a pronounced paedophile taste. *Recollections of the Yellow House* is an exemplary work of Monteiro's incarnation of a tramp living off odd jobs in a Lisbon boarding house, all of them unscrupulous. He extorts the last coins of his house-cleaner mother, does blackmail jobs based on fraudulent photographs and, in the film's central scene, steals from a prostitute, who has just died, all the savings she had hidden inside a rag doll to pay for her daughter's upbringing. In *Come and Go* the protagonist played by Monteiro, João Vuvu, actually kills his own son in a simulated accident.

True enough, the character's malignity is enacted through recourse to genre rules according to which criminals or monsters – such as

Nosferatu, one of Monteiro's obsessive referents – carry out their despicable acts with exquisitely refined, aristocratic manners. This generic code could also explain why an impressive retinue of beauties fall for the beast, in Monteiro's case a skeletal, balding middle-aged man, further adorned with a huge nose and big bulging eyes. The differential here is of course realism, that is, the fact that the acts in the fable are invariably performed outside the studio walls, most often in the streets, shops and houses of Lisbon, including carefully chosen real-life nymphets, whose unmade-up beauty is captured, à la Dreyer, in lengthy, epiphanic close-ups. In any case, whatever sympathy viewers may develop towards this character is regularly (and purposely) frustrated by the intervention of Monteiro's typical scatology, which includes, for example, an infamous delectation in amassing, classifying and even swallowing strands of female pubic hair (all of which are also, allegedly, real). Most notably, in *God's Comedy*, the character of João de Deus keeps a collection of female pubic hair samples, duly packed in small plastic sachets glued to the pages of an album called 'Book of Thoughts', in which each sample is identified, dated and accompanied by poetic captions. From a fellow collector in England, he receives a precious addition to his trove, left behind by Queen Victoria, which he duly salutes with a 'God shave the Queen!'

As far as ethics is concerned, let us first consider the issue of paedophilia by resorting to an example which could only approximately be defined as representational, given its degree of presentational authenticity. *God's Comedy* climaxes with the remarkable episode of João de Deus, the manager of Paraíso do Gelado ('Ice-cream Paradise' parlour), seducing one of his customers, Joaninha, the 14-year-old daughter of a butcher in João's neighbourhood, played by then 17-year-old Cláudia Teixeira. João invites her to his apartment where she opposes no resistance to the curious erotic ritual prepared for her. It includes her stripping off and changing into a kimono, then entering a milk bath while João takes care of sponging her private parts until he himself falls into the bathtub, making her jump and squeeze a few drops of urine (Fig. 7.1). She subsequently devours the ice-cream especially made by him for the occasion, served in a shell-shaped dish reminiscent of a vagina. João takes care of wiping up the cream drops that run down her chin and chest, uncovering, in the process, one of her developing breasts on which he places a delicate kiss. He then suggests an 'ancient' Portuguese remedy for her indigestion, consisting of a cornucopia filled with raw eggs which she breaks by sitting on them with her naked buttocks, before he dives his own head into the mess. After she

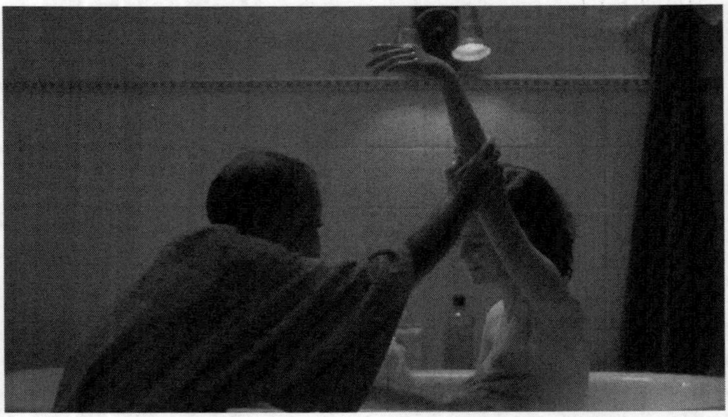

FIGURE 7.1 *God's Comedy*: the milk bath as part of João's erotic ritual

is gone, he filters the bath milk with a twofold purpose: to reuse the milk in ice-cream and to collect Joaninha's pubic hair, which he duly swallows. The extraordinary aesthetic effect of this long episode is inseparable from the ethical issue at its core, so I propose to start by examining the latter, first from a factual then from a philosophical point of view.

From a mere perceptual perspective, it would be perhaps legitimate to ask whether any film director would have the right to exercise his sexual fantasies on an adolescent who to that end has to expose her naked pubescence to a rolling camera. The right of reply should be given in the first place, of course, to Cláudia Teixeira herself. And what she has to tell us, in a testimonial collected nine years after the film's release, is a story of full personal involvement with the director for the sake of the film. When queried whether this could have caused a certain 'confusion' between life and fiction, she retorts that:

> There was no confusion. A fusion, yes. I can see it now. I think it is impossible to separate things. It is hard to say what actually happened: whether there was a transfer from life to film or from film to life. Isn't a work of art basically what a person is going through in life, a kind of inner journey from which the work results? (Teixeira, 2004, p. 146)

The candidness of this statement is only second to the innocence she attributes to the director himself. In her account, their relation started with him spotting her at a café, then having her, together with her mother, for dinner at home with his then wife (the actor and director

Margarida Gil), on which occasion the film project was discussed in detail. Her dithering on her acting abilities finally resolved itself with her 'throwing herself into his arms', saying: 'If you are confident, I will be confident' (p. 146). Throughout the film pre-production and shooting, Teixeira insists, Monteiro acted with 'a lot of propriety, a propriety that has been mostly lost these days' (p. 152). And if his method is 'potentially dangerous for him and those around him', this is because 'his purpose is the search for truth' (p. 150).

No doubt, such a respectful appraisal could be attributed to the actor's naivety – even nine years on, she was still only 24 – as much as to a need for self-protection. However, the same tone is adopted by many other collaborators, such as Manuela de Freitas, whose acting work alongside Monteiro for over three decades gives full credibility to her statement that Monteiro 'was of an extreme gentleness. He was very prudish, timid even' (2004, p. 142). Margarida Gil, his wife for 25 years and close collaborator in many films, equally highlights Monteiro's 'dignity', his attachment to 'order' and 'legitimacy', his 'ethical way of behaving' and his sense of 'discipline' (Gil, 2004, p. 97). But it is the filmmaker Manoel de Oliveira, now over 100 years of age, who comes closest to defining what the Monteirian ethics might be.

In a short article published in the homage book *João César Monteiro* (Nicolau, 2005), called 'César Monteiro: A Deontologically Exemplary Filmmaker', Oliveira states that his colleague abided by a peculiar 'cinematic deontology'. 'Deon' being the Greek word for 'duty', 'deontology' refers to a duty or rule-based ethics, according to which right action is predetermined by a moral command (as in Kantian ethics), as opposed to a consequentialist or teleological ethics, which defines right action according to its ends. Why Oliveira should choose 'deontology' to describe Monteiro's ethics is an interesting subject, as such an assessment would seem more appropriate to his own approach to cinema, as Johnson accurately observes:

> Oliveira's deontological posture derives, I would suggest, both from his reflections on the modern world, shaped in part by a combination of his religious formation and a perhaps more Kantian notion of ethics, and from intense reflection on the place and nature of film in its broader social and aesthetic context. (Johnson, 2008, p. 91)

Oliveira's and Monteiro's oeuvres run parallel to (and in competition with) each other in many ways, and there was a point where Oliveira invited Monteiro to star his *The Divine Comedy* (*A divina comédia*, 1991), but, by an intriguing coincidence, Monteiro had already entered pre-production for his own *God's Comedy* (Gil, 2004, p. 105). Each director was approaching Dante's cosmogony in contrasting, if not opposing, ways: the former, going back to the letter of the epic poem by positing a group of characters in a mental asylum who recite Dante's work; the latter, posing himself as the parody of a nonexistent god and rejecting Dante's Christian tripartite *Weltanschauung* altogether – Monteiro will return to the Christian cosmogony from an even more heretic perspective via Strindberg's autobiographical novel *Inferno,* the underlying text in *The Hips of J.W.* In any case, the reason why Oliveira had thought of him for a character in his asylum is to do with the fact that he considered Monteiro, in real life, a 'controlled schizophrenic', and here one is reminded that Monteiro had effectively been, in his youth, locked up for a brief period in a psychiatric institution, a fact fictionally reworked in *Recollections of the Yellow House.* Oliveira resorts to this schizoid personality split to explain Monteiro's cinema as a 'transcendental equivalence of his madness, which oscillates between the real and the metaphysical', hence as an ethical ('deontological') search for a lost, primeval unity, not least with the female, towards whom, according to Oliveira, he behaves at the same time as a predator and a submissive subject (Oliveira, 2005, p. 581).

In order to fully understand this split ethical subject, it is necessary to note that there is no explicit sex in any Monteiro films. How a self-reflexive split subject determines this fact I will explain shortly, but first let us establish that the absence of real sex is certainly not due to any prudery on the director's part – although it curiously chimes with Bazin's prohibition on filming the unique events of sex and death, so fiercely rejected by Oshima, as discussed in Chapter 5. This is because Monteiro's ethical realism is concerned with the reality of desire, rather than of its enjoyment. As Oliveira also observes, women in Monteiro's films are the 'object of temptation rather than pleasure' (2005, p. 581), that is, they are the source of desire, but not of its satisfaction. Here, a careful approach to Lacan's concept of the Real may be of help, despite this being, as Jameson warns us, the most complex element of his triadic order (the other two being the Imaginary and the Symbolic), and Lacan himself often being of little help in clarifying it (Jameson, 1977, p. 384). Zupancic, however, offers us a useful insight into this concept, which is entirely pertinent to this analysis:

> According to Lacan, the Real is impossible, and the fact that 'it happens (to us)' does not refute its basic 'impossibility'. . . . For Lacan, the accent is to be placed, first, on desire ('Have you acted in conformity with the desire which inhabits you?'), for it is desire that aims at the impossible, the Real. In his later work

> Lacan will come to conceive of desire, rather, as a defence against enjoyment – that is to say, as a compromise formation. In this later view we escape to the realm of infinite symbolic metonymy in order to avoid the encounter with the Real of enjoyment. (Zupancic, 2000, p. 235)

Monteiro's work seems to chime with this definition insofar as enjoyment in his fables is eschewed to the benefit of realistic descriptions of the workings of desire – or 'temptation' in Oliveira's Christian-inspired vocabulary. Indeed, the hero's physical interactions with the young beauties that populate his films invariably stop short of any carnal intercourse. To that end disruptive devices are purposely inserted in the form of comic, clumsy actions on the part of the seducer, as illustrated by his slapstick-style fall into the milk bath in the scene with Joaninha described above. If such a strategy could easily be defined as 'anti-illusionistic' in Brechtian terms, its function is much rather that of countering another kind of interruption, that of enjoyment, and allowing fantasy to continue its course.

One scene in *The Spousals of God* is particularly worth of note, as it provides the best example of Monteiro's lack of interest in real sex, while being at the same time the one in which he comes closest to it. João de Deus is going to have his nuptial night with Princess Elena Gombrowicz whom he has just won from Prince Omar Raschid in a poker match. They are both at João's rich estate (he is a millionaire at this point), which is a stunning real location, the Quinta da Bacalhoa, and she is having a bath in the ensuite bathroom, while he awaits her in bed. Sitting naked under the covers, he lifts them, looks down to his organ and recites a hilarious poem by the late eighteenth-century Portuguese erotic poet Manuel Maria du Bocage, in preparation for his possible failure:

> And you, relentless fucker,
> Who think you please the beautiful damsels
> Because you have a dick which, when stretched,
> Will touch your shins with its muzzle,
> Know you here, undeceived,
> That such dicks are not to their taste,
> As that which is beyond a hand and a half
> Cannot be pleasing to them.[1]

There follows a typically Monteirian and rigorously realistic static sequence shot, stretching for an excruciating five minutes, in which João de Deus, his full skeleton showing through his withered skin, tries from every possible position to perform sex with his gorgeous naked

FIGURE 7.2 *The Spousals of God*: 'life impedes love'

princess, never surpassing the stage of short kisses and licks here and there. It all finishes with João's sitting back and quoting the title of Guillaume Apollinaire's poem 'Vitam Impendere Amori', or 'a life devoted to love', by duly altering the verb to 'impedere', through which the meaning changes to 'life impedes love' (Fig. 7.2).

On the basis of this and so many other correlated scenes, Monteiro's autobiographical films have often been interpreted as variations on the theme of impotence. As Uzal puts it:

> Monteiro's cinema is a balance between excess and retention: excess of senses, retention of gesture. This retention is probably what makes Monteiro [to the eyes of some] an 'impotent'. . . . For Monteiro, desire does not necessarily need to end in consummation. . . . It is a way to counter the cult of efficiency and escape . . . the obligations of spectacle: prolonged desire rather than immediate enjoyment. (Uzal, 2004, p. 267)

What such an assessment evidences is that Monteiro's eroticism is pure onanistic exercise, requiring a subject's multiple splitting and mirroring into others. The harems of dazzling Lolitas and Venuses, blindly following a repulsive (albeit intellectually brilliant) aged man, real though they all might be, can only belong to the realm of fantasy, and this is where Monteiro meets the likes of Bocage and Sade, whose erotic writings are the quintessence of onanistic activity, stemming as they do, in both cases, from decades of isolation in prison. It is certainly not a coincidence that he had an aborted plan to adapt to the screen Sade's *Philosophy in the Bedroom,* going as far as recruiting crew and cast in France.

This send us back to Lacan and his famous essay 'Kant with Sade', which compares *Philosophy in the Bedroom* to Kant's ethics as laid out in his *Critique of Practical Reason.* According to Lacan, both texts are complementary in that Sade 'gives the truth of the *Critique*' (1989, p. 54). Monteiro was not alien to this argument, and in fact in the notes for his Sadian adaptation he highlights Sade's 'affinities with the German Aufklärung (Kant)' (Monteiro, 2005, p. 491), a remark that suggests, moreover, that he was aware, unlike Lacan, of the parallel between the two drawn by Adorno and Horkheimer in their *Dialectic of Enlightenment.* Lacan's main contention is that the 'right to *jouissance*' as defended by Sade is a natural consequence of the Kantian ethics, because, if all 'pathological', all 'progress, holiness, and even love, anything satisfying' is excluded from Kant's law of duty, the resulting disinterestedness is in every respect equivalent to Sade's apathy towards the pain inflicted on the other. Lacan further identifies a 'bipolarity' in the Kantian law hinging both on 'this radical rejection of the pathological . . . and the form of this law which is also its only substance, inasmuch as the will is only obligated to dismiss from its practice any reason which is not that of its maxim itself' (Lacan, 1989, p. 59). In this sense, for Lacan, 'the Sadian maxim, by pronouncing itself from the mouth of the Other, is more honest than appealing to the voice within, since it unmasks the splitting, usually conjured away, of the subject' (p. 59). By deriving Sade's philosophy from a radical understanding of the rights of man, Lacan states that it is 'the Other as free, it is the freedom of the Other, which the discourse of the right to *jouissance* poses as the subject of its enunciation', though this discourse, he completes, 'is no less determining for the subject of the statement' (p. 60). Monteiro seems to echo this assessment when he states that, for Sade:

> The emotion experienced by someone never touches the other, it is a curious form of autism which carries the brand of an irremediable self-confinement – negation of the other implying self-negation. (2005, p. 487)

It must be noted that Sadian fantasy based on enjoyment through the infliction of pain upon the other could not be further away from Monteiro's imaginary. However the subjective split associated with masturbatory isolation lies at the core of his ethical system, one which reasserts the absolute 'right to *jouissance*' upon the other as self-projection. As Lacan puts it, 'fantasy constitutes the pleasure proper to desire', and it is the reality of the pleasure of this desire that Monteiro's cinema aims at conveying, rather than its satisfaction. The self-reflexive character of this process is obvious, and this is why I believe his actors and collaborators never felt personally affected as the object upon which the director's fantasies were enacted. Critics seem to agree on this too, as does Paulo Monteiro, thereby again resorting, like Oliveira, to the idea of a personality split:

> Monteiro nurtures an intransigent fidelity to a super-ego, which has always controlled his exuberant ego: a constant cinematic and civic ethics . . . If his discourse draws on, or is even motivated by, ethical consideration, the drive that moves it is of the order of eroticism. He invents forms (and an ethics) to be able to film eroticism. (P.F. Monteiro, 2007, p. 206)

Monteiro has no qualms in qualifying himself as a self-centred misanthrope in the following terms:

> I am a ferociously individualist type who takes himself for the centre of the world and remains profoundly convinced that things to do with cinema or whatever you like must be traversed alone. (Monteiro, 2004, p. 35)

This trait is particularly noticeable in his autobiographical phase, one which is profoundly auteurist thanks to its centring on the director's ubiquitous presence before and behind the camera, and testifies to the multiplication of his persona through all his characters. Let us now examine how autobiography and authorship are shaped through an ethics of the real in Monteiro's films.

God's Autobiography

In an often quoted article, published in the May 1957 issue of *Arts* magazine, Truffaut prophesied that:

> The film of tomorrow appears to me as even more personal than an individual and autobiographical novel, like a confession, or an intimate diary. The young filmmakers will express themselves in the first person and will relate what has happened to them. . . . The film of tomorrow will resemble the person who has made it. (Truffaut, 1957, p. 4)

Truffaut was obviously wrong if he was referring to cinema as a whole, but entirely right with regard to the development in the last decades of a significant strand of independent auteur cinema towards a fusion of private and public spheres through which films become the mirror image of their directors. This ever-growing production has been variously identified as 'first-person film', 'film diary', 'I-movie', 'private documentary' and 'self-documentary', as examined in the previous chapter with reference to Hara and Kobayashi. As regards fiction cinema, the genre can be qualified as 'autofiction', 'mock' or 'fantasy' autobiography and related terms, all of which to lesser or major degrees apply to João César Monteiro's late output. Truffaut's quote, in fact, suits Monteiro's films to perfection, in that they bear the unmistakable stylistic mark of their director, on the one hand, and feature the director himself performing, at least in part, his own daily life, on the other. Let us examine each of these aspects in turn.

As far as authorship is concerned, Monteiro never left any doubts as to his authority to determine all aspects of his films. 'The photography must not participate in the drama', he insisted at every opportunity (Monteiro, 2003). Both crew and cast bear witness to the forceful quality of the director's style. For example, Mário Barroso, Monteiro's director of photography from *God's Comedy* onwards, when asked how much freedom he was granted by the director, answered categorically: 'None' (Barroso, 2003). This is because, according to Monteiro's strict code of practice, the camera must be kept at a considerable distance from its object, often static and unable to follow the characters' movements or gaze. Editors are also constrained to respect the extreme long takes and the near absence of reaction shots. Close-ups and detail shots are equally rare, but given pride of place, when, for example, there is a need to stress the plain beauty of an adolescent face. Natural light is always preferred over artificial lighting, regardless of the difficulties this entails for cinematographers and set designers. Although all sorts of sounds are added in the mixing process, voices and music must be diegetic and recorded on location. The music is more often than not played during the shoot itself, a procedure Monteiro branded as 'scenephony' (*cenofonia,* Monteiro, 2005, p. 480). If you add to such techniques the extensive use of non-professional actors, real outdoor and indoor locations and contemporary settings, the result is at once pure Bazinian realism and the very kind of personal cinema Truffaut and some of his *Cahiers* colleagues used to dream about.

Auteurism *Cahiers*-style was indeed purposely cultivated by Monteiro and received as such by the French. His kinship with the French is noticeable from his first film, *He Goes long Barefoot that Waits for Dead Men's Shoes* (*Quem espera por sapatos de defundo morre descalço,* 1970), an open homage to Godard and his self-reflexive tricks. Not surprisingly,

Monteiro became from the start a French idol, not only in the pages of the *Cahiers,* but also of the journal *Traffic,* directed by Serge Daney, who became close friends with the director. *God's Comedy* is dedicated to the memory of Daney, the author of the idea for *The Hips of J.W.* with a cinephile dream he told Monteiro about, in which 'John Wayne moves his hips wonderfully at the North Pole'. *Cahiers* critic Jean Douchet is another member of the Monteiro clique who performs minor parts in *God's Comedy* and *The Spousals of God.* In the former, he is a French businessman called Antoine Doinel, the name of Truffaut's alter-ego played by Jean-Pierre Léaud in a series of films, starting with the Nouvelle Vague milestone *The 400 Blows* (*Les Quatre cents coups,* 1959). Actually, the role should have been played by Léaud himself, who reportedly changed his mind at the last minute out of respect for Truffaut's memory (Douchet, 2004), originating a joke in the film: when João de Deus is introduced to the Douchet character, he says, in French, 'Je m'attendais quelqu'un d'autre' ('I expected somebody else') (Fig. 7.3).

Not by coincidence, a host of independent French producers poured money into Monteiro's films at different moments, in particular his mostly French-spoken *The Hips of J.W.* Also originally funded by the French, *God's Comedy* started as an expensive project, in scope format, with parts shot in Venice, a large crew and international cast. But a month into the shoot, Monteiro suddenly brought it to a halt, discarded the shot footage and restarted it from scratch in his own way, that is, on 35mm 4:3 format, with low budget, small crew, a Portuguese

FIGURE 7.3 Jean Douchet (centre) replacing Jean-Pierre Léaud as the character of Antoine Doinel: cinephilia in *God's Comedy*

cast and locations in Lisbon, as he had done for the first part of the trilogy, *Recollections of the Yellow House*. This confirms how Monteiro stubbornly stuck to his absolute auteurist power as celebrated in his self-enacted autobiographical films, in which he is defined as none other than god himself. What makes such megalomaniac pretention not only acceptable, but absolutely fascinating is, precisely, realism, which derives from Monteiro's addition to his onscreen persona of an entirely human, fallible, often repulsive and unethical element, which at the same time undermines and legitimizes his totalitarian pretensions as both director and actor.

One should not forget that Monteiro started to make films in 1970, the era par excellence of authorship denial, after Barthes had declared its death and Foucault reduced the author to a mere catalyst of social processes. Barthes, in fact, championed the deconstruction of the authorial institution, together with any ensuing unified meaning, as

> an anti-theological activity, an activity that is truly revolutionary since to refuse to fix meaning is, in the end, to refuse God and his hypostases – reason, science, law. (Barthes, 1977, p. 147)

Monteiro's self-deriding appellations to god by means of the composite names he adopts for his onscreen characters seem, at least at first sight, to conform to such a 'revolutionary' indictment of the authorial and authoritative god, if we just think of the parodic title *God's Comedy*, which immediately tells us that this is a comedy about god, and not any adaptation of Dante's religious epos. The humorous opening of the film leaves no doubt about this: over a shot of what seems to be an animation of the Andromeda Galaxy turning round (actually filmed at the Lisbon Planetarium) a child's voice announces: 'Joaquim Pinto presents *God's Comedy*, by João César Monteiro', and laughs when pronouncing the director's name. Still over the image of the turning galaxy, Monteverdi's 'Intonatio' from the Vespers of the Blessed Virgin irrupts with its bombastic horns and choir. This makes room for the introduction of Monteiro's character, João de Deus (John of God), the manager of the 'Ice-cream Paradise' parlour. The camera first focuses on two of the parlour's young female assistants standing at the parlour door, waiting for their boss to open it. They see him approaching off-frame with 'British punctuality' at a slow pace, and one of them observes: 'The slow movement is essentially majestic', while the other replies: 'For me it is a waste of time'. They giggle and then João de Deus enters the frame, now duly reduced to his earthly condition.

This is how the unified auteur is split into a double of omnipotence and insignificance in his screen reflection. At first sight, this would fit a Godardian model of self-inscription, according to which, as Sayad points out, the director's physical presence on screen 'constitutes an obstacle for closure', bringing 'instability to the classically conceived idea of the film as an isolated object depicting a world sealed off from reality' (2009). Monteiro's autobiographical work confirms this assessment insofar as the director's physical presence on screen undoubtedly establishes continuity between the reality of the fable and the profilmic world, the function of the latter being to deconstruct the former. There were even times Monteiro's filmmaking went down the route of an outright self-questioning mode, *The Hips of J.W.* being a typical example of crisis film. Its first quarter is a staging of Strindberg's *Inferno,* where characters, disposed in a vast warehouse, recite the Strindberg text around the Monteiro protagonist, the whole captured in extreme long shot with a stationary camera. Later, he disappears for a long spell, while characters, including a Pasolini-cum-Buñuel homage via Pierre Clémenti playing the stage director, rehearse what would have been the film's dialogue. Monteiro's character later reappears as a drunkard called Henrique or Max Monteiro, who tells another character called Jean de Dieu that he has 'surprised his wife in the arms of a socialite' and that he is in pain. The spontaneity of the director's acting at this point, and the successive glasses of (real) cognac he is downing, tell us about the reality of this experience, which is corroborated by crew testimonials, such as editor Vítor Silva Tavares's (2004, pp. 83–4) who enlightens us on the director's real marital crisis which led him to an alcoholic spell and heavily interfered with the film schedule, indeed determining its final fragmentary result. Monteiro's *Snow White* (*Branca de Neve,* 2000) is another, this time radically anti-cinematic crisis film, which has no images at all except for a few stills at the beginning, because the director was reportedly not satisfied with any of the images he had found to illustrate a text by Robert Walser, which is then simply read by the actors against a black background.

However, Monteiro's self-inscription is in most cases not at all aimed at decreeing the end of history and/or storytelling, in Godard's postmodernist way, but at injecting materiality and indexical value into the myth of the godly auteur, whose performing identity shares that of the director. As a result, the director's biography becomes inextricable from fiction and myth, a fact that locates Monteiro's late outputs at the intersection between three different genres: hagiography, in that they tell the 'lives' of holy figures (there is a Portuguese saint called São João de Deus), and even god and the devil; autobiography, because they obviously reflect the real life of the director; and autofiction, given their centring on an ordinary, albeit megalomaniac, fictional protagonist played by the director himself.

The process of attaching indexicality and historical depth to fiction and myth, and, conversely, mythologizing a simultaneously real and fictional index, is clearly intentional and made explicit through Monteiro's use of 'heteronyms' bearing part of his real name. The obvious example here is the character of João de Deus (John of God), at the centre of the John of God trilogy. This name has a number of historical resonances in Portugal, starting with João de Deus, the nineteenth-century lyric poet, who was also the author of a very popular reading and writing primer. It also alludes to São João de Deus (Saint John of God, 1495–1550), the founder of the order bearing his name. Finally, the surname 'de Deus', given to those of unknown family origin and preceded by a common forename such as 'João', suggests a 'Joe Bloggs', or a nobody. The merger of extreme irrelevance and almighty power, mediated by artistic imagination, is thus achieved through this humorous composite name, which adds mythical, historical and fictional complements to the real person of the film director. The function of naming as part of a performing self-identity reaches beyond the trilogy with João Vuvu, this name being an onomatopoeic reference to an African instrument with obvious obscene resonances in *Come and Go,* in which, after an African ritual, the hero is sodomized by a gigantic phallus (Fig. 7.4). Monteiro is also referred to as Max Monteiro, in a reference to the actor Max Schreck, who famously

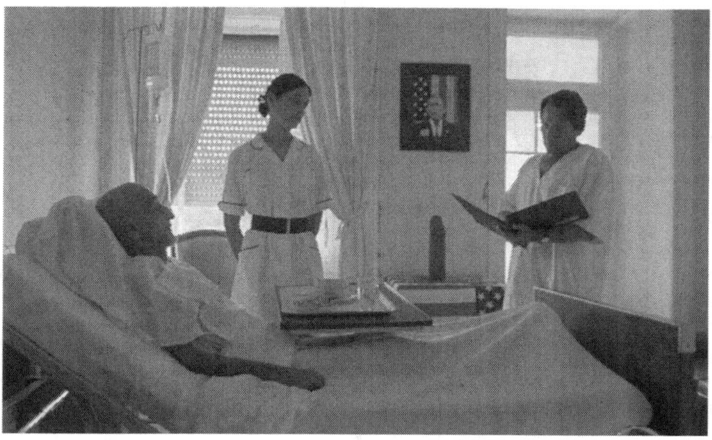

FIGURE 7.4 The hero is sodomized by a gigantic phallus and undergoes an operation in *Come and Go*

played Nosferatu in Murnau's *Nosferatu* (*Nosferatu, eine Symphonie des Grauens,* 1922), in the credits of *God's Comedy*. In *The Hips of J.W.*, the actor-director is multiplied into a plethora of different personas, starting with an elusive and strictly cinephiliac John Wayne, only shown in posters and through dialogue references, while the credits name the actor João César Monteiro as João, o Obscuro (John, the Obscure), in a reference to Thomas Hardy's novel, *Jude the Obscure,* in the role of the 'characters' of god and Max Monteiro, as well as that of Henrique. In this film, the director's identity is moreover interchangeable with that of his dead dog (also referred to as Max Monteiro) and of Lucifer, the latter a character in the film played by another actor (Hugue Quester) who introduces himself at a point as Jean de Dieu (John of God), in short: the filmmaker's alter ego is as omnipresent as god, but also as humane and ordinary as any common citizen or even a dog.

To return to Truffaut and the idea of auteurism as autobiography, critics, and Monteiro himself in interviews and writings, have explored to exhaustion the ways in which his own life is reflected in his films. According to these sources, the character of João de Deus, as depicted in the trilogy, is imbued with the intellectualism inherited by Monteiro from an anticlerical father, who provided him with first-class education, but died when he was a teenager. The constant falls of the character into extreme poverty, in their turn, would derive from his experience of deprivation alongside a widowed house-cleaner mother. Lastly, the films would reflect the intransigent adult turned film auteur, who rejected all compromise and often lived in dire poverty out of loyalty to his artistic principles. The obvious problem posed by such an interpretation is that autobiographies are necessarily based on past events, as illustrated by Truffaut's famous account of his own childhood in *The 400 Blows*. In Monteiro's case, however, real experiences are, as a rule, not *reproduced* but *produced* during the shoot. His motivation is not nostalgia or resentment, but desire, whose reality cannot be proved retroactively, but only through the here-and-now of the pro filmic event. However, the fulfilment of desire, that is, 'enjoyment' in Lacanian terms, is projected into an impossible future as a kind of Quixotic delusion often staged with the help of Monteiro's cinephilia populated by megalomaniac heroes, such as Erich von Stroheim and Charles Chaplin (who also starred their own films), as the following example shows.

In *Recollections of the Yellow House,* João de Deus is the penniless inhabitant of a boarding house, in which he struggles with bedbugs and an epididymis (sperm duct) inflammation, for which the doctor subscribes a painful treatment, the whole described in minute, often scientific detail, in real locations in Lisbon, with a real doctor and extras recruited from among the local population. As ever, João is an incorrigible womanizer, now stalking the boarding house owner's daughter, the young clarinettist Julieta, as well as courting his next-door prostitute lodger, Mimi. With both he manages to stage sexual encounters, but the actual intercourse is abruptly transferred from realistic staging to intermedial referencing. In the case of Mimi, the camera captures her as she starts rolling down her stocking with her foot posed on a chair, then, after a cut to João's face at the lower corner of the frame looking intently at her, it drifts left to focus on the bottom of a poster, on which we see a pair of empty female shoes and, next to them, a pair of legs in military boots. The camera dollies upwards on the poster to reveal the owner of the boots as the young Stroheim, one hand duly posed on the handle of the sword attached to his belt, the other holding a cigarette (two phallic metaphors), plus the infallible monocle (which Monteiro also sports at times in this and other films), in the role of Lieutenant Erich von Steuben in *Blind Husbands* (1919), in which the character, like Monteiro, preserves part of the director's real name – and no doubt personality. Meanwhile, sex foreplay is suggested by moans, which are soon interrupted by an off-frame dialogue:

Mimi: 'Well?'
João: 'Your nipples are covered with milk'.

Enjoyment is thus shown as the moment where sex escapes the realm of the hero's real, masturbatory fantasy in the present and is projected into strictly fictional (hence unrealizable) future. The next thing we learn is that Mimi has died from complications of a backstreet abortion, and João rushes to raid her room in search of her savings, which he finally finds inside a rag doll, definitely effacing, through realist enactment, any sense of fulfilled desire. As for sex with Julieta, this is again replaced by an abrupt image of a Beethoven bust, shot from João's point of view, while Beethoven's Fifth Symphony suddenly irrupts in the soundtrack, concomitant to João's assault at his prey. This actually does not get beyond his tearing off her bra which lands in the girl's mother's hands, as she enters the room and he escapes.

Beethoven's sudden intrusion in the sex scene, as if it were an extradiegetic interference under the character's diegetic command, is also illustrative of Monteiro's self-parody as a director whose 'conducting' skills are portrayed as the product of a fantasy-inflated ego. Indeed, the image of a delusional solitary conductor is Monteiro's most autobiographical emblem of his self-reflexive, and self-denying, authorial authority. A marvellous example of this is João de Deus's swimming lesson to Rosarinho, in *God's Comedy*. While she, lying face down on a raised board, moves arms and legs in swimming strokes, João rovers around her gesticulating as if he were conducting the 'Liebestod' aria of Wagner's *Tristan and Isolda* playing in the background – and actually in the shooting location, in Monteiro's 'scenephony' style (Fig. 7.5). That the conducting mania is nothing but solitary exercise, in every respect comparable to onanism, becomes clear in *The Spousals of God*. After losing the Princess Elena Gombrowicz, who has run away with his fortune, João de Deus is accused of hiding terrorist weaponry in his estate and sent to prison. Locked up in his cell, barefoot and bare-chested, João simultaneously 'conducts' and 'dances' to the sound of a *Traviata* aria playing on his portable stereo. He starts by juggling with an orange, then climbing up the ledge of his barred window, hanging there like a bat (in another allusion to *Nosferatu*), going back down to his stool, moaning when the music climaxes, until a prison guard knocks at the door and makes him stop (Fig. 7.6). What impresses in a scene like this is not so much the pathetic quality of such private emotions as the daringness of their unrestricted exposition to the camera. Monteiro's body language in his films (and I am not the first to note this) are those of an amateur dancer – often in citation mode of Max Schreck or Chaplin – or even of a choreographer, who wants to control

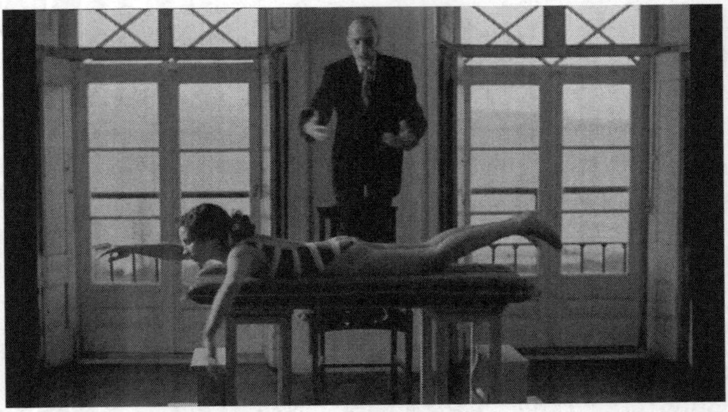

Figure 7.5 Conducting the 'Liebestod' in *God's Comedy*: an emblem of Monteiro's self-reflexive and self-denying authorial authority

FIGURE 7.6 *The Spousals of God*: the conducting mania is a solitary exercise comparable to onanism.

the movements of the world. Indeed, very often, he 'choreographs' the movements of his women while interacting with them, clumsy and invariably a failure as a teacher or initiator, or indeed a film director though he might be, as profusely illustrated in *God's Comedy*. One just needs to look at when he tries to teach Rosarinho to place an ice-cream ball on a cone, and smashes the cone in the process. His auteurist impositions thus include, beyond the author's absolutist stylistic power, the unrelenting effort to preserve the imperfectness of the director's autobiographical performances, including his hilarious, even at times embarrassing, failures. Here, I believe, lies the strength (and the ethics) of his realism.

The History Man

Indexical and realistic as he may be, Monteiro as self-performing auteur is nevertheless an 'unreliable narrator' as Sayad remarks about Godard and Allen's performing personas (2009). Indeed, other characters within the fable offer versions of the facts which radically differ from the one shown from João de Deus's ritualistic, fantasy-infused point of view. This is however intended less as a disruptive device of classical paradigms than a demonstration of the social workings of Portugal in reality. Interesting examples of this can be drawn from the

João de Deus trilogy. In *God's Comedy,* Rosarinho, the newly appointed assistant at the 'Ice-cream Paradise' parlour, a young beauty who is also an orphan of extremely poor background, is carefully initiated, through João's cultivated clumsiness, into the business of selling ice-cream, including lessons of hand washing and bathing in general, a favourite Monteiro trope. Later, however, João sodomizes her, in a scene where, typically in his films, discourse prevails over action: we only see their lower legs showing at the bottom of the short washroom doors, and hear her asking, among moans, 'Are you doggy-fucking me, Mr João?' There follows a scene, now in João's apartment, in which, perfectly composed, sitting in his bed, she reassures him that no real damage has been done to her anus. However, João is later accused by Judite, the ice-cream parlour's owner, of having 'torn the arse' of her best employee. The same is true of Joaninha, who, after joyfully going through all the stages of the bath and ice-cream rituals with Mr João, probably tells a very different story to her butcher father, who subsequently slashes the hero's face and sends him dying to hospital. In the police's version of the events, presented in *The Spousals of God,* João is a psychopath, already identifiable from the shape of his skull, who had been sent to a mental hospital (as shown in the first part of the trilogy, *Recollections of the Yellow House*) for having exposed his genitals to a seven-year-old girl in a public garden – a fact which is not staged in the film, but also not denied by the defendant. João's former boss Judite, in the ice-cream parlour, in her turn, is accused of recruiting underage girls for prostitution, one of them being precisely Rosarinho. All João has to say in his defence is that his misfortune was 'to have been born in Portugal', a phrase which is not simply a boutade restricted to the realm of fiction, but to which the director tries to give documentary evidence in all three instalments of the trilogy.

His time as homeless tramp, sleeping on garden benches and queuing up for charity soup kitchens, for example, gives Monteiro the opportunity to document, in *Recollections of the Yellow House,* the lives of the homeless elderly in Lisbon, among whom those scenes were shot. In *God's Comedy,* João's behaviour, unethical though it may seem, is nothing but the mirror of an entire society living off illegal activities. The innocent Rosarinho resides in a miserable district called Cambodja, a place scrutinized in documentary detail by the camera, where João meets children selling pictures of crimes to the press – and also of Rosarinho naked. The moralist butcher, who slashes João's face, sells black-market meat, falsifying the health inspection stamp with the help of his wife and daughters. This gives Monteiro the opportunity to document Lisbon's street markets and small businesses, including the detailed workings of the hands of a female fishmonger gutting a fish, whose innards are savoured by stray cats, and of a butcher skinning a lamb and chopping its head off.

This goes far beyond a mere indictment of a whole society, being rather an amorous confession of national identity and cultural belonging, irrespective of the moral or immoral qualities this nation and culture might contain. The most extraordinary means through which this confession acquires legitimacy in Monteiro's films are what could be defined as 'popular tribunals' staged at different points in the trilogy. *Recollections of the Yellow House* presents two brilliant examples. The first one shows Manuela de Freitas, in the role of Violeta, the boarding house owner, standing in the street, surrounded by neighbours all of whom were clearly recruited from the local community – old ladies, mothers with babies in their arms, idle men hanging around. She gives a speech in her defence, in reaction to the fact that one of her lodgers, Laurindo (a pimp to the prostitute Mimi), has just been taken away by the police. Her words are all aimed at assuring the honesty of her house and family, including her daughter, 'a straight Catholic girl, who plays the clarinet like an angel'. To this, a neighbour off-frame shouts: 'She was caught at the Arco de Jesus [Jesus Arch] blowing Messias' [Messiah's] clarinet!' As Violeta proceeds, neighbours offer their own views, one saying that Mimi is 'a very good girl, very generous', others shouting about Laurindo: 'He is a pimp!' Meanwhile, João, who is returning home after extorting the last pennies from his cleaner mother, roams around the gathered neighbours as if unconcerned, although he will be the next to be pilloried (Fig. 7.7). This happens at the second 'popular tribunal' scene, as follows. João has taken possession of the dead Mimi's savings and presently visits Julieta in her bedroom, allegedly to congratulate her on her performance with the military orchestra, but actually to propose to her a tour of Portugal and Spain, in a fully 'air-conditioned Puma bus', with Mimi's cash. There follows the love scene described above, interrupted by Violeta's arrival. João then throws all the cash he has over Julieta's half-naked body and makes his escape, racing down the stairs and into the street, overturning on the way a rubbish bin from which a cat jumps out. Violeta, after quickly collecting all the money spread over her daughter, rushes to her balcony and shouts: 'Police! Grab him, Grab him!' The neighbouring women immediately show at their balconies and windows too, the eldest of them asking: 'Grab what, grab whom?' The double meaning contained in this question is just a light introduction to an

FIGURE 7.7 Popular tribunal in *Recollections of the Yellow House*

FIGURE 7.8 'He must have a little thing like this': another popular tribunal in *Recollections of the Yellow House*

outright obscene altercation that develops among the neighbours. 'The hermaphrodite, he left her half strangled, my Julieta!', shouts Violeta, and the elder lady asks: 'Who, the long nose? He couldn't fuck his way out of a paper bag' (Fig. 7.8). Then one neighbour accuses another of being married to a queer, which she refutes by saying that she has 'calluses on her labia' caused by her husband's balls, to which yet another retorts that 'My man has got a dyke's dick', with a reply coming back as 'I like to feel them right up to the hilt like a cock crowing'. While middle-aged, even outright old women deliver themselves to this loud competition about their husbands, a black woman in a nightgown dances on her balcony, kids on another balcony giggle, Violeta crosses herself until a last lady appears at a high attic window beating a pan and shouting: 'Enough, enough!' sending everybody back inside. The scene closes with a street vendor passing by, playing a banjo and shouting: 'Girls, do you want bananas?'

As well as for its hilarity, this scene is striking for the naturalness with which these actors, clearly recruited among non-professionals, repeat these lines of erudite obscenity, displaying an array of synonyms for penis and vagina which certainly stems from Monteiro's encyclopaedic imagination and obsessive priapism, but here shown to derive from the low culture of the streets. This is why in the old lady's judgement João should be acquitted, because 'he couldn't fuck his way out of a paper bag' (according to the English subtitles, or, in a literal translation from Portuguese: 'He must have a little thing like this [moving the top of her finger], this wouldn't harm the girl').

A similar popular tribunal is staged at João's estate in *The Spousals of God,* when he is taken to prison and his former employees gather at the house steps to reflect on the justice of his fate. The butler is the first to speak: 'That was a disgrace! Her [the princess's] running around the estate showing her fanny and the weakling running and drooling after her, give me your cunt, give me your cunt!' A lower employee then expresses his sympathy, by saying that 'the Baron liked to give to the poor', and a woman concurs: 'He was a saint'. Another acquittal thus ensues equally based on João's inferiority to women and his lack of potency ('the linen was clean', notes one of the cleaners) (Fig. 7.9). Whether the fable clears João de Deus from any ethical trespassing is however less relevant than his demonstration through the film form of this ethics being firmly grounded in Portuguese culture. A popular composer and singer such as Quim Barreiros, whose song 'Chupa Teresa' ('Suck Teresa, suck, this delicious ice-cream is made of raspberry') is happily sung and danced to by the ice-cream factory worker, while she separates egg yolks from the white with her hands, in *God's Comedy,* is an asset of Portugal alone. Another even more indecent song ('Quero Cheirar teu Bacalhau/I Want to Sniff your Codfish') by Barreiros, played both in *God's Comedy* and *The Hips of J.W.,* does not fail to state that this is Portugal's favourite dish.

FIGURE 7.9 Popular tribunal in *The Spousals of God*

Finding the low, underground roots of high thought and high art is indeed the prevailing movement of Monteiro's cinema, noticeable not only in the equating of god and a tramp, of Dante and popular culture, but also in virtually all aesthetic choices in his films. The collection of pubic hair strands ('Ariadne's threads', he calls them), for example, is nothing but a realist translation of the traditional romantic lock of hair from the loved one. Another delicately staged reversal happens when Rosarinho, given by João a small hand mirror to check the damage done to her anus, checks on her face instead. Jean Narboni nicely summarises this aspect of Monteiro's work, by saying:

> He is a philosopher and a Parmenidean one, to the point of having low things proliferate deliriously in order to elevate them to the rank of Idea. To the filth, to the hair and the mud he adds the pubic hair, the menstruation, the fart, the sexual organs, holes in socks to be repaired on the surface of a raw egg and thousands of other inconveniences, reaching an apotheosis in *Come and Go* with the bearded and hairy woman who soon falls into a mythological and priapic dancing frenzy. (Narboni, 2004, p. 272)

It is also true, however, that all Idea gains corporeality in Monteiro's works. The 'sacrificial lamb' is a real lamb skinned by the butcher, which prefigures the slashing of João's face in *God's Comedy*. The metaphorical eggs, milk and eyes of Bataille, Buñuel and other surrealists, are also transported into a realist material world, where diners eat the eye out of a fish head (*Recollections of a Yellow House*), cooks immerse their hands in huge containers of raw eggs and Joaninha has a real bath in dozens of litters of milk (*God's Comedy*). Everyone is real, they eat, drink, urinate and fart, and expose themselves to a camera entirely aware of the seriousness of this exposure, as the actor Luís Miguel Cintra once brilliantly put it:

> I think that Monteiro had in common with Oliveira the awareness that to place the camera in front of someone was not to shoot fiction: it's to shoot someone alive, something which has to do with an exceptional life somehow. (Cintra, 2004, p. 117)

Making films, for Monteiro, is therefore making history, entailing change in the real life of cast and crew, and therefore producing an ethical reality.

NOTES

Chapter 1

[1] My option aims at better accuracy, given that the assumption of god as white and the devil as black, implicit in the English translation, is not at all a theme in the film, as I will explain later on in the analysis.

[2] For the Inuit names, I will be following the spelling utilized in Angilirk (2002), which differs considerably from that used in the titles and subtitles of the commercial DVD of *Atanarnuat, the Fast Runner.*

[3] *Anger of the Gods,* in fact, confirms Ouédraogo as part of a breed of new-wave filmmakers devoted to physical reenactments of the myth, the most eloquent illustration of them being Werner Herzog, notable for his predilection for adverse locations, ranging from the Sahara to Antarctica, coupled with extreme shooting conditions. One of Herzog's most notable characters, Don Lope de Aguirre, was equally prey to god's ire as enacted in reality by a perennially choleric Klaus Kinski in his all too physical confrontation with the Andes and the Amazon jungle, in *Aguirre, the Wrath of God* (*Aguirre, der Zorn Gottes,* 1972), a film bearing strong intertextual relations with Cinema Novo's works. Herzog's physical cinema and his Latin American trilogy, which includes *Fitzcarraldo* (1982) and *Cobra Verde* (1987), as well as *Aguirre,* all of which star Kinski in physical displays of metaphysical wrath, will be the subject of Chapter 2.

[4] *Cordel* is a traditional form of narrative poetry, illustrated by woodblock prints and published in leaflets, which are sold in street markets and other places across the northeastern states of Brazil.

[5] I have drawn a comparison between the closing scenes of *God and the Devil in the Land of the Sun* and *The 400 Blows,* under a different point of view, in the first chapter of *Brazil on Screen* (Nagib, 2007).

[6] In Portuguese, with metric and rhyme: '*Manuel e Rosa vivia no sertão, trabalhando a terra com as próprias mão*'. Unfortunately, none of this is translated in the English subtitled copies of the film available in the market.

[7] In the Portuguese original: '*Tinha todas as qualidades/ que pode ter um vivente/ era enfermeiro e parteiro/ falso, covarde e valente/ fraco igualmente ao sendeiro/ astuto como a serpente.*'

Chapter 2

[1] A very insightful study of authorial self-inscription in film, especially with regard to these two filmmakers, is currently being conducted by Cecilia Sayad.

[2] A more accurate translation of this title would be *The Power of Feelings.*

[3] The plot of *The 400 Blows* is detailed in Chapter 1.

[4] For further comparisons between *Even Dwarfs* and Buñuel's films (*The Exterminating Angel, An Andalusian Dog/Un chien andalous,* 1929, and *Beauty of the Day/Belle de Jour,* 1967), see Nagib, 1991, pp. 47ff. Emmanuel Carrère (1982, p. 20) also draws comparisons with *Land without Bread* (*Las hurdes,* Luis Buñuel, 1933).

[5] See Chapter 1, note 1, about my preferred translation for the title of Glauber Rocha's film *Deus e o diabo na terra do sol.*

[6] I am thankful to Peter B. Schumann for giving me the following important information: 'I organized the first overarching Cinema Novo retrospective for the Berlinale, in 1966. Then in 1967, a number of Brazilian films were shown on the ZDF channel, such as *Barren Lives* (*Vidas secas,* Nelson Pereira dos Santos, 1963), *God and the Devil in the Land of the Sun* (1964), *The Guns* (*Os fuzis,* Ruy Guerra, 1964), *Assault on the Paying Train* (*Assalto ao trem pagador,* Roberto Farias, 1962) and *The Obsessed of Catale* (*Vereda da salvação,* Anselmo Duarte, 1964). In 1968, the television channel WDR showed more Brazilian films as an illustration to my four documentaries about Cinema Novo, among them: *The Guns, God and the Devil, Barren Lives* and *Ganga Zumba* (Carlos Diegues, 1963). From 1969, Die Lupe (the distributor Art-House-Film) started to show the films by Glauber Rocha, including *God and the Devil, Land in Trance* (*Terra em transe,* 1967) and *Antônio das Mortes* (*O dragão da maldade contra o santo guerreiro,* 1969). In the same period, another Bavarian television channel, BR, started to show Glauber Rocha's work, including *Land in Trance, Antônio das Mortes, Cabezas cortadas* (1970) and *Der Leone Have Sept Cabeças* (1971). Finally the ARD (the first national channel) started to show Brazilian films from 1971, including *Hunger for Love* (*Fome de amor,* Nelson Pereira dos Santos, 1968), *The Heirs* (*Os herdeiros,* Carlos Diegues, 1970) and others.'

[7] This interview took place in São Paulo, on 27 July 1988, and remains unpublished.

[8] See Chapter 3, where I explain my preference for this title rather than other available English translations, such as *Land in Anguish* and *Earth Entranced.*

[9] Corrigan has raised the hypothesis that Herzog would have actually drawn the phrase from Roger Corman's *The Trip* (1967), 'a solidly Hollywood production which nonetheless offers a truly Herzogian sequence featuring a dwarf on a merry-go-round repeating Herzog's title again and again' (1983, p. 125). The dwarf and merry-go-round are indeed in this film, but not the phrase.

[10] See section on *God and the Devil in the Land of the Sun,* in Chapter 1, for the complex conceptualization of the term *sertão.*

[11] In an interview with me, Herzog stated that he was a friend of Rocha's and that once they spent a period in the house of a common friend in Berkeley (Nagib, 1991, p. 253), but I was unable to establish exactly when this happened. Rocha was in the US, including Los Angeles, in 1964, showing *The Turning Wind* (*Barravento,* 1962) and *God and the Devil.* He did not spend long periods in the US again before the 1970s. I am not aware of him ever mentioning Herzog in his abundant writings, though other Germans, such as Fleischmann and Straub, are constantly referred to.

[12] *Candomblé*: Afro-Brazilian religion, whose rituals are aimed at inducing trance and spiritualist communication with deities called *orixás* (orishas).

Chapter 3

[1] I thank José Carlos Avellar for providing me with details about Rocha's travels in 1965 and for granting me access to an unpublished version of the script for *América nuestra.* I also thank Eduardo Escorel, the editor of *Land in Trance,* for further information on the genesis of this film.

[2] I thank Mateus Araújo Silva for drawing my attention to a mention to this article in *Glauber Rocha: Scritti sul cinema* (Rocha, 1986, p. 219).

[3] See note about the title of this film in Chapter 1.

[4] For a long analysis of the opening of *Land in Trance,* under a different perspective, see my *Brazil on Screen: Cinema Novo, New Cinema, Utopia* (2007).

[5] See Chapter 2, note 12.

[6] Glauber Rocha's earliest mentions to *Que Viva Mexico!* are found in his articles on Elia Kazan, conflated in one piece and published in *O século do Cinema* (2006, pp. 89–98).

Chapter 5

[1] *Ai no koriida* has been translated as both *The Realm of the Senses* and *In the Realm of the Senses.* I will be using the former here, so as to avoid the constant clashing of the double preposition 'in *In the Realm of the Senses*'.

[2] As well as Johnston's book, other interesting accounts of Abe's life are included in Marran (2007) and Schreiber (2001).

[3] The British edition, released by Nouveaux Pictures, is uncut, however certain frames have been optically edited 'in accordance with BBFC guidelines'. A French edition released by Argos in 2003 is unaltered and even contains 6 minutes of edited-out scenes which the viewer can choose to watch or not within the complete film. It also includes interviews with producers and crew. In 2009, a special edition of the film has been launched on DVD by Criterion, which adds to the 2003 Argos materials an interview with Nagisa Oshima (sitting next to actress Eiko Matsuda, who only says a few words, and Tatsuya Fuji, who remains silent throughout), conducted in

1976 in Belgium, as well as a lengthy interview with Fuji conducted in 2008 and a booklet with an essay by Donald Richie.

[4] William Johnston, in his well-researched book on the Abe case, draws a comprehensive list of them (2005, pp. 156ff.).

[5] I here combine both the French and the English translations of Oshima's article for better accuracy.

[6] Sada Abe's story is itself sexually contagious, and there is an interesting anecdote in Johnston's book in this respect. It refers to the main judge in the trial, who confessed in his memories, published 20 years later, to have found himself sexually excited while reading the documents related to the case. In order to assure the other three judges would be able to lawfully release themselves, should they experience the same feelings, he discretely investigated the time when their respective wives were having their periods (sex during menstruation being a taboo in Japan in those days) so as to schedule the trial in a convenient moment for the three of them (Johnston, 2005, pp. 135–6).

[7] A thoroughly revised English version of this book was later published as *Reflexivity in Film and Literature* (Stam, 1985, first edition; 1992).

Chapter 6

[1] I would like to thank Alex King for making available the recording of the Q&A with Kazuo Hara and Sachiko Kobayashi, led by me, at the Leeds International Film Festival, on 10 November 2007. My thanks also go to Mika Ko who acted as interpreter of the Q&A. I am grateful to Sachiko Kobayashi, Kazuo Hara and Shisso Production for their invaluable help and support.

[2] It is common knowledge among critics that Kobayashi has been a partner in the making of all of her husband's films so far. Hara himself refers to his films as collaborative works with her. This notwithstanding, the authorship of their films continues to be attributed exclusively to him. This is probably due to the fact that Hara is the public face of the duo, endowed as he is with a charismatic personality and the power to articulate his creative ideas with impressive clarity in his interviews. Kobayashi is however an intellectual herself and, as much as Hara, makes a living partly out of teaching film. In this chapter, I have chosen to attribute authorial responsibility for their films to both of them.

[3] I have not included on this list *My Mishima* (*Watashi no Mishima,* 1999), as it is a collaborative work between Hara and a group of students from Cinema Juku, a filmmaking cooperative he founded, and would not therefore fit into the auteurist Hara-Kobayashi lineage I am analysing here. In the intervals between his films, Hara also worked as TV documentarian and assistant director in a number of important films, such as *Vengeance Is Mine* (*Fukushu suru wa sare ni ari,* Shohei Imamura, 1979) and *Sea and Poison* (*Umi to dokuyaku,* Kei Kumai, 1986).

[4] The viewer is not given the means to certify whether this event was produced before or after the divorce threat, within the profilmic chronology. It seems however to have taken place at the end of the shoot, as Yokota's final speech sums up his experience with the film – although again the asynchronous soundtrack brings a doubt about the simultaneous occurrence of image and sound.

Chapter 7

[1] I have altered the translation provided by the film's subtitles for better accuracy of Bocage's original poem, which goes: 'Agora vós, fodões encarniçados,/Que julgais agradar às moças belas/Por terdes uns marsapos que estirados/Vão pregar com os focinhos nas canelas:/Conhecereis aqui desenganados/Que não são tais porrões do gosto delas;/Que lhes não pode, enfim, causar recreio/Aquele que passar de palmo e meio'.

BIBLIOGRAPHY

Abe, Sada (2005), 'Notes from the Police Interrogation of Abe Sada', in William Johnston (ed.), *Geisha-Harlot-Strangler-Star: A Woman, Sex, & Morality in Modern Japan*. New York: Columbia University Press, pp. 163–208.

Allen, Don (1985), *Finally Truffaut*. London: Secker & Warburg.

Andrew, Dudley (2006), 'An Atlas of World Cinema', in Stephanie Dennison and Song Hwee Lim (eds), *Remapping World Cinema: Identity, Culture and Politics in Film*. London: Wallflower, pp. 19–29.

—(2010), 'Time zones and jetlag: the flows and phases of world cinema', in Natasa Durovicova and Kathleen Newman (eds), *World Cinemas, Transnational Perspectives*. New York/Abingdon: Routledge, pp. 59–89.

Angilirk, Paul Apak (ed.) (2002), *Atanarjuat, the Fast Runner*. Toronto: Coach House Books/Isuma Publishing.

Appiah, Kwame Anthony (2006), *Cosmopolitanism: Ethics in a World of Strangers*. London: Penguin.

Arrigucci Jr, Davi (1995), 'O mundo misturado: romance e experiência em Guimarães Rosa', in Ana Pizarro (ed.), *América Latina: Palavra, literatura e cultura vol. 3, Vanguarda e Modernismo*. Campinas: Editora da Unicamp.

Atanarjuat, the Fast Runner (n/d), DVD, ICA Projects.

Aufderheide, Patricia (1997), 'Public intimacy: the development of first-person documentary', in *Afterimage*, July-August, available on http://findarticles.com/p/articles/mi_m2479/is_n1_v25/ai_20198552/print?tag=artBody;%20col%201, accessed on 14 August 2008.

Badiou, Alain (2002), *Ethics: An Essay on the Understanding of Evil*, translated by Peter Hallward. London/New York: Verso.

—(2007), *Being and Event*, translated by Oliver Feltham. London/New York: Continuum.

Bakari, Imruh and Mbye Cham (eds) (1996), *African Experiences of Cinema*. London: BFI.

Barker, Jennifer M. (2009), *The Tactile Eye: Touch and the Cinematic Experience*. Berkeley/Los Angeles: University of California Press.

Barlet, Olivier (1996), *Les cinémas d'Afrique noire: le regard en question*. Paris: L'Harmattan.

Barney, Stephen A. (1979), *Allegories of History, Allegories of Love*. Hamden, Connecticut: Archon Books.

Baron, Jeanine (1989), 'Entretien avec le réalisateur: L'aide humanitaire renferme un mépris inconscient', in *Yaaba* press release.

Barreto, Luiz Carlos (2006), Interview in the extras of the DVD *Terra em transe*. Rio: Versátil Home Video.

Barroso, Mário (2003), testimonial in the extras of the DVD *A comédia de Deus*, Lisboa, Madragoa Filmes.

Barthes, Roland (1970), *L'Empire des signes*. Paris: Champs/Flammarion.

—(1977), *Image-Music-Text*, edited and translated by Stephen Heath. London: Fontana.

—(1982), *Camera Lucida*, translated by Richard Howard. London: Vintage.

Bastos, Othon (n/d), Interview in the extras of the DVD *Deus e o diabo na terra do sol*.Rio de Janeiro: Versátil Home Video/Riofilme.

Bataille, Georges (1967), 'La Notion de dépense', in *La Part maudite*. Paris: Les Éditions de Minuit.

—(1970), *Œuvres complètes I: Premiers Écrits 1922–1940*. Paris: Gallimard.

—(1985), *Visions of Excess: Selected Writings, 1927–1939*, edited and translated by Allan Stoekl. Minneapolis: University of Minnesota Press.

—(1986), *Erotism: Death & Sensuality*, edited and translated by Mary Dalwood. San Francisco: City Lights Books.

Baudry, Jean-Louis (1986), 'Ideological Effects of the Basic Cinematographic Apparatus'; 'The Apparatus: Metapsychological Approaches to the Impression of Reality in Cinema', in Philip Rosen (ed.), *Narrative, Apparatus, Ideology: A Film Theory Reader*. New York: Columbia University Press, pp. 286–318.

Bax, Dominique (ed.) (2005), *Glauber Rocha—Nelson Rodrigues*. Paris: Magic Cinéma/Cinémathèque Française.

Bazin, André (1967), *What Is Cinema?* vol. 1, essays selected and translated by Hugh Gray. Berkeley/Los Angeles/London: University of California Press.

—(1982), *The Cinema of Cruelty: from Buñuel to Hitchcock*, edited and with an introduction by François Truffaut; translated by Sabine d' Estrée with the assistance of Tiffany Fliss. New York: Seaver Books.

—(1985), 'On the *politique des auteurs*', in Jim Hillier (ed.), *Cahiers du Cinéma: The 1950s: Neo-Realism, Hollywood, New Wave*. Cambridge, Massachusetts: Harvard University Press, pp. 248–59.

—(1997), *Bazin at Work*, translated by Alain Piette and Bert Cardullo, edited by Bert Cardullo. New York/London: Routledge, pp. 211–19.

—(2003), 'Death Every Afternoon', translated by Mark A. Cohen, in Margulies, Ivone (ed.), *Rites of Realism: Essays on Corporeal Cinema*. Durham/London: Duke University Press, pp. 27–31.

—(2005), *What Is Cinema?* vol. 2, essays selected and translated by Hugh Gray. Berkeley/Los Angeles/London: University of California Press.

Benjamin, Walter (1999), 'The Image of Proust', 'The Work of Art in the Age of Mechanical Reproduction', in *Illuminations*, edited by Hannah Arendt, translated by Harry Zorn. London: Pimlico, pp. 197–244.

—(1999), 'On Some Motifs in Baudelaire', in *Illuminations*, edited with an introduction by Hannah Arendt, translated by Harry Zorn, London: Pimlico, pp. 152–90.

Bentes, Ivana (1997), 'Introdução', in Glauber Rocha, *Cartas ao mundo*, edited by Ivana Bentes. São Paulo: Companhia das Letras.

Bergala, Alain (1980), 'L'Homme qui se lève', *Cahiers du Cinéma*, n. 311, May, pp. 25–6.

Bergson, Henri (1968), *Durée et Simultanéité.* Paris: Presses Universitaires de France.

Bernardet, Jean-Claude (2007), *Brasil em tempo de cinema: ensaio sobre o cinema brasileiro de 1958 a 1966.* São Paulo: Companhia das Letras.

Bloom, Harold (1975), *The Anxiety of Influence: A Theory of Poetry.* London: Oxford University Press.

Bonitzer, Pascal (1976), 'L'Essence du pire (*L'Empire des sens*)', *Cahiers du Cinéma,* 270, September–October, pp. 48–52.

Bovier, François (with Cédric Flückiger), 'Danger, chute de Dieu!', *Decadrages: Cinéma, à travers champs,* 10, Spring 2007, pp. 43–51.

Boughedir, Férid (1995), 'Cinema africano e ideologia: tendências e evolução', in Luciana Fina, Cristina Fina and Antônio Loja Neves (eds), *Cinemas de África.* Lisboa: Cinemateca Portuguesa/Culturgest, pp. 22–9.

Brewster, Ben (1974), 'From Shklovsky to Brecht: A Reply', *Screen,* vol. 15, n. 2, pp. 82–101.

Buisson, Dominique (2001), *Le Corps japonais.* Paris: Hazan.

Buruma, Ian (1982), 'Bad Boy', *The New York Review,* 8 October, pp. 40–2.

Brecht, Bertolt (2001), *Brecht on Theatre: The Development of an Aesthetic,* edited and translated by John Willett. London: Methuen.

Burch, Noël (1979), *To the Distant Observer: Form and meaning in the Japanese cinema.* Berkeley/Los Angeles: University of California Press.

—(1990), *Life to those Shadows.* Berkeley/Los Angeles: University of California Press.

Bush, Annette and Max Annas (2008), *Ousmane Sembène: Interviews.* Jackson, Mississippi: University Press of Mississippi.

Butterfly, Élisabeth (2004), *François Truffaut: Le Journal d'Alphonse.* Paris: Gallimard.

Cahoreau, Gilles (1989), *François Truffaut: 1932–1984.* Paris: Julliard.

Campbell, Joseph (2008), *The Hero with a Thousand Faces.* Novato, California: New World Library.

Carrère, Emmanuel (1982), *Werner Herzog.* Paris: Edillig.

Carroll, Noël (1998), *Interpreting the Moving Image.* Cambridge: University of Cambridge Press.

—(1998), *Mystifying Movies: Fads and Fallacies in Contemporary Film Theory.* New York: Columbia University Press.

Ching, Erik, Christina Buckley and Angélica Lozano-Alonso (2007), *Reframing Latin America: A Cultural Theory Reading of the Nineteenth and Twentieth Centuries.* Austin: University of Texas Press.

Chun, Kimberly (2002), 'Storytelling in the Arctic Circle: An Interview with Zacharias Kunuk', *Cineaste,* 28:1, Winter, pp. 21–3.

Cintra, Luís Miguel (2004), 'Luís Miguel Cintra, Acteur', in Fabrice Revault d'Allonnes (ed.), *Pour João César Monteiro: contre tous les feux, le feu, mon feu.* Crisnée: Yellow Now, pp. 114–29.

Corrigan, Timothy (1983), *New German Film: The Displaced Image.* Austin: University of Texas Press.

—(ed.) (1986), *The Films of Werner Herzog: Between Mirage and History*. New York/London: Methuen.

Cressole, Michel (1988), 'Les hauts et les bas de *Yaaba*', *Libération,* 22 July, pp. 25–6.

Crime Delicado DVD (n/d), extras. Rio de Janeiro: Videofilmes.

Cronin, Paul (ed.) (2002), *Herzog on Herzog*. London: Faber and Faber.

Cunha, Euclides da (1995), *Rebellion in the Backlands,* translated by Samuel Putnam. Basingstoke: Picador.

Daney, Serge (1993), *L'Exercice a été profitable, Monsieur.* Paris: P.O.L.

Daney, Serge and Narboni, Jean (1980), 'Intervista con Nagisa Oshima', in Nagisa Oshima, *L'impero dei sensi di Nagisa Oshima,* translated by J.P. Manganaro. Milan: Ubulibri, pp. 79–85.

Dauman, Anatole (1989), *Souvenir-Ecran.* Paris: Centre Georges Pompidou.

De Baecque, Antoine (1990), 'Idrissa Ouédraogo', *Cahiers du cinéma,* n. 431–2, May, p. 13.

De Baecque, Antoine and Serge Toubiana (1996), *François Truffaut.* Paris: Gallimard.

Debs, Sylvie (2002), *Cinéma et literature au Brésil: Les myths du Sertão: émergence d'une identité nationale.* Paris: L'Harmattan.

Deleuze, Gilles (2002), *L'Île déserte: textes et entretiens 1953–1974.* Paris: Les Éditions de Minuit.

—(2004), 'Immanence: A Life', in Michael Drolet (ed.), *The Postmodernism Reader: Foundational Texts.* London: Routledge, pp. 178–80.

—(2005), *Cinema 1: The Movement-Image,* translated by Hugh Tomlinson and Barbara Habberjam. New York/London: Continuum.

—(2005), *Cinema 2: The Time-Image,* translated by Hugh Tomlinson and Robert Galeta. New York/London: Continuum.

Diawara, Manthia (1992), *African Cinema: Politics and Culture.* Bloomington/Indianapolis: Indiana University Press.

Doane, Mary Ann (2002), *The Emergence of Cinematic Time: Modernity, Contingency, the Archive.* Cambridge, MA/London: Harvard University Press.

—(2003), 'The Object of Theory', in Ivone Margulies (ed.), *Rites of Realism: Essays on Corporeal Cinema.* Durham, NC/London: Duke University Press, pp. 80–9.

Doll, Susan, 'Kazuo Hara' (2007), in the leaflet included in the DVD case of *Goodbye CP.* Chicago: Facets Video.

Downing, Lisa and Libby Saxton (2010), *Film and Ethics: Foreclosed Encounters.* London/New York: Routledge.

Eisenstein, Sergei (1985), *Immoral Memories: An Autobiography,* translated by Herbert Marshall. London: Peter Owen.

—(1991), *Selected Works Volume II, Towards a Theory of Montage,* edited by Michael Glenny and Richard Taylor, translated by Michael Glenny. London: BFI.

—(1993), 'Imitation as Mastery', in Ian Christie and Richard Taylor (eds), *Eisenstein Rediscovered.* London/New York: Routledge, pp. 66–71.

Elsaesser, Thomas (1996), *Fassbinder's Germany: History, Identity, Subject.* Amsterdam: Amsterdam University Press.

—(2009), 'World Cinema: Realism, Evidence, Presence', in Lúcia Nagib and Cecília Mello (eds), *Realism and the Audiovisual Media*. Basingstoke: Palgrave, pp. 3–19.

Evans, Peter (1999), *The Films of Luiz Buñuel: Subjectivity and Desire*. Oxford: Oxford University Press.

Freitas, Manuela de (2004), 'Manuela de Freitas, Actrice', in Fabrice Revault d'Allonnes (ed.), *Pour João César Monteiro: contre tous les feux, le feu, mon feu*. Crisnée: Yellow Now, pp. 130–43.

Galvão, Maria Rita and Jean-Claude Bernardet (1983), *O nacional e o popular na cultura brasileira: cinema*. São Paulo: Brasiliense/Embrafilme.

Gaston, Sean (2005), *Derrida and Disinterest*. London/New York: Continuum.

Gaut, Berys (2007), *Art, Emotion and Ethics*. New York: Oxford University Press.

Gil, Margarida (2004), 'Margarida Gil, Ex-compagne/Assistante', in Fabrice Revault d'Allonnes (ed.), *Pour João César Monteiro: contre tous les feux, le feu, mon feu*. Crisnée: Yellow Now, pp. 94–106.

Gillain, Anne (ed.) (1988), *Le Cinéma selon François Truffaut*. Paris: Flammarion.

—(1991), *Les 400 coups: François Truffaut*. Paris: Nathan.

—(1991b), *Fraçois Truffaut: Le Secret perdu*. Paris: Hatier.

Gaudreault, André (1997), 'Film, Narrative, Narration: The Cinema of the Lumière Brothers', in Thomas Elsaesser (ed.), *Early Cinema: Space, Frame, Narrative*. London: BFI, pp. 68–75.

Grant, Kim (2005), *Surrealism and the Visual Arts: Theory and Reception*. Cambridge: Cambridge University Press.

Greenberg, Alan (1976), *Heart of Glass*. Munich: Skellig.

Greenblatt, Stephen J. (1981), 'Preface', in S.J. Greenblatt (ed.), *Allegory and Representation*. Baltimore/London: The Johns Hopkins University Press, pp. vii–xiii.

Gregor, Ulrich (1976), 'Interview', in Ulrich Gregor and others, *Herzog/Kluge/Straub*. Munich: Hanser.

Grodal, Torben (2002), 'The Experience of Realism in Audiovisual Representation', in Anne Jerslev (ed.), *Realism and 'Reality' in Film and Media*. Copenhagen: Museum Tusculanum Press/University of Copenhagen, pp. 67–91.

Gunning, Tom (1997), 'The Cinema of Attractions: Early Film, Its Spectator and the Avant-Garde', in Thomas Elsaesser (ed.), *Early Cinema: Space, Frame, Narrative*. London: BFI, pp. 56–62.

—(2000), *The Films of Fritz Lang: Allegories of Vision and Modernity*. London: BFI.

Hall, Stuart (2003), 'Introduction', in Stuart Hall (ed.), *Representation: Cultural Representations and Signifying Practices*. London/Thousand Oaks/New Delhi: Sage/The Open University, pp. 1–11.

Hallward, Peter (2002), 'Translator's Introduction', in Alain Badiou, *Ethics: An Essay on the Understanding of Evil*. London: Verso, 2002.

Hansen, Miriam (1996), Preface to Oskar Negt and Alexander Kluge, *Public Sphere and Experience: Analysis of the Bourgeois and Proletarian Public Sphere*. Bloomington: Duke University Press.

Hansen, Miriam Bratu (1997), 'Introduction', in Siegfried Kracauer, *Theory of Film: The Redemption of Physical Reality*. Princeton, New Jersey: Princeton University Press, pp. vii–xlv.

Heath, Stephen (1986), 'Narrative Space', in Philip Rosen (ed.), *Narrative, Apparatus, Ideology: A Film Theory Reader.* New York: Columbia University Press, pp. 379–420.

Hemingway, Ernest (2000), *Death in the Afternoon.* London: Vintage.

Hill, John (1986), *Sex, Class and Realism: British Cinema 1956–1963.* London: BFI.

Hayward, Susan (2002), 'Framing National Cinemas', in Mette Hjört and Scott Mackenzie, *Cinema & Nation.* London/New York: Routledge, pp. 88–102.

Herzog, Werner (2004), *Conquest of the Useless: Reflections from the Making of* Fitzcarraldo. New York: HarperCollins.

Holmes, Diana and Robert Ingram (1997), *François Truffaut.* Manchester: Manchester University Press.

I Am Cuba (n/d), Distribution press-book, available on http://www.milestonefilms.com/pdf/Iamcuba.pdf, accessed on 01/01/2010.

Jameson, Fredric (1977), 'Imaginary and Symbolic in Lacan: Marxism, Psychoanalytic Criticism, and the Problem of the Subject', in *Yale French Studies,* n. 55/56, pp. 338–95.

Jeong, Seung-Hoon and Dudley Andrew (2008), 'Grizzly ghost: Herzog, Bazin and the cinematic animal', *Screen,* 49:1, Spring.

Jerslev, Anne (ed.) (2002), *Realism and 'Reality' in Film and Media.* Copenhagen: Museum Tusculanum Press/University of Copenhagen.

Johnson, Randal (2008), 'Manoel de Oliveira and the Ethics of Representation', in *Dekalog 2: On Manoel de Oliveira,* guest editor: Carolin Overhoff Ferreira. London: Wallflower Press, pp. 89–109.

Johnston, William (2005), *Geisha-Harlot-Strangler-Star: A Woman, Sex, & Morality in Modern Japan.* New York: Columbia University Press.

Karetnikova, Inga in collaboration with Leon Steinmetz (1991), *Mexico According to Eisenstein.* Albuquerque: University of New Mexico Press.

Kawatake, Toshio (1990), *Japan on Stage: Japanese Concepts of Beauty as Shown in the Traditional Theatre,* translated by P.G. O'Neill. Tokyo: 3A Corporation.

King, John, Ana M. López and Manuel Alvarado (eds) (1993), *Mediating Two Worlds: Cinematic Encounters in the Americas.* London: BFI.

Klompmakers, Inge (2001), *Japanese Erotic Prints: Shunga by Harunobu & Hokusai.* Leiden: Hotei.

Kluge, Alexander (1973), *Lernprozesse mit tödlichem Ausgang.* Frankfurt am Main: Suhrkamp. English edition: (1996) *Learning Processes with a Deadly Outcome.* Durham, NY: Duke University Press.

—(1975), 'Die realistische Methode und das sog. "Filmishe" ', in *Gelegenheitsarbeit einer Sklavin – Zur realistischen Methode.* Frankfurt am Main: Suhrkamp.

Kracauer, Siegfried (1997), *Theory of Film: The Redemption of Physical Reality.* Princeton: Princeton University Press.

Lacan, Jacques (1989), 'Kant with Sade', translated by James B. Swenson, Jr., *October* vol. 51, Winter, pp. 55–75.

—(2004), *Le séminaire de Jacques Lacan. Livre 10, L'angoisse,* edited by Jacques-Alain Miller. Paris: Seuil.

MacCann, Richard A. (ed.) (1966), *Film: A Montage of Theories*. New York: EP Sutton.

Magalhães, Ioná (n/d), Interview in the extras of the DVD *Deus e o diabo na terra do sol*. Rio de Janeiro: Versátil Home Video/Riofilme.

Malanga, Paola (1996), *Tutto il cinema di Truffaut*. Milan: Baldini & Castoldi.

Mandiargues, Pieyre de (1989), 'Propos recueillis par Ornella Volta', in Anatole Dauman (1989), *Souvenir-Ecran*. Paris: Centre Georges Pompidou, pp. 236–8.

Margulies, Ivone (ed.) (2003), *Rites of Realism: Essays on Corporeal Cinema*. Durham, North Carolina/London: Duke University Press.

Marks, Laura U. (2002), *Touch: Sensuous Theory and Multisensory Media*. Minneapolis/London: University of Minnesota Press.

Marran, Christine L. (2007), *Poison Woman: Figuring Female Transgression in Modern Japanese Culture*. Minneapolis: University of Minnesota Press.

Mellen, Joan (2004), *In the Realm of the Senses*. London: BFI.

Metz, Christian (1982), 'The scopic regime of the cinema', in *The Imaginary Signifier: Psychoanalysis and the Cinema*. Bloomington: Indiana University Press, pp. 61–5

Mitchell, Stanley (1974), 'From Shklovsky to Brecht: Some preliminary remarks towards a history of the politicisation of Russian Formalism', *Screen*, vol. 15, n. 2, pp. 74–81.

Monteiro, João César (2004), 'Auto-entretien, Extraits', in Fabrice Revault d'Allonnes (ed.), *Pour João César Monteiro: contre tous les feux, le feu, mon feu*. Crisnée: Yellow Now, pp. 30–6.

—(2005), 'IV A Filosofia na Alcova – Textos de João César Monteiro in *Uma Semana Noutra Cidade*', in João Nicolau (ed.), *João César Monteiro*. Lisboa: Cinemateca Portuguesa, pp. 476–512.

Monteiro, Paulo Filipe (2007), '*A comédia de Deus*, João César Monteiro, 1995', in Carolin Overhoff Ferreira (ed.), *O cinema português através dos seus filmes*. Porto: Campos das Letras, pp. 203–13.

Mulvey, Laura (1989), *Visual and Other Pleasures*. London: Macmillan.

Murphy, David and Patrick Williams (eds) (2007), *Poscolonial African Cinema: Ten Directors*. Manchester: Manchester University Press.

Nagib, Lúcia (1982), '*Fitzcarraldo*, a selva ao som de Caruso', *Folhetim, Folha de S. Paulo*, 30 May, pp. 6–7.

—(1988), 'A Negação de Si', interview with Nagisa Oshima, in *Folha de São Paulo*, 3 June, pp. B-5–7.

—(1991a), *Werner Herzog: o cinema como realidade*. São Paulo: Estação Liberdade.

—(1991b), 'Diretor de *O tambor* retorna com adaptação de Frish em *Voyager*', 'Locações impressionam escritor', 'Cineasta tentou "imitar" Glauber' (articles and interview with Volker Schlöndorff, in Tokyo), *Folha de S. Paulo, Ilustrada*, 15.10.1991, p. 5–1.

—(1995), *Nascido das cinzas: autor e sujeito nos filmes de Oshima*. São Paulo: Edusp.

—(1996), 'In the Realm of the Individual: An Analysis of Nagisa Oshima's *In the Realm of the Senses*', in Nevena Dakovic, Deniz Derman and Karen Ross (eds), *Gender & Media*. Ankara: Med-Campus Project, pp. 156–74.

—(1998), 'Entrevista com Idrissa Ouédraogo', *Imagens,* n. 8, May–August.

—(2001), 'Ouédraogo and the Aesthetics of Silence', in Russell H. Kaschula (ed.), *African Oral Literature: Functions in Contemporary Contexts.* Cape Town: NAE, pp. 100–110.

—(2006), 'Teoria experimental do realismo corpóreo baseada nos filmes de Nagisa Oshima e da nouvelle vague japonesa', in Christine Greiner and Claudia Amorim (eds), *Leituras do Sexo.* São Paulo: Annablume.

—(2006), 'Towards a positive definition of world cinema', in Stephanie Dennison and Song Hwee Lim (eds), *Remapping World Cinema: Identity, Culture and Politics in Film.* London: Wallflower, pp. 30–7.

—(2007), *Brazil on Screen: Cinema Novo, New Cinema, Utopia.* London/New York: I.B. Tauris.

—(2007), Q&A with Kazuo Hara and Sachiko Kobayashi, translated by Mika Ko, 10 November. Leeds: Leeds International Film Festival, unpublished.

Nagib, Lúcia and Cecília Mello (2009), 'Introduction', in Lúcia Nagib and Cecília Mello (eds), *Realism and the Audiovisual Media.* Basingstoke: Palgrave, pp. xiv–xxv.

Narboni, Jean (2004), *Les exercices spirituels, et autres, de João César Monteiro,* in Fabrice Revault d'Allonnes (ed.), *Pour João César Monteiro: contre tous les feux, le feu, mon feu.* Crisnée: Yellow Now, pp. 270–81.

Nichols, Bill (1991), *Representing Reality: Issues and Concepts in Documentary.* Bloomington/Indianapolis: Indiana University Press.

—(2001), *Introduction to Documentary.* Bloomington: Indiana University Press.

Nietzsche, Friedrich (1964), *Beyond Good and Evil: Prelude to a Philosophy of the Future,* translated by Helen Zimmern. New York: Russell & Russell.

Nornes, Abé Mark (2003), 'Private Reality: Hara Kazuo's Films', in Ivone Margulies (ed.), *Rites of Realism: Essays on Corporeal Cinema,* pp. 144–63.

—(2007), *Forest of Pressure: Ogawa Shinsuke and Postwar Japanese Documentary.* Minneapolis/London: University of Minnesota Press.

Odin, Steve (2001), *Artistic Detachment in Japan and the West.* Honolulu: University of Hawaii Press.

Oliveira, Manoel de (2005), 'César Monteiro cineasta deontologicamente exemplar', in João Nicolau (ed.), *João César Monteiro.* Lisboa: Cinemateca Portuguesa, pp. 581–3.

Oricchio, Luiz Zanin (2006), 'A crítica posta em crise em *Crime Delicado,* do diretor Beto Brant', *O Estado de São Paulo,* 12 February, p. D6.

Ortiz, Renato (1994), *Cultura brasileira e identidade nacional.* São Paulo: Brasiliense.

Oshima, Nagisa (1980), 'Le Drapeau de l'Eros flotte dans les cieux', *Cahiers du Cinéma,* 309, March, pp. 9–12.

—(1980), *L'impero dei sensi di Nagisa Oshima,* translated by J.P. Manganaro. Milan: Ubulibri.

—(1992), *Cinema, Censorship, and the State: The Writings of Nagisa Oshima,* edited by Annette Michelson, translated by Dawn Lawson. Cambridge, Massachusetts/London: MIT.

Pasolini, Pier Paolo (2005), *Heretical Empiricism,* translated by Ben Lawton and Louise K. Barnett. Washington, DC: New Academia Publishing.

Pflaum, Hans Günther (1979), 'Interview', in Hans Günther Pflaum and others, *Werner Herzog*. Munich: Carl Hanser Verlag.

Prager, Brad (2007), *The Cinema of Werner Herzog: Aesthetic Ecstasy and Truth*. London: Wallflower Press.

Proença, Manoel Cavalcanti (ed.) (1986), *Literatura popular em verso: antologia*. Belo Horizonte: Itatiaia.

Proust, Marcel (1981), *Remembrance of Things Past*, vol. III, translated by C.K. Scott Mondrieff and Terence Kilmartin. New York: Vintage.

Rancière, Jacques (2004), *Aesthetics and its Discontents*. Cambridge: Polity.

—(2006), *Film Fables*. Oxford/New York: Berg.

—(2009), *The Emancipated Spectator*. London/New York: Verso.

Renov, Michael (2005), 'Investigando o sujeito: uma introdução', in Maria Dora Mourão and Amir Labaki (eds), *O cinema do Real*. São Paulo: Cosac Naify, pp. 234–46.

Richie, Donald (1996), *Public People, Private People: Portraits of Some Japanese*. Tokyo/New York/London: Kodansha.

Roberts, David (1983), 'Alexander Kluge und die deutsche Zeitgeschichte: *Der Luftangriff auf Halberstadt am 8.4.1945*', in Thomas Böhm-Christl (ed.), *Alexander Kluge*. Frankfurt am Main: Suhrkamp.

Rocha, Glauber (1960), '*Quando voam as cegonhas*', *Diário de Notícias*, Salvador, 12 June.

—(1985), *Roteiros do Terceyro Mundo*, edited by Orlando Senna. Rio de Janeiro: Alhambra/Embrafilme.

—(1986), *Glauber Rocha: Scritti sul cinema*. Venice: XLIII Mostra Internazionale del Cinema.

—(1995), 'An Esthetic of Hunger', in Robert Stam and Randal Johnson (eds), *Brazilian Cinema*. New York: Columbia University Press.

—(2003), *Revisão crítica do cinema brasileiro*. São Paulo: Cosac Naify.

—(2004a), *Revolução do cinema novo*. São Paulo: Cosac Naify.

—(2004b), 'Eztetyka do Sonho 71', in *Revolução do Cinema Novo*. São Paulo: Cosac Naify, pp. 248–51.

—(2004c), 'Teoria e prática do cinema latino-americano 67', in *Revolução do Cinema Novo*. São Paulo: Cosac Naify, pp. 83–7.

—(2004d), 'Tricontinental 67', in *Revolução do Cinema Novo*. São Paulo: Cosac Naify, pp. 104–9.

—(2006), 'Elia Kazan', in *O século do cinema*. São Paulo: Cosac Naify, pp. 89–98.

Rodowick, D.N. (2007), *The Virtual Life of Film*. Cambridge, Massachusetts/London: Harvard University Press.

Rosen, Philip (2003), 'History of Image, Image of History: Subject and Ontology in Bazin', in Ivone Margulies (ed.), *Rites of Realism: Essays on Corporeal Cinema*. Durham/London: Duke University Press, pp. 42–79.

Ruoff, Jeffrey and Kenneth Ruoff (2007), 'Reception History: Japanese Memories of the War', in the leaflet included in the DVD case of *The Emperor's Naked Army Marches On*. Chicago: Facets Video.

Ruoff, Kenneth (1993), 'Japan's Outlaw Filmmaker: An Interview with Hara Kazuo', *Iris: A Journal of Theory on Image and Sound*, 16, Spring, pp. 103–13.

Sai, Yoichi (2003), Talk in the extras of the DVD of *L'Empire des sens*. Argos Films—Arte France Développement.

Said, S.F. (2002), 'Northern Exposure', *Sight & Sound,* February. Available online on www.bfi.org.uk/sightandsound/feature/71.

Sant'Anna, Sérgio (1997), *Um crime delicado*. São Paulo: Companhia das Letras.

Saraceni, Paulo César (1993), *Por dentro do Cinema Novo: minha viagem*. Rio de Janeiro: Nova Fronteira.

Sartre, Jean-Paul (1943), *L'Être et le néant*. Paris: Gallimard.

—(1951), *Le Diable et le bon dieu*. Paris: Gallimard.

Scarry, Elaine (2006), *On Beauty and Being Just*. London: Duckworth.

Schreiber, Mark (2001), *The Dark Side: Infamous Japanese Crimes and Criminals*. Tokyo/New York/London: Kodansha.

Screech, Timon (1999), *Sex and the Floating World: Erotic Images in Japan 1700–1820*. London: Reaktion.

Sharp, Jasper (2008), *Behind the Pink Curtain: The Complete History of Japanese Sex Cinema*. Godalming: FAB.

Shaviro, Steven (2006), *The Cinematic Body*. Minneapolis/London: University of Minnesota Press.

Shohat, Ella and Robert Stam (1994), *Unthinking Eurocentrism: Multiculturalism and the Media*. London/New York: Routledge.

Smith, Murray (1996), 'The Logic and Legacy of Brechtianism', in David Bordwell and Noël Caroll (eds), *Post-Theory: Reconstructing Film Studies*. Madison: University of Wisconsin Press.

Sobchack, Vivian (1984), 'Inscribing Ethical Space: Ten Propositions on Death, Representation, and Documentary', *Quarterly Review of Film Studies* 9(4), pp. 283–300. Reprinted in Sobchack, Vivian (2004).

—(2004), *Carnal Thoughts: Embodiment and Moving Image Culture*. Berkeley/Los Angeles/London: University of California Press.

Stadler, Jane (2008), *Pulling Focus: Intersubjective Experience, Narrative Film, and Ethics*. New York/London: Continuum.

Stam, Robert (1981), *O espetáculo interrompido: literature e cinema de desmistificação,* translated by José Eduardo Moretzsohn. Rio de Janeiro: Paz e Terra.

—(1982), '*Land in Anguish*', in R. Stam and Randal Johnson (eds), *Brazilian Cinema* (expanded edition). New York: Columbia University Press, pp. 149–61.

—(1992), *Reflexivity in Film and Literature: From Don Quixote to Jean-Luc Godard*. New York: Columbia University Press.

Stanislavski, Constantin (2003), *An Actor Prepares*. New York/London: Routledge.

Steiner, Peter (1984), *Russian Formalism: A Metapoetics*. Ithaca/London: Cornell University Press.

Stoller, Paul (1992), *The Cinematic Griot: The Ethnography of Jean Rouch*. Chicago/London: University of Chicago Press.

Tavares, Vítor Silva (2004), 'Vítor Silva Tavares, Ami/Éditeur', in Fabrice Revault d'Allonnes (ed.), *Pour João César Monteiro: contre tous les feux, le feu, mon feu*. Crisnée: Yellow Now, pp. 70–93.

Teixeira, Cláudia (2004), 'Cláudia Teixeira, "Non-actrice" ', in Fabrice Revault d'Allonnes (ed.), *Pour João César Monteiro: contre tous les feux, le feu, mon feu.* Crisnée: Yellow Now, pp. 144–53.

Todorov, Tzvetan (1989), *Nous et les autres: la réflexion française sur la diversité humane.* Paris: Seuil.

Thompson, Kristin (1986), 'The Concept of Cinematic Excess', in Philip Rosen, *Narrative, Apparatus, Ideology: A Film Theory Reader.* New York: Columbia University Press, pp. 130–42.

Truffaut, François (1957), 'Le Cinéma crève sous les fausses légendes', *Arts* 619, 9 May, pp. 3–4.

—(1975), *Les Films de ma vie.* Paris: Flammarion.

—(1988), *Le Cinéma selon François Truffaut,* textes réunis par Anne Gillain. Paris: Fammarion.

Turim, Maureen (1998), *The Films of Oshima Nagisa: Images of a Japanese Iconoclast.* Berkeley/Los Angeles/London: University of California Press.

Ukadike, N. Frank (1991), '*Yaaba*', *Film Quarterly,* 44(3), Spring, pp. 54–7.

Uzal, Marcos (2004), 'L'Infini des sensations', in Fabrice Revault d'Allonnes (ed.), *Pour João César Monteiro: contre tous les feux, le feu, mon feu.* Crisnée: Yellow Now, pp. 256–69.

Varga, Darrell (2006), 'Atanarjuat: The Fast Runner', in Jerry White (ed.), *The Cinema of Canada.* London: Wallflower, pp. 225–33.

Veloso, Caetano (1997), *Verdade tropical.* São Paulo: Companhia das Letras.

Viany, Alex (ed.) (1965), *Glauber Rocha: Deus e o diabo na terra do sol.* Rio de Janeiro: Civilização Brasileira.

Visconti, Luchino (1996), 'Cinema Antropomorfico', in Lino Micciché, *Luchino Visconti: Un profilo critico.* Venice: Marsilio, pp. 100–2. Originally published in Cinema, VIII, n. 173–4, 25/09–25/10/1943, pp. 108–9.

Wakamatsu, Koji (2003), Talk in the extras of the DVD *L'Empire des sens.* Argos Films – Arte France Développement.

Wheatley, Catherine (2009), *Michael Haneke's Cinema: The Ethic of the Image.* New York/Oxford: Berghahn.

White, Jerry (2005), 'Frozen but Always in Motion: Arctic Film, Video, and Broadcast', *The Velvet Light Trap,* n. 55, Spring, pp. 52–64.

—(2007), 'Zach Kunuk and Inuit Filmmaking', in George Melnyk (ed.), *Great Canadian Film Directors.* Edmonton: University of Alberta Press, pp. 347–60.

Willemen, Paul (2010), 'Fantasy in Action', in Natasa Durovicova and Kathleen Newman (eds), *World Cinemas, Transnational Perspectives.* New York/Abingdon: Routledge, pp. 247–86.

Williams, Linda (1999), 'The Ethics of Intervention: Dennis O'Rourke's *The Good Woman of Bangkok*', in Jan M. Gaines and Michael Renov (eds), *Collecting Visible Evidence.* Minneapolis/London: University of Minnesota Press, pp. 176–89.

—(2008), *Screening Sex.* Durham/London: Duke University Press.

Williams, Raymond (1977), 'A Lecture on Realism', *Screen* 18(1), Spring, pp. 61–74.

—(1978), 'Recent English Drama', in Boris Ford (ed.), *The Pelican Guide to English Literature 7: The Modern Age.* Harmondsworth: Penguin.

Wollen, Peter (1998), *Signs and Meaning in the Cinema.* London: BFI.

Xavier, Ismail (1997), *Allegories of Underdevelopment: Aesthetics and Politics in Modern Brazilian Cinema.* Minneapolis/London: University of Minnesota Press.

—(2000), 'O cinema brasileiro dos anos 90', an interview, *Praga,* n. 9, pp. 97–138.

—(2008), Interview in the extras of the DVD of *O dragão da maldade contra o santo guerreiro,* Versátil Home Vídeo.

Yampolsky, Mikhail (1993), 'The essential bone structure: mimesis in Eisenstein', in Ian Christie and Richard Taylor (eds), *Eisenstein Rediscovered.* London/New York: Routledge, pp. 177–88.

Zavattini, Cesare (1966), 'Some Ideas on the Cinema', in Richard A. MacCann (ed.), *Film: A Montage of Theories.* New York: EP Sutton, pp. 216–29. Originally published in *Sight and Sound,* October 1953, pp. 64–9, edited from a recorded interview published in *La Revista del Cinema Italiano,* December 1952.

Zupancic, Alenka (2000), *Ethics of the Real: Kant, Lacan.* London: Verso.

Zylinska, Joanna (2005), *The Ethics of Cultural Studies.* London/New York: Continuum.

INDEX